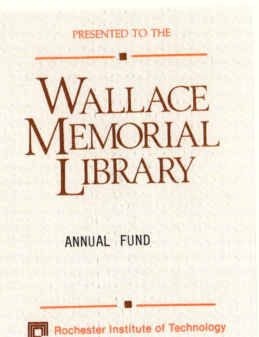

Open & Distance Learning: Case Studies from Industry and Education

Open and Distance Learning Series
Series Editor: Fred Lockwood

OPEN AND DISTANCE LEARNING SERIES

Open & Distance Learning: Case Studies from Industry and Education

Edited by
STEPHEN BROWN

KOGAN PAGE

Hardback edition first published in 1997
Paperback edition published in 1999

Kogan Page Limited
120 Pentonville Road
London N1 9JN, UK

Sylus Publishing Inc.
22883 Quicksilver Drive
Stirling, VA 20166, USA

© Stephen C. Brown, 1997, 1999

British Library Cataloguing in Publication Data

A CIP record for this book is available from the British Library.

ISBN 0 7494 2934 8

Typeset by Kate Williams, London
Printed and bound in Great Britain by Biddles Ltd, Guildford and King's Lynn

Contents

Glossary of abbreviations

ACOL	Analytical Chemistry by Open Learning
ACTOR	Application of ISDN Technologies to Extend Out-Reach project
ADC	Academic Development Committee (University of Sheffield)
BAG	Broadcasting Action Group (University of Sunderland)
BT	British Telecom
BTechEd	Bachelor of Technological Education
CAL	computer-assisted learning/computer-aided learning
CALMAT	Computer-Aided Learning in Mathematics
CATS	Credit Accumulation and Transfer System
CBE	Computer Based Education
CBT	computer-based training
CGA	computer graphics adapter
CMLR	customized menu learning resource
CSCW	Computer-Supported Collaborative Working
CTI	Computers in Teaching Initiative
DACE	Division of Adult and Continuing Education (University of Sheffield)
DENI	Department of Education, Northern Ireland
DES	Department of Education and Science
DLC	Distance Learning Centre (Lloyds Bank)
DLG	Distance Learning Group (Abbey National, BT)
DLU	Distance Learning Unit (BT)
EMF	Educational Media Facility (QUT)
ERDU	Educational Research and Development Unit (QUT)
FEFC	Further Education Funding Council
FLC	Flexible Learning Centre (University of South Australia)
FPC	Financial Planning Certificate (TSB)
FSA	Financial Services Act (1986)
HEFCE	Higher Education Funding Council for England

HEFCW	Higher Education Funding Council for Wales
HMI	Her Majesty's Inspectorate
HNC	Higher National Certificate
ISDN	integrated services digital network
IT	information technology
ITCO	information technology curriculum officer (WMC)
IV	interactive video
LAN	local area network
LRC	learning resource centre (TSB)
LTDO	learning technology development officer (WMC)
MIS	Management Information Services (University of Sheffield)
MSP	Management Skills Programme (TSB)
NCC	National Computing Centre
NHS	National Health Service
NVQs	National Vocational Qualifications
OLDU	Open Learning Development Unit (University of Sunderland)
OMR	optical mark reader
OU	Open University
PBT	paper-based training
PC	personal computer
PCC	Personal Communications Computer
PGDQA	Post Graduate Diploma in Quality Assurance
PIA	Personal Investment Authority
PLU	Programmed Learning Unit (Lloyds Bank)
QUT	Queensland University of Technology
R&D	research and development
RAM	random access memory
SACAE	South Australian College of Advanced Education
SAIT	South Australian Institute of Technology
SHEFC	Scottish Higher Education Funding Council
SIB	Securities and Investment Board
SLS	Student Learning Support
SMEs	small and medium-sized enterprises
SRHE	Society for Research into Higher Education
STAR	Special Telecommunications Action for Regional development
TBT	technology-based training
TDG	Training Development Group (Lloyds Bank)
TILT	Teaching with Independent Learning Technologies
TLTP	Teaching and Learning Technology Programme
TNA	Training Needs Analysis
TSB	Trustee Savings Bank
UKI	UK and Ireland (Reuters)
WAN	wide area network
WICAT	World Institute for Computer-Aided Training
WMC	Wirral Metropolitan College
WWW	World Wide Web

Series Editor's Foreword

Are you facing the prospect of becoming involved in some form of technology-based open, distance or flexible learning in your institution – be this as a teacher or trainer, manager or administrator, in a big company or small department? Do you wonder about the introduction and impact of the new technologies on teaching and training – growth of the Internet and multimedia? Are you interested in how others, in industry, commerce and education have responded to these challenges – finding out what has gone horribly wrong and wonderfully right? Are you interested in learning from the experience of others? If so, this could well be the book you have been looking for.

Stephen has assembled a collection of case studies, written by those who were intimately involved in the teaching/training initiatives, that draw upon open and distance learning strategies. The case studies themselves, and the stories they tell, are very different and are drawn from different parts of the world. They range from multimillion pound organizations to modest institutions. They illustrate different training initiatives from banking to telecommunications, from teaching mathematics to teaching Portuguese. They reflect on the pressures upon teachers and learners to managers and administrators; they reflect on the process of curriculum and cultural change.

The case studies are fascinating in themselves. However, the major contribution this book makes, for anyone either about to become involved in open and distance learning – be it in industry, commerce, the social services or education, is the analysis Stephen offers. His final chapter distils the years of effort of his contributors and blends it with his own considerable experience. It offers valuable insights to anyone working in, or about to work in, this growing field. However, those hoping for a simple recipe are going to be disappointed. In his concluding chapter he says: 'Despite the commonality of themes, the case studies show that there is no simple algorithm which can be applied to the introduction of open/distance learning into a conventional face-to-face context.'

After considering his analysis of the impact of information technology, human factors, cultural changes, as well as the issues that emerge from the case studies, it is likely that any initiative you are associated with will have a much better chance of success.

Fred Lockwood

Acknowledgements

I decided to try to assemble a useful, practical guide to implementing open and distance learning after a chance conversation with Fred Lockwood in 1995. The resulting product is due to his encouragement and guidance during the long gestation period that followed. His help has been very much appreciated. I am very grateful too for all the hard work put in by the individual chapter authors, for the many hours of spare time they have spent and their generous sharing of precious experience. I wish to thank also the organizations described in this book for allowing themselves to be written about so openly. Throughout I have had unswervingly cheerful assistance and professional guidance from Sally Ann Mitchell. Thank you.

Introduction

Should you be reading this book?

Fashions come and go in all branches of human endeavour. The activities formerly known as 'teaching' and 'training' are now commonly referred to both individually and collectively as 'learning' and 'development', reflecting a change in philosophy from teacher-centred to student-centred processes. Along with this change there has been a growing emphasis on the design of more 'open' or 'flexible' learning experiences, which allow learners to work at times and in ways that better suit their individual needs and situations. New technologies have often been the drivers, or at least the enablers, for new learning strategies whereby learners and teachers are not necessarily all in the same place at the same time, ie open/distance/flexible learning.

This book is aimed at people who may be considering trying to introduce some element of technology-based open or distance learning into their organization, or are currently grappling with the problems of trying to do so, and may be wondering where to find practical guidance and help. Ideally, in this situation one would turn to some trusted colleague who had been through it all before and ask for advice. The problem is in finding the right person to ask. Despite increasing interest in open and distance learning methods since the 1960s, most education and training is still dominated by traditional face-to-face methods, so the chances of finding someone experienced in your own organization are probably slim.

The body of literature on education, educational technology, educational psychology, training and development etc, is huge, but books about educational theories, while of academic interest and value, can be difficult to apply directly to real learning situations. Case studies and reports are periodically published that describe in some detail developments in a particular company or institution, but again there are potential barriers to transferability of results because of differences in organizational contexts, structures and processes. This book sets out to overcome the twin problems of over-generality versus over-specificity. Drawing on real, practical, examples from education and industry, it reviews some of the important and broadly applicable lessons to be learned from trying to integrate distance learning strategies with established face-to-face teaching methods and organizations.

The kinds of readers therefore most likely to derive benefit from this book will be decision makers, decision influencers and practitioners. Typically they will include:

- training managers of large corporates;
- personnel directors;
- managers with staff development responsibilities;
- trainers;
- chief executives of small and medium sized enterprises;
- university vice-chancellors, deans and heads of department;
- school and college heads;
- lecturers and teachers.

This book should help you to think in new ways about the delivery and support of learning and provide practical guidance on the implications of trying to introduce distance learning methods into more traditional learning contexts and organizations. In particular it addresses the following questions.

- Is there evidence that open learning can enrich and enhance the cost-effectiveness of more traditional programmes of education and training?
- What options do companies and educational organizations have in fostering the development and implementation of such approaches?
- What are the likely pitfalls and how can they best be avoided?

Why bother with open learning?

The obvious question to be asked when considering the introduction of open learning into an established learning environment is 'why bother?' Traditionally, for most people and most subjects, learning has taken place in a face-to-face environment, led by a teacher, instructor, or whatever. However, pressures are now growing that serve to undermine the traditional structure of learning provision across all sectors. Relative to other competing nations, western countries (the UK and USA in particular) exhibit low levels of attainment in schools, low levels of participation in HE, and under-skilled and inflexible workforces, with shortages of key skills apparent even in times of recession. There is an increasingly urgent need for cost-effective, rapid retraining of the European workforce. Factors contributing to this need include: general competitive pressures to cut costs; the need to cope with different work patterns (encompassing job sharing, part-time working, tele-working and career breaks); a skilled labour shortage due to the decline in birth rate and under-utilization of women and minority workers; rapid changes and advances in technology; rising unemployment and the consequent increased competition for jobs; decentralization and globalization of corporate resources; and increased labour mobility within the EC. Thus there are imperatives not only for more cost-effective learning methods, but for wider access to learning services and higher quality results. The learning sector environment is clearly changing in a way that makes it more receptive to new approaches.

The case studies in the following chapters explain how open/distance/flexible learning has been taken up by a variety of public and private sector organizations in response to these sorts of pressures. The reasons given for initiating change differ in detail from context to context but the underlying motivations are similar:

- increased student access to learning;
- reduced learner drop-out rates;
- enhanced learning quality and learning strategies;
- wider range of learning available;
- more effective use of skilled tutors;
- reductions in costs;
- reduction/elimination of time and place dependence for interactions between learners and material, learners and tutors, learners and peers.

While much of the activity in the open/distance learning field is carried out via 'low tech' media, in particular printed texts, there has been a rapid increase in the everyday use of technology stimulated by the increasing availability and familiarity of items such as video cassette recorders, microcomputers, CD-ROMs and, most recently, Internet-based services. This is having an impact on education and training as the case studies in this book show. However, it is important to recognize that the history of new technology in teaching has not been a great success (Ely and Plomp, 1989). Successive waves of new learning media (print, audio, video, interactive video, computer-based training (CBT), CD-ROM, etc) have met with difficulties and in many cases, after the initial enthusiasm/funding has been exhausted, the particular innovation has been quietly abandoned, resources reallocated and 'business as usual' reinstated.

Not all of the developments described in the following chapters have been unalloyed successes; see for example the chapters on BT and Abbey National. If new learning technologies are so crucial to future success then it is important that we get their introduction right and learn from the experiences of others who have already worked their way up the learning curve.

For instance, it is tempting to view the introduction of open and distance learning methods simply as changes in teaching technology. Each new wave of technological development is accompanied by a drive to apply it to education and training, as in the current rush to launch courses on the Internet. From a technical viewpoint, each new wave brings with it a different set of problems to be addressed. However, practitioners who have ridden more than one of these waves will recognize that, although challenging, the technical problems are ultimately resolvable, as demonstrated by the examples of Wirral Metropolitan College and Barclays Bank; or the technology moves on and a new set of problems is thrown up, as in BT and Abbey National. At a time when the processing power of most hardware is doubling roughly every 18 months, the main issues tend to be related to human factors rather than technical feasibility or even cost – ie the availability and willingness of individuals to get involved and promote new approaches and the capability of organizations to adapt to changing needs, opportunities and pressures. This book shows that there are recurring themes across a wide range of organizational types, learning delivery technologies and at different levels of study. It draws out of these observations on the preconditions for success and reports on successful adaptive coping strategies for newcomers and existing practitioners alike.

How to get the best out of this book

Depending on your needs, there are different ways in which the contents of this book might be accessed. To get the most out of it, it may be helpful to understand the underlying model that has guided the selection and ordering of the chapters. The chapters are all case studies exemplifying a range of different contexts and technologies with varying degrees of impact and transferability.

Within this broad framework the chapters address the following range of topics:

- costing models and investment strategies;
- user expectations and reactions;
- role of the tutor/trainer;
- methods of integration;
- leadership and the role of champions in the organization;
- dissemination of expertise;
- staff development and student learning support systems;
- cultural change and vested interests;
- scalability and rates of change;
- evaluation strategies and techniques;
- collaboration and competition;
- models for priority setting, planning and resource allocation.

Contexts

The book is organized into two main sections: commercial and educational, presenting case studies on innovations in teaching and learning within the following organizations:

Commercial
- Abbey National plc
- Barclays Bank
- British Telecommunications plc (BT)
- Lloyds Bank
- Reuters
- Trustee Savings Bank (TSB)

Educational
- Glasgow University, UK
- Queensland University of Technology, Australia
- Sheffield University, UK
- Sunderland University, UK
- University of South Australia, Australia
- University of Ulster, UK
- Wirral Metropolitan College, UK

The first four commercial case studies cover the pioneering period referred to in the title of the Abbey National case study: 'From pioneers to settlers'. The mid 1980s were exciting times for training departments in many large corporates, with new technology driven opportunities (the first PCs, interactive video discs, direct broadcast by satellite), expanding budgets and a growing consensus that non-traditional target audiences such as managers and sales staff could benefit from alternative training methods. It is interesting to note how important different organizational contexts and practices seem to have been in determining the success or otherwise of these ventures. In the TSB for instance, the system whereby all training was developed by a single in-house group, regardless of subject matter, and delivery was largely carried out by contract staff, meant that a move towards distance learning was not the problem that it became in other organizations such as BT, Lloyds or Abbey National.

The next two chapters, 'Implementing distance learning in Barclays Bank' and 'Open learning in Reuters' represent more recent developments. Here are examples of organizations that have had time to learn from the experiences of the earlier pioneers and it is interesting to note the emphasis they both place on accessibility and learning support. The learning point here is one of timeliness, a theme running through most of the examples in this book and brought out particularly in the Abbey National and TSB examples. Clearly the availability of a particular technology that enables a particular approach to be adopted is a necessary but insufficient precondition for success. The time has to be ripe in the sense that there is a real, recognized, need that matches closely with the characteristics of the proposed innovation.

The educational case studies begin at the micro level with two examples of course-specific innovations from Glasgow University, both employing computer-assisted learning (CAL). The first of the two, 'Integrated courseware in language learning', reports in detail on the experiences of the course team developing, implementing and evaluating its own integrated approach, while the second, 'Conversion of a mathematics course to tutor-supported computer-assisted flexible learning', examines the issues raised when introducing materials developed elsewhere. Glasgow University was one of the few universities in the United Kingdom to be funded by the Teaching and Learning Technology Programme (TLTP) to evaluate how teaching and learning can be made more productive and efficient throughout the entire institution. The two different strategies adopted in these examples illustrate the range of alternatives possible on the one hand, and the commonality of issues on the other.

The broader institutional-wide theme is taken up in the next two case studies, 'Champion for change: Learning development at the University of Sunderland' and 'Innovation in a traditional setting at Sheffield University'. Whereas the Glasgow examples describe a kind of 'bottom up', self-help, approach, whereby teachers themselves plan, design and implement the innovation, these next two case studies report on the growing professionalization of learning technologies within their institutions and the evolution over a longer time period, of organizational structures to support the development and of open and distance learning methods. They are set in the context of a 'new' university (ie, a former polytechnic) and an 'old' university, dealing with undergraduate and postgraduate level studies respectively. Yet despite these differences, the issues raised and the responses made are broadly similar. The following chapter, 'Computer-based education at Queensland University of Technology', describes a similar process at an Australian university, although here there is greater emphasis on developing centralized production facilities and the institutional focus is restricted to delivering and supporting only materials produced in-house.

METTNET® is the registered name of Wirral Metropolitan College's college-wide area network, at once shifting the context to further education and broadening the focus from the stand-alone developments described so far. Infrastructure and staff development issues, very similar to those raised by the commercial case studies, take precedence here. The University of Ulster takes the network theme a stage further with their ACTOR project in 'Technologies to extend out-reach', describing how ISDN-based communications can be exploited to extend the access to learning beyond the physical boundaries of the institution and nation state. Again, infrastructure and staff development feature strongly. This chapter also returns to the earlier theme of institutional change, examining the potential impact of new technologies not only on traditional teaching roles but also on the wider operations of the host organization in terms of space utilization, rapid response, collaboration and management.

The final study in this chapter, 'Flexible learning as university policy', from the University of South Australia, takes these themes further and closes the loop back to the institutional policy issues that set the context for the opening two chapters. This time the perspective is that of the senior manager attempting to mould institutional behaviour and encourage and facilitate the kind of course specific development described in the Glasgow case studies.

What is interesting is the frequency with which authors from both sectors have commented on the emergence and significance of cultural and organizational issues even where these have not been explicitly addressed, eg Reuters, BT, Abbey National, Lloyds Bank, Ulster, Wirral Metropolitan College, Sheffield and Glasgow University. This key theme is taken up again in the concluding chapter of the book, which summarizes the experiences described in the earlier chapters and offers some guidelines on how best to proceed with planning and implementing an open learning strategy.

Technologies

The cases selected span a broad range of different technologies, old and new, ranging from print-based materials, video and stand-alone computer-based learning (CBT, interactive video, CD-ROM) through to computer-mediated communications, videoconferencing, Internet and satellite technology. However, this is not a book about technology *per se* and the technical details have been kept to a minimum. This is partly because the rate of technology change rapidly renders specific solutions obsolete and hence details of their implementation redundant. In many of the cases described here, externally driven technological developments rendered the carefully planned infrastructure obsolete and/or excessively costly, resulting in major technology upgrades (Barclays) or complete changes to the original strategy (Abbey National, Lloyds Bank).

What is perhaps more useful than the specifics of the different technologies used is to note the general observation quoted by Doughty *et al.* in the Glasgow maths case study:

'What performs more or less well is not some material or medium (a lecture, a book, a computer program) but the whole teaching and learning episode managed by the teacher who employs [the educational innovation] as one element.' (Draper 1994)

In other words the technology itself is relatively unimportant. Of course, different technologies have different characteristics that can be exploited to enhance particular kinds of learning, but the underlying determinant of success or failure appears to be the quality of the learning design itself, rather than the vehicle.

If you are interested in reading about specific technologies, you can use the index at the back of the book to locate the item of interest. Further information about any of the technologies referred to in the following chapters may also be obtained directly from the individual authors themselves (see The Contributors, p.197).

Impact

Each case is significant in terms of its impact on one or more of the following:

- learners;
- tutors;
- managers;
- organizational performance;
- organizational structures and practices;
- budgets.

Teaching innovations cannot be simply an add-on to an otherwise unchanged learning environment. There has to be a fundamental restructuring of learning that implies shifts in roles and responsibilities of the key participants: teachers and learners (Laurillard, 1993). Not surprisingly, the educational case studies tend to emphasize more the changing roles of teachers and learners (eg Glasgow University, Wirral Metropolitan), while the examples from commerce and industry inevitably take managers more into their consideration (eg TSB, BT, Reuters). Nevertheless, this distinction is not entirely clear-cut. The TSB, Abbey National and Reuters case studies all emphasize the need for learners to be more autonomous and for trainers to accept the role of facilitator rather than teacher. Equally, the authors of the Ulster and South Australia case studies mention explicitly the impact on management structures and processes.

Most of the case studies are concerned in some way with organizational performance, structures and practices, whether at the micro course level (Glasgow, TSB) or the strategic institutional level (Ulster, South Australia, Abbey National, Lloyds). In many cases these concerns centre on strategic positioning within the sector: being seen to be a modern, high-tech company (Abbey National, BT), anticipating legislative change (TSB, Abbey National), or seeking to extend influence regionally (Wirral Metropolitan, Ulster and University of South Australia). Nevertheless, costs are an important consideration in all cases and four of the examples provide cost comparative data in some form: Barclays, BT, Abbey National and Glasgow University. Despite fierce reductions in the unit of student resource, the educational organizations tend to be less concerned with cost reduction and concentrate more on extending access to and enhancing the impact of their programmes within existing resource constraints. The industrial/commercial organizations' reports reveal a greater emphasis on cost measurement and control in this sector, trying to achieve the same results with fewer resources in most cases. This is not surprising since the core business of the educational institutions is teaching and revenue from increased student numbers is a primary goal. Within the companies, training is a support service that needs to be carried out as cost-effectively as possible, but which is not generally targeted to grow year on year, hence the emphasis on cost reduction. Unfortunately this difference in orientation makes comparisons between the two sectors difficult and detailed analyses such as that reported from BT are rarely found.

Transferability

Although there is considerable variation between the target audiences, the subjects and levels taught, the organizational contexts and so on, the purpose of assembling this collection of case studies is to identify the key ideas and strategies underlying each case that can be generalized to different situations. These general lessons are drawn out and discussed in the concluding chapter of the book. If you would like an overview to help you assimilate the case studies, you may find it helpful to read the concluding chapter first. Alternatively, it might suit you better to build up the picture more gradually, focusing on those aspects that interest you most or are most relevant to your own situation. Either way, I hope this Introduction has given you enough pointers to enable you to pick your own route through the case studies and to draw your own conclusions. The cases themselves are distilled from over 200 person-years of empirical activity and are rich in real practical detail. In offering them, the authors sincerely hope that you can learn and profit from their experiences.

References

Draper, S, Brown, M I, Henderson, F P and McAteer, E (1996) 'Integrative evaluation: an emerging role for classroom studies of CAL', *Computers in Education,* **26,** 17–32.

Ely, D P and Plomp, T (1989) 'The promises of educational technology: a reassessment' in *Computers in the Human Context,* T Forrester (ed.), Blackwell, Oxford.

Laurillard, D (1993) *Rethinking University Teaching: A framework for the effective use of educational technology,* Routledge, London.

Part 1

Commercial case studies

Chapter 1

Lloyds Bank
and multimedia

Howard Hills

Introduction

In 1984, Lloyds Bank took a major step forward in the technology of training delivery and bought 1,500 interactive video (IV) systems. At that time most of the clerical training in Lloyds Bank was delivered with eight track audiotapes and workbooks. The subject content was entirely procedural, concentrating on processes done by junior staff such as cashiering and processing standing orders. The aim was to replace the audiotapes and workbooks used by that target group.

This chapter summarizes what happened within Lloyds Bank since that decision was taken and highlights some of the lessons learned in the development of multimedia over a period of 12 years. The most significant lesson is that a learning culture is needed to exploit multimedia for training purposes and that it takes a whole organization to establish such a culture rather than just the training department on its own.

1984: Formation of the Video Unit

In 1984, many conditions within Lloyds Bank looked right for the introduction of a new training technology. Branch-based study for procedural training was well established. Programmed Learning was an established means of delivering training into the Branch network and had been so since 1968. The Programmed Learning Unit (PLU) existed with all the facilities needed to produce audiotapes and amend and reprint workbooks. The unit was well resourced and able to keep on top of the continuous amendments that were necessary. The replacement of the multiple-track tape recorders by interactive video seemed a natural extension of the training strategy. In establishing the use of interactive video and the unit that would support it, Lloyds made some implicit assumptions. These were:

1. Interactive video was a suitable medium for procedural training.
2. No other training media for procedural training would be required.
3. The existing staff of the PLU was sufficient to project manage the development of new courses in the new technology.
4. Within two years, all existing programmed learning courses could be converted to interactive video.
5. The funding for those programmes would be forthcoming from the business in the normal course of events.
6. The technology would be long lived and stable.
7. Branch-based training was well managed and appropriate benefit was being extracted.

These are interesting assumptions and, with hindsight, all can be seen to be flawed in some way.

During the first two years a regular sequence of new courses came out. A typical course would follow a 'lesson' format.

A scene setter as a business rationale
↓
Introduction highlighting what the course would achieve
↓
The main body interposed with questions and tests
↓
A summary of what had been learned

A typical production sequence would proceed through

- establish the learning points;
- prepare a brief for commercial tender;
- commission a video production company;
- write the script (and obtain approval from the various interested parties within the bank);
- shoot the scenes;
- press the laser disc;
- write the Microtext software that would control the programme.

The major part of the investment was in the video production. Most courses used either half-an-hour or an hour of video. This was determined by the size of IV disks rather than the required content. The video scripting and production content influenced the design of the material to a very great extent. The principal reason why was that this was the outsourced element and the attention of both sponsors and designers focused on this element. The Microtext programming environment was very simplistic, as was the computer element of the IV workstation. The graphics standard was CGA (computer graphics adapter) with only four colours available. All this added up to an environment in which the video element of the material was much more sophisticated than the computer element.

Evaluation

Late in 1987 the National Physical Laboratory was commissioned to complete a usability study of some of the material that had been produced. Their main recommendations focused on improving the computer element of the design by increasing the interactive density, formatting the structure with menus and increasing the user control.

Notwithstanding these comments, several of these courses were absolute stars with the users. The medium was new and attractive. The visual presentation was excellent. Although the computing element was very basic, at that time the only competition for cheap single user computing was the BBC computer. So even the computing element was impressive to most users. From a branch perspective, the training appeared to be a great success, so why didn't Lloyds re-invest and upgrade the technology?

Problems

There were three key factors that caused Lloyds to re-think its approach to the delivery of training within the branch network. Firstly, the pace of change within the UK clearing banking accelerated. The Interactive Video equipment had been seen as the means by which procedural training would be delivered. But in 1986 Lloyds stated its intention of converting from paper-based processing to entirely computerized processing. At a stroke, the new training delivery medium was rendered obsolete, embedded CBT would be needed rather than stand-alone IV.

The second key factor was fundamental change in the delivery technology. Lloyds were pioneers in the use of the new IV medium. In 1984 the total UK IV sales were 2,500, of which Lloyds Bank represented 1,500. However, within one year of its installation, the specification of the Bank's IV system was below that accepted as the generic standard by the industry. No economical upgrade route was available from the suppliers.

Thirdly, the assumption that business units would fund development of IV packages led to some very curious choices for programme priority. This is best illustrated by Cashpoint training. The Cashpoint installation that the Bank undertook in 1985 was a major programme with some very significant expenditure. A training budget of £400,000 was a very small percentage of this installation programme. This led to four IVs being produced in what was a very minor area of branch procedural activity, although at the time one that had a major customer impact. In addition, at least two of these programmes were better defined as communication and should have been produced on linear videotape at much lower cost. At the same time, training that should have been developed wasn't; for example: a basic introduction to the bank, banking, and the operation of the procedural systems. Because there was no strategy for the development of IV-based training products, the Video Unit had its resources taken up by those departments who were prepared, and able, to pay. Also, since it was not part of the Training Department, there was no integration with face-to-face training or workbooks. The nature of the funding meant that the two-year target for replacing programme learning courses was not achieved.

The rate of business change had its biggest impact within the branch network. The programmed learning courses had been relatively well managed within a stable environment. The ability to manage training in a highly volatile environment had to be learned by branch management and the amendment of training material had to proceed at a faster rate. This was difficult because IVs were more expensive to update than the programmed learning courses. The workbooks accompanying the programmed learning courses had been despatched from the centre and could be updated relatively easily. The video discs were stored in the branches with no accompanying written material. The number of staff in the video unit was insufficient to keep pace with maintenance of existing material and create new programmes at the pace required.

1987: formation of the Distance Learning Centre

In 1987, the Video Unit became part of the Training Department, its title changed to Distance Learning Centre (DLC) and its remit was extended to include all distance learning material. This enabled workbooks to be integrated with IV material (and with CBT delivered to every Branch IT workstation). The design of face-to-face training remained separate. Shortly after this, a method of delivering computer-based training on to the rapidly expanding Branch Information Technology system was introduced. The intention was to use this for the training in application usage, and hence much of the procedural training. This placed CBT on the desk of every member of staff who used the main IT system. (At that time about one in three staff although the ratio has steadily risen.)

The DLC invested in a standard authoring template for both IV and CBT. This was developed in Tencore and provided a consistent look and feel to the material. The template gave a standard menu structure, consistent use of forward and back keys, exit key, glossary functions, etc. Although courses varied in purpose and content, a similar design approach was used that mirrored much of the material produced in the first two years of the IV platform. This was directive in nature rather than exploratory. Although users had full control over which bits of a course were visited, the design assumption was that users would work through relevant stages in a serial fashion. The improved programming environment did allow more formal testing and record keeping to be introduced.

After the organization change, the Distance Learning Centre produced a much wider range of products. Paper increased in volume, the IV platform was used as a means of delivering CBT, and some minor use was made of videotape material. Very rapidly, IV moved into the position of being used less frequently than other methods of delivery. Part of the reason for this was the high cost of materials production (£20,000 to press, package and distribute in 1988). Another reason was that the limitations of the computer meant that most of the video material had to be filmed, then transferred to video, which was also expensive.

So that the DLC budget could be maximized, much of the project management was brought in-house. The internal staff were expanded in both quantity and quality. Heavy use was made of contractors working on an individual basis rather than contracting out complete projects. This mix of internal and external resource has proved to be a winning formula. We also endeavoured to use distance learning for topics other than procedural training. A management guide to managing distance learning was produced and very well received. However, there were still three missing ingredients.

1. No access to generic training packages

Neither the Bank's IV system nor the computer-based training (CBT) transmission system would accept generic material. The original computer specified with the Bank's IV (Multimedia Interactive Control – MIC) system was a very early generation PC. It had twin 3¼" disk drives, no hard disk and a MIC 2000 Video Adapter. Lloyds Bank had specified 3¼" disk drives that differed from the 3¼" diskette standard introduced later by IBM. This was a minor limitation but did create some challenging programming problems. The biggest limitation was the MIC 2000 card produced by Videologic, which was the earliest generation and only accepted four colours on the computer screen. The display adapter was also very limited (CGA). The combined result was a very low standard of graphics display and a limited choice of fonts. Several unacceptably expensive modifications to the equipment would have been required to enable the generic material available in 1989 to run on the IV workstation. The CBT transmission system had some very tight design constraints. For the system in use in 1989 no course could exceed 250k of magnetic storage or use more than about 250k of virtual memory. In addition, all screen interface design had to conform with the then IBM Common User Access Standards. At the time no generic course could meet these rigorous technical standards.

2. Lack of integration with face-to-face training

The development and delivery of face-to-face training was managed and staffed separately to the development of distance learning. Distance learning development was heavily staffed by external specialists; traditional training was staffed by line bankers who were spending part of their career in the training environment. This presented an artificial organizational barrier that needed to be removed.

3. A perception that distance learning could not be used for soft skills training

This was contrary to the situation in most other organizations where Interactive Video was being used for management training and soft skills such as listening, presentation and stress management.

1991: Formation of the Training Development Group

In 1991, Lloyds integrated the development of face-to-face training and distance learning. This unit was called the Training Development Group. The TDG was composed of a mixture of traditional trainers (mostly drawn from a Bank career) and specialist designers of flexible learning materials.

At the start neither group readily appreciated the value of the other. The TDG took on the responsibility of supporting the regional teams of trainers, and for producing new courses, for delivery within the training centre as well as by the regional teams. There was a growing realization by traditional trainers that the design of study materials, particularly technology-based, did require specialist skills and that these could best be organized and deployed in a specialist unit. However, a more fundamental reason for establishing the TDG was to enable the distance learning materials to be seen to be part of, and supporting, face-to-face training. It took approximately three years from 1991 to reach this goal. The integration of one team to be responsible for all training development irrespective of media has proved to be a key ingredient in making multimedia successful.

Even at this stage (1991), there was still an assumption within the Bank that interactive video was best employed for the training of junior staff in procedural tasks even though the use of IV in most other companies was primarily for soft skills and supervisory skills. Also CBT had not been widely introduced in Lloyds until after the use of IV and was considered to be more sophisticated and advanced than IV. Certainly the means of delivering CBT was very effective and a considerable amount of work had been done to produce training material of an exceptionally high quality. If multimedia was to be used in the way in which other companies were exploiting it, this perception had to be overcome. There had to be a demonstration of the ability of multimedia to train managerial and interpersonal skills. The decision was taken within central training to develop a multimedia course for training in Sales Management (Anon, 1994). The partially completed product was demonstrated to the top management of the Retail Bank. As a result of that demonstration, an immediate decision was taken to purchase 20 multimedia systems, closely followed by a further 40. The equipment was carefully specified to be able to run generic IV material as well as making available CD-ROM, a likely source of future training material.

The CBT and IV produced in the 1980s was very didactic in its learning style. Increasingly the design of material became more consultative. This has been seen in many products produced generically as well as inside other organizations. It has been coupled with the use of multimedia as a database of visual objects. The concept of a 'learning resource' had been introduced in the late 1980s and this is now reflected in the design of current (1996) training material.

Preparing for the full-scale adoption of multimedia

Most of the initial assumptions made in 1984 had (in 1992) been revisited and actions taken:

1. Interactive video would not be used for procedural training. Three core Lloyds Bank's programmes demonstrate IV's ability to familiarize soft skills and management training.
2. Extensive use is made of paper and CBT for the delivery of procedural training. These have been the main methods of introducing new computer applications to the network. More recently (1993 onwards), in-branch trainers have been used to introduce changes in procedures. The change has been so rapid that using a cascade approach of training teams centrally and sending them out to branches has been the best way of helping branches through the recent major transitions. The effort applied to this is being reduced.
3. The Training Development Group is now of a similar size to that which the Programme Learning Unit was in 1968. However, the quality and expertise of staff is much higher. There is a heavy emphasis on the ability to project manage the development of training across a wide range of media. Training development is now involved in all the major initiatives that the Retail Bank undertakes.
4. The final programmed learning course was converted to CBT and text in 1990, four years later than originally envisaged. Most of the procedural and lending training is now in a format that can be more readily updated.
5. Funding has now moved full circle and in 1994 Training Development

was back to being a zero-based budget. However, discussions about annual spend are now held at a very much higher level within the organization. We should be better placed to ensure that training spend is properly balanced and more appropriately aligned to its leverage on the business. The next few years should see whether this will work properly.

6. The technology is not long-lived or stable and the pace of innovation remains an irritant. However the CD-ROM market is much bigger than the IV market, and it is hoped that it will be more stable. The growth of good quality generic titles is producing some sort of stability. The market has expanded beyond that of training, which is excellent news, and it has been possible to convert existing Laser Vision material to CD-ROM ready for an upgrade of our training delivery platforms.

7. The final assumption was that branch-based training was well managed and appropriate benefit was being extracted. In 1988, an extensive survey showed this had ceased to be the case. This still remained an issue in 1992 and indeed had not been fully resolved in 1994. The first step along the road of ensuring the effective management of branch-based training was to place it on the agenda of local training managers. The 60 multimedia platforms situated around the country became a means for enabling this to happen. The range of courses on the systems had a higher profile than the earlier interactive videos. Several of the topics were more closely associated with face-to-face courses that were being run in local centres. Also, in a time of recession, the investment in hardware and courseware was more noticeable. Between 1984 and 1986 the Bank spent £8,000,000 on procedural training courses and the equipment by which to deliver them. In 1990, the expenditure of half a million pounds on training for junior managerial staff attracted more attention.

Local management attention has been focused on the use of multimedia as a means of providing training throughout the branch network. We now have locally based flexible learning coordinators whose main responsibility will be to ensure that flexible learning, including the use of multimedia, is well managed at branch level. Also, a number of key products have been developed that improve the information available to local managers, and are aimed at enabling them to extract appropriate benefit from training material available to them and their staff. In a geographically dispersed organization, this remains a vital key in fully developing the available human resource. The proper management of training in almost 2,000 locations, in most cases, with less than ten staff in each location, is a difficult challenge.

The 60 multimedia systems had expanded to 132 in 1995; 60% of those were used at a rate above that of the break-even figure in 1995. This break-even figure is calculated as the cost comparable with providing locally based non-residential face-to-face training. It makes no allowance for the reduced travel costs or the reduction in staff time. In the second quarter of 1994, there was a 100% increase in the usage rate. We have developed a Supervisory Management course that utilizes face-to-face training, paper-based workbooks, generic CD-ROM and CBT, all as a fully integrated package. There is now much greater support from the training community as to the value of multimedia. In 1996 there are 250 multimedia systems in use within the Lloyds Bank part of Lloyds TSB.

Lessons learned

The introduction of multimedia is a change process. To be successful a clear vision is needed; individuals will resist that change and they will be confused as to what is required. It is very challenging for a support function, like training, to introduce a compelling vision that the business relates to. The visions that can support the use of multimedia are:

- reduced training time for staff;
- reduced cost;
- increased throughput;
- an alternative to increase the choice of staff and their managers;
- a more immediate training response available.

Increasing the responsibility of line managers in coaching and developing their people is also an important business driver (and integral to Investors in People). The first lesson is to ensure that training meets the needs of the business and as a responsibility of every manager.

Multimedia is (still) a complex technical area. Successful implementation requires the technical issues to be managed – almost managed away from the user. This must not be done in a patronizing manner but the technical problems (in either development or delivery) cannot be allowed to detract from the user's appreciation of the system. The problem is slightly different to the usual IT problem since many courses come from small suppliers who do not seem to understand fully that their material operates with lots of other software on the same platform. I see no possibility of common technical standards being used, therefore integration of courses on to common systems will continue to be an issue for users to manage.

The final lesson (and the most simple) is that courses must:

- meet the current business need;
- be relevant to the business environment;
- be ready on time
- be flexible (and not didactic in design);
- make full use of a range of learning approaches and styles, including using visual, aural and feeling senses to the full.

Conclusion

The period 1984 to 1996 has seen significant changes in the way training is delivered in Lloyds Bank. Training has moved out of training centres towards local trainers and flexible learning. Informal training in the workplace has remained a major method of delivering training but is now much more formalized with various support tools provided. What has been the impact of these changes?

Learners are provided with more training at lower cost. The training is nearer the point at which it is needed both in time and in place. Learners are less 'spoon fed'. They must be much more active in their own development and much more focused in what they need to learn. There is a greater reliance on the part of individuals to drive their own development but this is better supported by more available products.

Trainers are now faced with more challenging course content. Whereas in the late 1980s and early 1990s most face-to-face training courses dealt primarily with the transfer of knowledge and some skills practice, now most courses deal with skills practice or the introduction of major change initiatives. Skills practice requires close observation and high quality feedback. Higher orders of training skills are needed in the syndicate room as multimedia takes over the more mundane transference of knowledge and skills. The introduction of major new initiatives requires trainers who can defuse emotionally charged situations. No one likes change and the trainers frequently find themselves in the 'front line'.

Managers are being asked to take on more responsibility for training and developing their staff. Of course this is not a product of introducing multimedia training; multimedia training is an enabler that helps managers deliver this key management activity. Investors in People is very clear about defining the responsibility for training and developing people and this rests clearly and unequivocally with the manager. Guidance and support is provided to help them do this. Training modules in coaching, developing people, managing training have all been produced for line managers in the last four years (1992–96).

Organizational performance has clearly improved. This is evident in business terms and training has supported many of the business initiatives that are showing a better return. A recent survey of staff attitudes (Lloyds, 1995) shows an improvement in the organizational 'climate'. Staff 'feel better trained and believe both that there are more training opportunities available to them, and that they are given greater encouragement to take advantage of these'. More feel that 'they have the opportunity for personal development in the Bank than previously'. Of course, multimedia training is only part of the support that has enabled this change in perception, nevertheless it has contributed to it.

Finally we can show a return on the investment both in specific instances and globally. Two specific examples are:

- A cost saving of £26,000 by using a technology-based training solution to replace a two-day locally run course in balance sheet interpretation. This saving is based on five sites with 150 users per annum with hardware costs shared across users of other courses at 40 users per month.
- A cost saving of £110,000 for training 76 users at a regional office and a saving of £33,400 for training 53 users on three sites in a rural area, using a CD package to replace external trainers.

Globally a total of 5,500 days of multimedia training is delivered at a cost of £970,000 (based on average figures through 1994 and 1995). This annual cost is based on the full administrative costs, hardware depreciation and maintenance and a percentage of the courseware costs. This percentage assumes a shelf life of two to four years for the generic and bespoke products. This compares with a traditional training cost of £825,000. However the usage of open learning is steadily increasing *at no increase in cost*. By the end of 1995, 60% of the multimedia systems were showing a positive return on investment. This return is independent of any additional savings made from reduced travel costs.

In 1996 the introduction of a library for courseware will significantly reduce the per hour participant costs, even though the number of multimedia workstations will increase. Clearly there has been benefit to the organization.

The future

The 'super highway' is bound to change the way in which organizations work. Within the training community, the most likely concept is that of the 'online tutor'. Examples already exist of the Internet being a 'college'. This will add the dimension of a remote 'interpersonal interaction' to flexible learning materials. It remains to be seen whether this will be used only to enhance existing topics of whether this type of training will move into topic areas in which flexible learning is not well represented currently. One thing remains certain, it will become increasingly important to provide more training and support within the workplace. Work groups will become smaller and people will be ever more reliant on technology to support their development.

References

Anon (1994) 'Moving to multimedia', *IT Training*, April/May, 17–23.
Anon (1994) 'Multimedia in training', *Banking & Financial Training*, January, 14.
Anon (1994) 'Learning at the workplace', *Audio Visual*, November, 12–14.
Lloyds (1995) *Lloyds Bank UKRB*, internal report, September.

Chapter 2

Integrated learning in the TSB

Peter Higgins

Introduction

Over the early part of 1996, TSB Group merged with Lloyds Bank to form the Lloyds TSB Group. The integration of the two bank's systems and processes continues to be reviewed and policies and strategies defined. At the time of writing these have not affected, to any great extent, the usage of open and distance learning strategies previously adopted within the TSB.

The following is a discussion of TSB's experience with open and distance learning, and in particular its use in the accreditation of sellers with the Financial Planning Certificate (FPC). This will focus on the activities undertaken by TSB Bank plc before its merger with Lloyds Bank.

Following the production of a consultative paper by the Personal Investment Authority (PIA) that indicated that all sellers of regulated products and their supervisors needed to complete Financial Planning Certificates 1, 2 and 3 and to demonstrate sales competence by 30 June 1997, TSB needed to formulate action plans to equip some 3,000 bank managers and sellers with the skills necessary to meet this requirement.

To understand how the bank tackled this issue and the role of open and distance learning strategies this report will briefly discuss TSB Group and TSB Retail Bank. It will also consider the resources available to design and deliver the training, through the bank's Retail Training Department, together with the bank's previous experience of Open Learning strategies.

The major part of the discussion will focus on the open learning strategy used to ensure that the bank complied with the PIA's designated completion time scale. It will be seen that the bank has been successful in its approach to FPC accreditation and adapted its strategy to accommodate both business needs and those of the sellers.

TSB Bank plc

From its founding as a Savings Institute in 1810, TSB evolved into a highly focused financial service group, with some 1.1 million individual shareholders and 7.5 million customers. TSB Group's core business is conducted through TSB Bank. The major part of this operation is TSB's Retail Bank, which employs some 16,000 staff and has a national network of 1200 branches.

The bank's desire to be 'more professional and innovative than its competitors' led TSB to review its products, service and distribution channels. This resulted in TSB fully integrating its retail banking and insurance business to become the UK's leading Bancassurer. The move to Bancassurance, ie merging the identities, structures and sales forces of the banking and insurance businesses to form a fully integrated financial service, enabled the bank to market more effectively its life, pension and general insurance products to its large customer base.

TSB's training resources

In support of TSB's branch network, the bank's training resources were held under the control of its Retail Training Department. The design and production of the bank's core training solutions were primarily developed by an in-house team of 18 with flexibility to enlarge the group to 25 to accommodate peaks in demand for training materials.

Retail training requirements were identified by a sponsor (often a senior branch network representative). The 'Training Need' was then passed to the design team, who conducted a training needs analysis. This analysis established whether the 'need' could be solved by training and where appropriate, recommended the best training solution. Upon agreement with the sponsor that the proposed solution met their objectives, the design team produced and distributed the completed training solution. This distribution was either to the delivery team (where 'face-to-face' training was required) or directly to the end users (via a central mailing system).

TSB's delivery team had just over 100 designated trainers. These trainers formed teams, each team being responsible for a specific area of training. The main teams consisted of five regional teams (each with 14 trainers) who delivered local 'face-to-face' training. Management skills training was delivered through ten trainers and a central team of 15 delivered regulated sales training.

To deliver residential training, the TSB principally relied upon its college facilities at Solihull, Telford and Andover. Telford, the largest residential facility, had a bedroom capacity of 90 and had eight lecture rooms and 12 syndicate rooms. This site had primarily been used to deliver TSB's sales and distribution training. Solihull Group Management College was of similar size to Telford, with 79 bedrooms, seven lecture rooms and 11 syndicate rooms but focused upon the delivery of management skills training. The remaining residential facility, Andover, was somewhat smaller with 32 bedrooms. This site had also been used for the delivery of sales training.

To take training closer to the learner and to supplement the college facilities, the bank had also set up and utilized 20 non-residential local training sites located throughout the UK. TSB had also made use of local hotel facilities, to cater for demand, when appropriate and convenient. A major objective of Retail Training's strategy was the need to develop increased flexibility in training delivery to support the changing working patterns seen in the branch network. To achieve this the Retail Training Department needed to:

- Reduce the reliance upon the use of residential training.
- Increase the flexibility of training design.
- Increase the use of learning resource centres.
- Make greater use of technology.

To achieve these objectives, Retail Training saw open learning and distance learning methodologies as a development priority, particularly as these offered increased emphasis on productivity and efficiency of both trainer and trainee. This approach would reduce the need to take people out of the business for training (reducing the associated opportunity costs), and could maximize the value provided from Retail Training's budget.

TSB's existing open learning delivery methods

Besides the residential facilities at Solihull, Telford and Andover and the regional training sites, TSB had used a range of open learning and distance learning methods to provide training support to its branch network. These had been used either as stand alone items or in combination with other methods. These strategies had included:

- learning resource centres;
- computer-based training;
- workbooks;
- audio.

Learning resource centres

Following initial development in 1989, TSB launched its learning resource centres (LRCs). These LRCs enabled the bank to take training out to the learner and also built upon the staffs' comfort with the use of new technologies. The LRCs were located throughout the UK and by 1994, 150 training packages were locally available. The packages were delivered through 120 multimedia workstations, 80 interactive videos and a range of linear videos, computer-based training and compact discs (CD-ROM).

Local LRC administrators were appointed for each LRC. These administrators were responsible for maintaining the currency of the training packages available at the LRC. This involved receiving and actioning centrally produced new material and updates. They also controlled the booking of LRC time for local staff and provided advice on what material was available to satisfy the individual's learning need.

Computer-based training

TSB had used a variety of computer-based training (CBT) since the late 1980s including CBT interactive video and computer-aided learning (CAL). These have supported other training and development initiatives, for example, training on branch processes and systems. Many of these packages have been developed in-house. With the exception of training on the in-branch computer systems, most CBT packages have been delivered through the LRCs.

Workbooks

Workbooks have been used to compliment LRC material or as stand-alone packages that have been primarily used in the branch network. Most of these workbooks have been produced internally and their complexity has varied according to the content. The bank had principally utilized workbooks to accommodate the need to train a large, geographically dispersed audience, within tight time scales.

Audio

Audio had limited usage within TSB as a distance learning strategy. When used, it had only supported other training methodologies, for example, being included as part of a study support pack.

Financial Planning Certificate (FPC) in TSB

The need for FPC accreditation for regulated sellers

The Financial Services Act (FSA) of 1986 was designed to provide investor protection. The Securities and Investment Board (SIB), as an agent of the Chancellor of the Exchequer, was delegated most of the powers of this Act. The SIB in turn recognized and supervised self regulatory organizations and professional bodies. These acted as the main source of authority for banks to be able to conduct investment business.

For TSB, the Personal Investment Authority (PIA) is the regulatory body that controls and monitors the standards relating to the sale of regulated products, such as life assurance, pensions and investment products. The PIA has also regularly validated and assessed the training and competency schemes used by the TSB to support its distribution network.

To meet the PIA's standards of competency, sellers of regulated products and their supervisors needed to complete FPC1, 2 and 3 and demonstrate sales competency by the 30 June 1997.

In view of the extensive and lengthy training requirements imposed, the PIA agreed transitional arrangements that allowed sellers to retain their 'competency' (and continue to sell) providing they subsequently met all other criteria, ie achievement of the FPC1, 2 and 3 examinations, by 30 June 1997.

From 1 July 1997 the PIA will not allow further criteria exceptions. Therefore sellers that had not met the PIA's requirements by this time would not be able to continue to sell, without 'direct supervision', after that date. This condition had clear implications for both the bank and the individual seller.

To ensure that the bank met the PIA's competency requirements, significant commitment was required from both TSB and it's 3,000 sellers. This commitment was particularly vital as during completion of the training programme, agreed business and personal objectives still needed to be achieved.

The Bank's FPC training strategy

TSB's retail training department was charged with providing materials and support to enable TSB's Bank Managers and Regulated Sellers to complete the required FPC training. The requirement for FPC training covered some 3,000 geographically dispersed bank managers and sellers at TSB branches throughout the UK.

Following usual design analysis, the bank reviewed a range of delivery strategies for FPC training, including traditional residential 'face-to-face' training.

It was concluded that 'face-to-face' teaching methods were inappropriate for a number of factors including cost, disruption to business continuity and training resource limitations. In view of the enormity of the FPC training requirements, it was clear that the bank did not possess sufficient numbers of in-house trainers to support such a huge programme.

On the other hand, Open Learning methods did seem appropriate because:

- As previously indicated, changing work patterns in the branch network resulted in the need for training delivery systems to compliment the needs of the business.

- The training requirements for FPC were considered to be relatively stable and primarily knowledge-based.
- Some of the target population for FPC training had already experienced the benefits of an open learning approach. Open learning had been successfully introduced within TSB before implementation of the FPC studies, for example, on a programme designed to develop inexperienced managers in core management skills (Management Skills Programme).
- The use of open learning also provided the individual with a choice of time, place and method of study. This enabled the learners to obtain some control over their learning and was generally welcomed.

The primary training solution chosen from this review therefore was open learning. This would enable nationally dispersed bank managers and sellers to complete their FPC training to time and within cost constraints, and it presented the bank with an opportunity to deliver its objectives.

The FPC open learning package: solution 1

The initial launch of FPC training was via workbooks and six satellite TV broadcasts transmitted to TSB branches. To improve the speed and quality of communications to the branch network, TSB had installed satellite links to many of its branches. With the satellite infrastructure already in place and paid for, Retail Training was able to take advantage of satellite TV for FPC training at a relatively low cost.

The workbooks were bought in from the Chartered Institute of Insurers and provided most of the training. They were supported by TSB produced broadcasts of up to one hour in duration. These incorporated a 'question and answer' session conducted by FPC trainers. Video recordings of the broadcast were also made available to all bank managers or sellers who were unable to view the original broadcast.

In the early stages of the FPC1 studies, Retail Training issued workbooks to bank managers and sellers and advised them of their examination date. This date was typically a few weeks ahead.

The requirement to complete the FPC1 examinations within a tight time frame resulted in:

- Concentrated study sessions being completed during office hours, at work or at home. This reduced the productivity of the bank managers and sellers. It also placed increased pressure on them as they were still expected to meet their personal objectives.
- The initial despatch of FPC1 material not being prepared specifically for TSB and additionally it was not produced in open learning format. It was therefore not easy to read or to assimilate within the allowed time.
- Individuals being unable to control the speed of their learning. This

posed a problem for some sellers who needed more time to assimilate the FPC material.

- The potential of the TV satellite broadcast not being fully realized as it was difficult to adequately cover the subject matter over six short broadcasts.

The FPC open learning package: solution 2

In the light of these results, Retail Training reviewed its strategy as regard FPC training and established the following fundamentals:

- to ensure that the bank was regulatory compliant;
- to ensure that the PIA principles of 'best advice' were promoted;
- to meet the PIA's competency standard within the set time scale;
- to provide bank managers and sellers with FPC accreditation and portable skills;
- to support changing work patterns seen in the branch network;
- to recognize that individuals have different learning preferences.

The last point formed a major objective within Retail Training strategy. It was thought important to provide flexibility of training delivery via a range of methodologies so that individuals had an opportunity to 'mix and match' to suit their needs. The delivery of the training solution was extended therefore to include, in addition to workbooks and satellite broadcasts, audiotapes, computer-based training, revision days and support. Trainees were also offered extended examination dates and allowed a more flexible approach to exam venue.

Workbooks

After evaluating the comments received on the suitability of the initial FPC1 workbook it was clear that the TSB needed to find an alternative to the generic, 'off-the-shelf' FPC material previously used.

Retail Training therefore decided to jointly develop new FPC material with an external company. This new material would draw on the comments received from the early FPC1 material and would be more 'user friendly' and produced in a format and style similar to that being used within the Management Skills Programme (MSP). This encouraged the learners to feel comfortable with the workbooks as it was not necessary for them to become accustomed to any differences in production style and presentation.

Workbooks were supplied to each bank manager and seller as they progressed through their remaining FPC examinations. These workbooks were held in an A4 ring binder that allowed amendments to be inserted when required to reflect budget or syllabus changes. Additionally, the material was designed in a sufficiently generic manner to allow them to be sold externally to help defray the initial development costs.

Satellite TV

Satellite TV was used to deliver 'face-to-face' training. This time broadcasts separately covered each module in the workbook. The integration of open learning with established face-to-face methods allowed bank managers and sellers to take advantage of their own preferred learning style. In addition, the TSB agreed to fund college courses of up to six months (one night per week) to support the attainment of FPC2 should this be the learners preferred learning style.

Audiotapes

One feature of today's working environment is the need to travel either to and from work or between office locations. This is considered by some to be time wasted. To utilize this time for the benefit of the learner, production of easy listening audiotapes offered an alternative and convenient method of study.

To take advantage of this opportunity, each TSB branch was provided with a presentation case containing audiotapes covering all three FPC examination papers. Bank managers and sellers were then able to access these audiotapes when required to supplement their FPC studies. Line managers and LRCs were also issued with additional copies for reference purposes.

Computer-based training

Computer-based training (CBT) on the FPC was made available through the TSB's national network of LRCs. This method of learning had been used for a range of other training initiatives and had proved to be highly successful. Again the learners' familiarity with the technology encouraged its usage and acceptance.

Revision days

To support preparation for the FPC examinations, revision days were provided for each learner some seven to ten days before the examination date. These revision days were available at a number of locations throughout the country and facilitated by an expert FPC trainer. The revision days were designed to supplement the previous learning and allow the learner to achieve the extra marks that could ensure examination success. They also provided a forum to raise questions and allay concerns. Brief revision notes were issued at these events. External trainers were used for this purpose.

Examination preference

An important feature of the open learning package was the choice of examination date and venue. This increased flexibility was well appreciated by the students as it facilitated a planned approach to the study, allowing for consideration of business and or domestic issues. Line managers and central control units of course monitored progress to ensure completion of examinations.

Miscellaneous support

A central library of recommended reading was created and made available to students who wished to undertake wider reading on the subject.

A non-technical helpline was also established to deal with logistical issues and remove an area of concern for students. A technical fax helpline was also established to receive and respond to individual content queries that the learner could not resolve. This helpline worked within a guaranteed response time and was available to all TSB managers and sellers.

Benefits of an open learning approach

Benefits to TSB

This approach to open learning maximized in-branch productivity and reduced the study time taken in the branches, for example, by using audiotapes while travelling to and from work. The supportive approach generated goodwill amongst bank managers and sellers. This was particularly beneficial in helping individuals achieve their personal goals.

The completion of FPC through open learning methods significantly reduced the number of FPC designated trainers that would have been needed by the bank, and in turn reduced Retail Training's overall budgetary requirements. In addition, as the training could be completed locally, further cost savings accrued on travel expenses (as there was no need to travel to residential facilities). Furthermore the in-house design and production of training material proved significantly cheaper than the cost of purchasing externally produced, generic training material.

The initial population targeted for FPC training were bank managers. After they experienced the benefits of using the LRCs, the bank managers were better able to take the lead in encouraging their own staff to study at the LRC. Therefore, the bank managers' influential position in the branch network led to a great number of branch staff using the LRC facilities for FPC training and to satisfy their other personal development needs. The support offered by line management for FPC training and their willingness to release people to complete the training further embedded the training culture in the branch network.

The design of open learning material enabled individuals to complete the learning in their own time by choice. This reduced potential resistance to the learning process as it allowed individuals to learn at home should they prefer this option. Examination results were considerably better than initially antici-pated by the bank, allowing the bank to move toward the achievement of the PIA's competency requirements within the designated time scale.

The FPC materials were produced in the same style and livery as the MSP materials, causing it to be seen by some bank managers as part of their con-tinuing management development. This not only fostered a 'corporate' iden-tity for the training material but, more importantly, drew upon the positive perceptions of MSP, which in turn made reactions to the FPC material favour-able. The provision of study and learning support for a portable qualification was appreciated by bank managers and sellers and it supported the perception of the bank being a caring organization.

Benefits to the learner

The use of open learning minimized the time bank managers and sellers were taken out of the business for study. This therefore enabled them to maximize the time they could spend on the achievement of their personal objectives. The flexibility of examination time scales and study options ena-bled the learner to take charge of the process and feel empowered. This approach catered for individual learning styles and maximized individual commitment.

These choices and options encouraged a 'personal development' atmos-phere as opposed to a 'teaching' environment. The benefits of this can be seen in the considerable number of people continuing their studies beyond FPC3 to Advanced FPC as part of their continuing personal development.

Consideration of the individuals' personal commitments by the use of flex-ible learning options has resulted in staff feeling valued. It has also shown that support is available from the TSB if needed (as evidenced in the provision of two 'help lines'). Should an individual fail their FPC examination using one method of study, they can of course draw on other forms of study not previ-ously used. The TSB also allowed bank managers and sellers who failed their FPC examinations to attend a one week, residential course to assist their preparations for a re-sit. The revision days proved to be a highly successful aid to study and certainly gave confidence to learners. Weaknesses highlighted on the revision days could be resolved in time for the examination. Popularity of the revision days increased as the word spread of their value to the student.

Commitments required by an open learning approach

From the TSB

The provision of a variety of study options caused additional administrative work for the bank, particularly in the recording and delivery of learner preferences. The flexibility provided to the learners also resulted in the need for close monitoring of examination passes. This monitoring was essential to ensure that the PIA time scales were met. Obviously the costs of providing a comprehensive range of flexible learning solutions were greater than that which would have been incurred by simply providing a single training solution. However, recoveries from selling the FPC material to other companies, combined with the benefits of the increased pass rates generated, clearly outweighed the higher setting up costs.

From the learners

Initially some learners, who had only experienced imposed, planned training programmes, found the freedom to choose and arrange their own FPC study plan difficult to manage. However, once the benefits of the new approach became apparent and the need for self discipline established, most learners welcomed the situation. Because of other business pressures, study sometimes needed to be completed away from work and in the students' personal time.

Reactions to the use of open learning

Trainers

Because the FPC training fell outside the normal remit of in-house trainers, use of open learning techniques, as opposed to traditional residential training, did not pose a threat to the TSB's existing trainer population. Furthermore, the trainers were not technically equipped, in sufficient numbers, to provide national FPC training coverage. Therefore the in-house trainers accepted the use of open learning methods without resistance.

Bank managers and sellers

As the FPC training was launched, TSB was undertaking a restructure of its Retail Banking operation. The bank's move to a Bancassurance structure strongly suggested that individuals with Bancassurance skills would be highly prized in the reformed organization. Therefore the attainment of the FPC examinations was seen by bank managers and sellers as vital to their future career development. This factor, and the desirability of obtaining a portable qualification overcame sellers' concerns regarding the high level of commitment required to achieve the necessary FPC qualifications, particularly when they still had to achieve personal and business objectives.

Others

Line managers in the branch network welcomed the use of open learning to support the attainment of FPC accreditation, especially as it minimized reductions in the productivity of bank managers and sellers during their study periods. Indeed many line managers decided to take advantage of the quality of the material and support provided by completing the FPC examinations themselves. This situation was replicated in other functional departments and in various business units, as managers and staff saw success in the FPC examinations as beneficial to their own personal development.

Validation and evaluation of TSB's approach

Validation

Validation of the FPC materials can be assessed by comparing the success enjoyed by TSB with FPC examination passes to those rates achieved by others within the insurance industry. When assessing the results and making comparisons it must be noted that TSB's target populations for FPC training were 'traditional bankers', as opposed to the usual industry population of experienced insurance salespeople. In addition, many of the TSB sellers were quite young and inexperienced when compared to long-term sellers of insurance.

In these circumstances the results obtained from the TSB would be expected to be significantly lower than those experienced from insurance

Table 2.1   Financial planning certificate pass rates (%).

	FPC1	FPC2	FPC3
TSB pass rate	67	63	73
Narrow fail (within 10% of pass)	17	32	17
National industry average pass rate	74	69	60

companies. However, the results at the TSB compare very favourably as indicated in Table 2.1.

Evaluation

Full and meaningful evaluation can only occur after a reasonable time but early indications are that the quality of the TSB's regulated sales business has improved and increased. This would suggest that the sellers now have greater self confidence and moreover, better product knowledge.

The support given to students and the flexibility of study offered has generated high levels of goodwill amongst staff. Evidence is coming through of people developing themselves beyond the minimum PIA requirement. This indicates that the learning process was well received and coordinated. The TSB of course continues to provide support to the individuals as appropriate.

Conclusions

The PIA requirement to complete FPC training amongst the TSB's regulated sales force by 30 June 1997 imposed a considerable commitment on both the bank and its sellers. The main commitment for the bank has been the cost of developing the FPC training solutions, together with the opportunity cost of taking its sellers out of the business for periods to complete their studies.

However, this cost should be compared to what would have been the cost, in terms of actual pounds sterling and disruption to the business, if the FPC training had been conducted by traditional 'face-to-face' residential courses. Moreover, the training has ensured that the PIA's requirements have been met. This has provided the TSB with a highly motivated and more skilled sales force who are better able to provide 'best advice' to their customers and importantly has allowed the TSB to retain its licence to sell regulated products.

With this in mind, open learning has proved to be a highly effective and relatively inexpensive method of training large numbers of bank managers and sellers, in a short period of time. The bank has also been able to sell the FPC material it has developed, recouping some of the initial development costs.

Some of the major preconditions for success of the bank's FPC training strategy were:

- the training strongly supported the bank's move to Bancassurance and provided the learners with skills vital to their continued career development;
- the organizational structure was such that training deliverers (who might have felt threatened by open learning methods) were not normally involved in the training development process;

- the scale and nature of the task was not one that the conventional trainers could take on;
- the training solutions provided met the needs and learning preferences of the target population;
- the bank decided not to take people out of the business (whenever possible) during completion of their FPC studies;
- the encouragement and support provided to line managers for the completion of their own FPC studies ensured they appreciated the complexity of the material and the study needs of their direct reports. This in turn increased line managers' support to bank managers and sellers.

The TSB's approach to FPC studies has developed staff learning skills and reinforced open learning as a preferred learning methodology for both the business and staff. The re-focusing of strategy after the initial FPC1 material launch not only showed the TSB's ability to develop its own open learning material but more importantly, that the views and needs of the learners were valued and acted upon.

Since the roll out of the FPC material, the lessons learned have been successfully incorporated into other in-house training solutions, building upon the experience gained from the FPC programme.

Chapter 3

Corporate context and cultural change: distance learning in BT

Stephen Brown

Corporate context

BT is an organization that has experienced massive change over the last decade. Prior to 1984, BT enjoyed the position of an almost total monopoly supplier of telecoms services to the UK market. Since then the pressures of aggressive competition, regulation, and economic recession have required the company to invest significantly in new technology, to reduce staff levels dramatically, to restructure massively and to overhaul completely its attitudes to customers and service. These changes have required new skills, attitudes, knowledge and ways of working with an almost continuous need for updating and retraining of the workforce, including managers and customer facing staff, as well as engineers.

Traditionally, BT training needs were met largely through conventional face-to-face training, but from the early 1980s this began to change. In an organization this size (250,000 employees in total in 1984) it was not difficult to make the case for a distance learning training strategy based on the economics of mass training. From the early 1980s, the company gradually built up an extensive in-house distance learning design, production, distribution and support capability: a national network of over 300 workstations spread over 39 learning centres and business units throughout the UK and a financial investment of around £30 million. At its peak there was a dedicated full-time staff of over 40 people, producing distance learning packages for all kinds of staff: clerical, administrative, management, sales, engineering, research, etc, covering a wide range of subjects, skills and issues. The range of media included printed text, audio and video cassette, satellite broadcast TV, CBT, interactive video (IV) and CD-ROM-based multimedia. By 1995 this had been disbanded as part of a company wide down-sizing process, although in 1996 there were signs of regrowth. This chapter reviews the circumstances that brought about such changes and tries to draw some lessons from them.

Although BT (formerly the Post Office) had a long tradition of media-based learning, including printed text, video, and computer-based materials, distance learning in BT had two separate and distinct origins, reflecting the then structure of BT Training. In the early 1980s BT Training was made up of three separate colleges dealing with Technical, Management, and Sales and Marketing training respectively. The colleges were largely autonomous, located on widely separated sites and had very different traditions and values. Nevertheless the way in which they related to the business and developed training courses was broadly similar. Business units, anticipating a need for training, for example to launch a new product, would approach the relevant college(s) and request a new training programme. The colleges were subdivided into design and delivery teams along subject specialist lines and the sponsor would therefore approach a particular subject team directly.

The colleges were responsible for developing, publicizing and delivering the training. Other business units would contract to send their staff on these training courses once the latter were available. Sponsors were expected to pay for course development, while users were expected to pay for course delivery. Management training was slightly different in that senior managers within the college themselves took a view about some of the training needs and initiated courses centrally. But within the college the system of specialist teams working to identified business units was much the same. In addition, the central training activity was supported and supplemented by local trainers within each of the BT regional districts. Local trainers helped to identify training needs in their part of the organization, sourced training courses from within and outwith BT and developed and delivered courses of their own, tailored to local demands.

Not surprisingly, the technical college was the first to seriously consider exploiting the potential of computer-based learning to provide routine training and assessment for large numbers of technical apprentices. In the early 1980s it established a computer-based training (CBT) design and production unit in-house. A few years later the management college came to a similar conclusion and established its own separate distance learning group, based on interactive video (IV) technology which at that time was just becoming available in the UK. Apart from the use of computers to support training, the two units had little in common.

The Technical CBT unit, which numbered 20 people at its peak, was set up to produce and manage in-house courses tailored to the specific needs of BT technical people. It employed a proprietary hardware and software system: WICAT (World Institute for Computer-Aided Training). Training packages were designed in outline on paper by a team of designers, with reference to a system of computer-based templates that rendered the process highly efficient. Paper designs were passed to a larger team of keyboard specialists, or 'inputters', who had detailed working knowledge of the WICAT authoring system, for processing into working programmes. The finished courses were held on servers and students accessed them via terminals in dedicated learning centres on site at the technical college. Requests for CBT courses came mainly from the other subject specialist training units within the college. The courses were carefully designed in conjunction with these units to be integral components of larger programmes of study. Students were scheduled through a series of lectures, practical workshops and CBT sessions.

The courses themselves were of the drill-and-practice type. Students were required to answer successfully multiple choice questions at the end of each section within a course. Failure to achieve a specified threshold of correct responses resulted in the learner being routed back to the beginning of the section in question for restudy. Three successive failures caused the programme to lock the student out and refer them to their course tutor. As such therefore, these courses were not really distance learning or open learning, more programmed learning, but a good example of embedded or integrated technology-based training.

Staff within the CBT unit were drawn mainly from existing BT Technical Training personnel, each with their own subject specialism and a track record in training. They in turn had been recruited mainly from business units within the company. So all of the members of the unit were well known to their colleagues in the other training units within the college and respected by them. The Distance Learning Unit (DLU), as set up in the BT Management training college, was not conceived initially to be a production unit. The idea was that IV training packages would be designed and produced by external companies, working to specifications provided by BT and managed by in-house project managers. The unit was established originally as a small (two person) team consisting a BT trainer with a long career record in BT and a new manager recruited directly from education, ie with no company background, or previous track record within the Management college.

The medium of interactive video helped to distinguish the product in the minds of the target audience from the kinds of CBT used by non management grades and it was felt the 'multimedia' (the term was not then in common use) properties of IV would lend themselves well to management training tasks. In the early 1980s the IBM PC was not yet available, so the first experimental IV systems that were introduced were based on BBC desktop computers.

The first few titles developed were on generic topics, such as the BT network or safety. Unlike the technical training CBT courses, they were not produced to standard templates. External companies were contracted for their design and production and so each ended up with quite a different feel. Also, they were not conceived as an integral part of conventional courses and, although they included self-assessment questions, these were for personal feedback only, and failure to answer the questions correctly did not result in the learners being barred from further progress. Learners could study the different sections in any order and as often as they liked, dipping in and out of sections as they felt appropriate. The underlying model of learner behaviour was quite different from the philosophy applied to technical training. The prevailing view in technical training was that technical grades needed to be told what they should learn, then taught it in a straightforward, didactic way, then tested on their recall and understanding and either passed as competent, or referred back for revision. The management training philosophy was that managers were responsible for their own development needs; were capable of making judgements about what they needed to learn, when, how much and at what pace. Management training therefore was much better suited to an open or distance learning approach, whereas technical training was modelled more on a programmed learning approach.

Within their own environments each approach was judged to be a success. The CBT unit became firmly established as a component part of the technical training provision, while the initial IV trials were regarded sufficiently positively to justify further investment. A decision was taken to switch to PCs as the delivery platforms, to establish delivery workstations in some of the regional training centres and to develop an application that for the first time would be targeted at a core area of training.

Appraisal and counselling

Within the context of so much organizational change, regular and effective appraisal and feedback on staff performance was essential, yet evaluations of appraisal and counselling practice revealed unacceptable shortcomings in the quality of the process. In 1987 it was decided to redesign the BT management Appraisal and Counselling training course. The original course was run as a three day face-to-face event. Students would travel from all over the UK to a residential training location for a series of lectures, seminars and workshop sessions. After redesign, the course was presented as a multimedia package comprising an interactive video disc with a video cassette introduction and a one day follow-up workshop delivered locally with further video and text elements. To facilitate local delivery, a new infrastructure of interactive video workstations was installed in BT training locations around the UK, under the control of local training managers.

The introductory video cassette gave potential students and their line managers an overview of the course and a feel for what the interactive video component would be like. A presenter showed extracts from the IV and explained how to navigate around in it. The interactive video introduced the purpose and principles of appraisal and counselling, it explained the procedures involved and the knowledge and concepts relevant to the subject and provided opportunities for skills practice through question and answer sessions. The follow-up workshop gave managers an opportunity to review and discuss the main points presented in the IV, to relate them to their own particular circumstances and to practise their skills through role plays.

The new course was evaluated thoroughly during the first year of presentation via a combination of postal questionnaires, structured interviews with users and follow up analysis of the impact of the training on performance. It was clear from the user surveys that the course was well received by both managers (as trainees) and local trainers. A majority of managers felt that they had gained much from the course in terms of its four stated aims and almost 90% of respondents felt that the training was 'highly' or 'very' appropriate to their needs. Over 80% of managers felt that the course had increased their confidence and ability to appraise and counsel their staff.

Approximately half the respondents said the course as a whole was interesting and fun, they liked learning from the IV. Trainers with experience of using the course also felt very positive about it and considered the methods to be effective in preparing managers for their appraisal and counselling activities. Even managers with many years' experience of appraisal and counselling reported that something new had been learned from this course (Kirkwood, 1991).

It is not unusual to get favourable feedback shortly after a training course has been completed; it is another matter to discover how effective the training has been. After 18 months a follow up study was conducted to assess the actual impact of the appraisal and counselling course. Comparative analysis of appraisal forms completed before and after training showed a significant improvement in the way in which appraisals have been conducted, with much more and better quality information being recorded on the forms. Managers interviewed about their recent experiences of appraising and counselling indicated that the value and purpose of the process had become much clearer as a result of the training. Most had tried to make the counselling interview more positive and forward looking than had previously been the case and were able to report new ways in which they planned, conducted and reported on the interview sessions. Some had given their staff a clearer explanation of the purpose of the interviews in order that they should approach the situation more positively and be better prepared for participation (Kirkwood, 1993).

Cultural change

The success of the appraisal and counselling IV was apparent even before the evaluation study was complete. It was shown that, compared with the previous face-to-face version of the course, the new course had saved the company approximately £1.8million in the first 18 months (Brown, 1990). This success became the trigger for BT to expand its programme of interactive video-based training packages and its in-house design and production capacity. Again the new recruits came from outside the company and were selected on the basis of their understanding of learning design issues, technical computing skills and knowledge of interactive video, not their knowledge of telecommunications or BT. The intention was that the new recruits would work in the same way as the original members of the unit, managing externally placed contracts. In fact, the addition of the new members began to change the character of the unit and the way in which it worked.

Although external contracts were still placed for all projects, more of the design, and then production work, began to be undertaken in-house. This was partly a direct consequence of employing specialists with design, computing and teaching skills and partly due to the need to control the costs and quality of the training packages being produced by the external contractors. The unit also began to expand its remit, developing materials in print, audio and video initially and then looking at the possibilities of CD-ROM as a replacement for interactive video. An in-house desktop publishing team was recruited and trained and a video production unit was incorporated from another part of the management college. The team began to establish links with BT research laboratories looking at the potential of digital video storage for networked delivery (the beginnings of 'video-on-demand'), and with an outside development house to design and produce an 'audio plinth' that would enable sound to be added easily to the PCs (this was before the first 'off-the-peg' sound cards were produced).

Throughout the late 1980s the unit continued to expand through amalgamation with other teams, culminating in 1990 with a merger with the Technical training college CBT unit, which introduced into technical training new ideas about training design, new technologies and a new pioneering spirit. Steps were taken to migrate the technical training CBT products from WICAT to PC-based systems; new, industry standard, authoring tools were introduced, external production companies were brought in to assist with design and production and the role of the 'inputters' was radically changed, converting most of them to desktop publishers. In other words, the values and working methods of the management college were transposed to the technical college. Not surprisingly this was not an entirely smooth process, and some responded more favourably to these changes than others.

By this time the Distance Learning Group (DLG), as it was then known, had grown to around 40 members and there were over 130 IV workstations in over 50 different UK locations throughout BT Training, local training units and within various business units (see Figure 3.1).

Yet despite this apparent success, or perhaps because of it, all was not well. Within management training there were growing signs of resistance to distance learning. For example, despite the proven effectiveness of the revised appraisal and counselling course, the training group responsible for appraisal and counselling training went on to make further changes to the course that, while they were improvements, it could be argued that they did not add significantly to its overall effectiveness. Other training groups showed a reluctance to allow parts of their courses to be converted to distance learning format, and when pressed, offered up only peripheral elements of their training programmes for conversion. Arguments used against distance learning were: that learners preferred face-to-face events, line managers found it

Interactive Video (IV) Workstations in BT

Key

● IV workstations location

Figure 3.1   Interactive video workstations in BT

difficult to manage a situation where someone was present at their desk or at least in the same building, but was not available for work because they were training on a distance learning package, sponsors did not like having to fund the heavy, up-front, delivery costs of distance learning and trainers felt that while it may be suitable for other topics, their own was best delivered by conventional means.

Progressive selling

In fairness, not all of the IV training packages were well received. Later designs were increasingly ambitious in their design, entirely replacing face-to-face courses, catering for various kinds of learners, maximizing choice of study routes, offering varieties of types of assessments and moving beyond teaching facts, concepts and procedural skills into subtler areas to do with interpersonal communication skills. For example, an interactive video called 'Progressive Selling' was developed to replace a centrally delivered training course for experienced sales staff. The stated learning objectives were to teach more advanced sales techniques based on an understanding of human behavioural types. There was, however, a hidden agenda. It was believed by the training sponsor that although many sales team leaders were in need of refresher training, they would not be willing to acknowledge this need in case it affected their status and authority. Secondly it was thought that although team leaders should be more involved in the development of their staff, this objective would meet resistance if stated explicitly.

The training package was developed as a scenario in which learners were asked to imagine themselves as a new member of a sales team. It had four sections intended to simulate items and events that are part of normal best practice in a sales team:

- *coaching sessions* provided straight tuition on topics related to the learning objectives of the package, followed by multiple choice tests;
- *observation exercises* allowed learners to watch and comment on a series of sales visits;
- *simulation exercises* provided learners with opportunities to manage their own sales interviews.

Feedback was given as:

- numerical scores and commentary on answers to the quizzes in the tutorials;
- feedback on comments made during the observation exercises;
- outcomes of the simulation role plays;
- commentary on the dialogue choices made during the simulation role plays.

Progressive selling was trialled with around 30 BT sales people across several sales groups in the south of England. Pilot groups were initially only lukewarm to the idea of a technology-based training package, questioning the likely learning effectiveness of computer-based materials in the context of sales skills training. Line managers anticipated difficulties with scheduling their staff through the package and had reservations about the possibly disruptive effect of the training on the smooth workings of their sales teams. During the trials it became apparent that there were a number of significant barriers to successful learning.

1. Faced with a choice between following up a new sales lead, or visiting a BT learning centre, most sales staff could be expected to look to their bonus and cancel their training booking. To deal with this problem an alternative set of six workstations was established in the pilot areas for sole use by the sales force, but in the event these were so widely spaced that distance became a barrier to convenient access.
2. Sales training events were usually held in quality hotel venues, with recreational facilities, good meals and the opportunity to mix with colleagues. Attendance at such events was viewed by many delegates as a reward for good performance. Technology-based learning offered no such attractions and was mildly threatening for most sales staff who had little or no experience of using computers.
3. The package was intended to encourage self reliant, exploratory, experiential learning, in line with BT management values. But learners experienced difficulties in knowing where to start and what to do next. They also got confused about the differences between each of the various sections and what they were required to do in each section.
4. Finally, few sales people could agree on how best to tackle any of the scenarios included. Selling turned out to be a much more idiosyncratic and personal process than was possible to encapsulate on an IV disc.

Corporate context revisited

Despite occasional setbacks such as progressive selling, the DLG went on to produce over 30 hours of interactive video-based training materials, workbooks, audio and video cassettes. Several of the products won national training media design awards, the group became well known in human resource circles as a centre of excellence, received many visitors and was even consulted by the UK Government Cabinet Office for advice on technology-based learning. Yet this success was against a background of major corporate changes. In 1987 the company employed 250,000 people. By 1994 that total had been reduced to 150,000, with further reductions targeted over the following five years. It had not been possible to reduce staff numbers so dramatically without considerable structural reorganization and reallocation of responsibilities and this inevitably had a knock-on effect on the training needs of the organization. It temporarily depressed demand for training while business units restructured and so added to the pressures on BT Training to downsize. Management training was moved to another part of the corporate structure, leaving the DLG behind in BT Training, which was effectively under the control of Technical training. A business process re-engineering exercise rapidly followed that aimed at integrating the DLG with the rest of training. Functions such as management and support of the national network of learning centres were hived off, managers with more conventional BT career histories were introduced and the pioneering specialists brought in from outside by the management college were encouraged to seek broader career paths outside the unit.

Lessons learned

By 1994 the Distance Learning Group had been disbanded, all the externally recruited specialists had left the company and the materials themselves were relatively little used. To understand why, it is useful to examine the situation from a variety of viewpoints:

- learners;
- line managers;
- training sponsors;
- trainers;
- the company perspective.

Learners

Despite general enthusiasm for technology-based training, learners nevertheless have some reservations. *Isolation* is a problem. BT people have frequently reported that they do not like studying on their own because of the lack of social contact and learning support. *Time off* for self study is harder to obtain than time off for residential or day schools. *The credibility* of self teach packages is not as high as face-to-face training events. *The reward element* of a few days away from the pressures of work at a comfortable hotel or training centre is lacking. Learners expect the *delivery infrastructure* to be sufficiently well developed to provide *convenient access*. Learners don't like to be presented with *too many choices* about the learning event. They prefer to be told what to study and how to study it. *Learner support* should be readily available for those who need help or who disagree with part of the course.

Line managers

Credibility of self teach methods is an issue for line managers too. They are concerned that they may be drawn into the training and assessment activity and *acquire unwelcome extra responsibilities*. Distance learning *cannot be used to reward* good employees in the way that residential courses in an attractive hotel can.

Training sponsors

Training sponsors in BT commission new courses, have the budget to pay for their creation and commit the target audience to study them. Delivery is paid for by the operational unit sending its people for training. From the sponsor's point of view therefore: distance learning is *expensive* compared with face-to-face training because the *development costs* of face-to-face training are much lower than for distance learning, even though the delivery costs are much higher.

Trainers

Trainers are concerned that distance learning may *de-skill their roles* and lead to *redundancies*. Alternatively, some trainers are concerned that if their honed and polished pet lecture is revamped in multimedia format, freeing them up for more individual tuition, then their *jobs will become more demanding*.

   Trainers need to *trust* their distance learning colleagues. The levels of trust in technical training were high because the conventional trainers and the CBT designers were well known to each other, shared the same career experiences and company values and collaborated closely to produce a product that supplemented the face-to-face training activity rather than threatened it. The situation in the management college was quite the reverse.

The company perspective

The value of technology-based learning in a company the size of BT is unquestionable. However, the costs and benefits really only show up when a company-wide perspective is taken. For example, studies in BT have shown that distance learning, when used appropriately, can be much cheaper per student day than face-to-face tuition (Brown, 1994). Table 3.1 summarizes the cost comparisons of different media used for training in BT, compared with the *per diem* cost of conventional tutor led training.

   However, because of the high development costs of technology-based training, use of this approach makes the training budget seem very high. The

Table 3.1   Comparison of daily costs of training by different media and size of audience (£).

Media	Number of people in the audience						
	100	500	1,000	2,000	3,000	5,000	10,000
Tutor-led delivery	158	158	158	158	158	158	158
Workbook	140	36	23	17	14	13	11
Workbook and audio	283	67	40	27	22	18	16
Workbook and video	355	83	49	32	26	22	18
Workbook, video and audio	498	114	66	42	34	28	23
CBT	434	98	56	35	28	22	18
CD-ROM	1,255	263	56	35	28	22	18
IV	1,860	388	204	112	82	57	39

problem lies in *the way costs and benefits are apportioned.* BT operates on the basis of local cost centres. The company has been downsizing for some years and so cost centres have been required to reduce their budgets. Under these circumstances the development costs of technology-based training stand out as *an obvious target for reduction.*

Despite these complicating factors, the economics are such that technology-based learning, used appropriately, cannot be resisted indefinitely and the emergence of cheap, high performance hardware is bringing the necessary infrastructure rapidly within reach of very large numbers of people. One has only to look at the phenomenal growth of the Internet to realize that we are only a short step away from being able to access learning materials on almost any topic from all around the world at the click of a mouse. When that happens, many of the organizational barriers to technology-based training will be set aside, freeing us up to concentrate on the real learning issues.

References

Brown, S (1990) 'It ain't what you do, it's the way that you do it', in *Computers in Education,* A McDougall, and C Dowling (eds), Elsevier Science Publishers BV, Holland.

Brown, S (1994) 'Turbulence, training and telematics', *Journal of Educational Television,* 20(3), 135–50.

Kirkwood, A (1991) 'Interaction upon interaction: combining interactive video and group sessions in management training', *Computers in Adult Education and Training,* 2(3), 174–85.

Kirkwood, A (1993) 'Bearing fruit: the longer-term effects of management training using interactive video', *Educational and Training Technology International,* 30(4), 343–53.

Chapter 4

From pioneers to settlers: the Abbey National

Julian Wakeley

Introduction

This case study reviews the eight-year implementation and development process in Abbey National of a Distance Learning approach. By the mid eighties Abbey National was Britain's number two building society with assets exceeding £14 billion and 12,000 staff in 700 locations. At this time the building society movement was under considerable strain. Competition by the Government for funds meant increasingly competitive National Savings issues, putting banks under pressure to seek more secure and high yielding forms of lending, as opposed to risky corporate finance. Banks responded by becoming more active in the home lending and personal savings arenas.

While pressure from the banks and other institutions meant that the traditional markets of the building societies were being eroded, the industry was constrained by the Building Societies Act 1962, which restricted the sources of funds and the types of loans building societies could make to the public. A new Act was proposed and was enacted upon in 1986, which freed building societies to offer personal loans, operate 'proper' current accounts and enter the area of corporate finance.

About the same time, the Abbey National head office was relocated to Milton Keynes and key, experienced, employees left the company. The resulting serious gaps in the company knowledge and expertise base threw the demand for centralized, consistent, training into sharp relief. It is in this context that Abbey National became interested in other forms of learning. Abbey National had had positive experiences of using computers in the human resources field; it was one of the first companies to have computerized succession planning done in a systematic way and the then Personnel General

Manager was keen to apply computers to training. Up until 1985 Abbey National had used traditional forms of learning, either conducted internally on residential training courses in hotels or in the Head Offices in London and Milton Keynes. Unlike most of the other, larger, banking institutions, they did not have a Management Development Training Centre, though from time to time this had been considered, then rejected on the grounds of cost. By mid-1985 it had become apparent that within Abbey National that there were various training issues that were not being communicated as effectively as possible due to the widely dispersed nature of the employee base, limitations on the availability of locations and the commitment of some local management. On top of this, the 1986 Act opened up opportunities for Abbey National to move into new ventures, which would increase the amount of training required still further.

A new training director was appointed who saw migration to distance learning as a way of possibly catching up on training provision and of moving forward with new ways of learning. The decision was taken to investigate whether distance learning, using computer-based training (CBT), could be a viable addition to the traditional training methods employed at the time, or even in some instances an acceptable alternative. At this stage CBT was seen as a supplement to existing, mainly technical, training provision.

1986: the pilot project

An internal training development budget was established and work commenced with the UK National Computing Centre (NCC) to produce a project plan for a six-month pilot, starting in early 1986. The pilot would investigate:

- Was CBT an effective training mechanism (did it work)?
- Was CBT appropriate for the culture in Abbey National (would it work in Abbey National)?
- What type of programmes would be suited to CBT?
- What authoring systems or languages would be best?
- What platform would be best, given Abbey National's platform strategy?

Two alternative proprietary CBT development and delivery systems were reviewed. One was a videotext system similar to PRESTEL. This employed what was then a new authoring package called DISC TUTOR to generate text and graphics that could be displayed on a screen. The other was a DOS-based authoring package called TenCORE that could generate applications that ran on high performance (by 1986 standards) personal computers. At the time, Abbey National, along with many other financial organizations, used PRESTEL to deliver insurance quotations to dedicated proprietary terminals in branches. The PC route was actually a higher risk as no one in Abbey National had really used PCs at that time.

Over the six month period of the pilot, two courses were developed in parallel to run on both systems; one on insurance, the other on health and safety. At the end of this period they were each installed into 12 sites located around the country for user trials. After three months trialling in each location staff were interviewed and the results fed through and collated together with views of the developers of both systems.

It was found that whilst the PRESTEL system was effective on the trials and also offered facilities for software distribution and learner management, the level of graphics, the amount of data corruption in the information, as well as inconsistency in display speeds meant that it was not practical for a wider roll out (sometimes response was slow, at other times it was fast). The result was that Abbey National went forward with purchase of dedicated PCs for training, using TenCORE as the authoring system. With hindsight, this fitted with the long-term strategy of the business in terms of a move towards PCs, even though in 1989 the wider adoption of PCs into the mainstream business was still some three years away.

Following selection of appropriate computer hardware and a consulting company to co-develop some titles, production began. The list of titles was drawn up from meetings with trainers in the business, as well as from a 'shopping list' of courses needing to be addressed that had been in existence for some time. Care was taken to ensure that trainers were never given the impression that CBT was going to replace the way most courses were run at that time. There were a lot of new training topic areas that needed to be addressed that did not affect the existing trainers apart from in the areas of IT and procedural/technical training. At this time there were only two Abbey National staff directly involved plus a few consultants and it was envisaged that most of the development work would be carried out externally. The internal staff reported to the training manager as part of the technical training area, but were housed in a completely separate building some five miles away. This caused some 'them and us' tensions as the team grew and began to attract publicity from the training and computer press. Over the next eight years the team expanded to 15 staff and, at various times, tens of consultants, eventually taking over technical training when more training was going out by CBT than by conventional means.

1987–90: implementation

Abbey National was one of the first organizations in the UK to move from overnight batch processing to a real-time computer network. By the mid-1980s a complex network had been installed that enabled the branch mini-computers to communicate directly with the central computer facility in Milton Keynes on a real-time basis, with updates to software and operating systems happening overnight, or in some instances during the working day.

However the terminals connected to the branch processors were not suitable for delivery of the new CBT materials. The new training delivery platforms were to be separate, dedicated, stand alone PCs, located in 400 of the larger offices where they could be accessed fairly easily by staff from smaller locations. They were not linked to the head office because there was not any PC-based communication path in the IT system, and modems were rather hit and miss at this time. Even if there had been a suitable network path, it is likely that it would have been one way – from the centre out to the locations – as opposed to from the locations back to head office. As a result Abbey National relied on floppy disks as the means of software distribution and retrieval of local performance and management data on students and courses. As most branches of the company had between ten and 50 staff only (not the 100 or so that could be in a clearing bank) the numbers of machines per location were kept low (up to a maximum of three). Location of the PCs was left to local management. Rather than being placed in a special learning centre environment configuration, they were allocated on a floor by floor basis, depending on location and need. In some instances the machines were placed in corridors. In some other cases managers relocated the machines to their own offices so that they could re-purpose them for their own needs. This was possible because the new machines were dedicated solely to CBT delivery, so there was plenty of disk space to accommodate other software (eg word processing, databases) and there were significant periods of time when the equipment was idle. As it happened, the business case for the equipment had been justified over a period of three years, based on five major training initiatives, so this down time was still cost effective. But it soon became apparent that dedicated equipment was not the appropriate way forward.

This realization coincided with the introduction of other personal computers into the branch network for business purposes by mid 1988. In many ways this was a stroke of luck. The company could just as easily have opted for a UNIX environment, leaving the CBT PCs isolated. However, this was the opportunity to implement a more coherent approach to distance learning and CBT, linked to business applications on the branch PC network. A PC menu was created to allow the running of CBT programmes on the new business machines, removing the requirement for so much dedicated equipment. Hence the plan to roll out a dedicated CBT PC to each of the 700 locations was shelved mid way through 1988, and for the remainder of the period of this study Abbey National concentrated on developing solutions to run on these business machines.

Aligning the training delivery platforms to a business system meant that the resources of the company IT systems area could then be utilized properly for the first time, for example for testing and software distribution. There were disadvantages as well as gains from this strategy. Since testing had to include proper systems testing with live applications, this meant restricting when a program could be released since it had to pass various conformity tests. This had not been a problem previously. Moving to non dedicated platforms created a new set of problems concerning software and hardware conflicts between the requirements of the different applications and creating the right conditions for learning. It also meant that the CBT group had to liaise more closely with the business IT team.

Up to this point the major thrust was to get CBT programmes out as fast as possible in order to get to a critical mass. This was understandable at the time but with hindsight it was recognized that along with the development of CBT packages, Abbey National needed to ascertain whether students were:

- taking the courses;
- able to access the programmes in the most efficient and simple way possible;
- passing the programmes, or having difficulties.

In retrospect this mix of priorities was incorrect and more time should have been spent in creating a learner management system that would work across networks from the start. Instead Abbey National had to re-write the system several times, while retaining backwards compatibility with previous course programs and management systems and hardware configurations. However, the end result of this painful process of evolution was an effective learning management system where the cost of development was probably only 1% of the actual cost of the software (CBT programs) that it supported.

It later transpired that the data that was captured by the learning management system was not being used at a local level and, when it was reviewed, indicated that local utilization of CBT was poor. As a result there was a period in mid 1989 when the whole issue of its viability could have been brought into question. Fortunately this period coincided with two key events. Firstly the publication of a Coopers and Lybrand report on the costs of computer-based learning (Coopers & Lybrand, 1989) showed that the cost of CBT at Abbey National was only £4 per topic (or £25 if you included the PC), compared to between £75 and £150 for an equivalent programme delivered traditionally by a trainer. Great play was also made of the 'fire station' analogy: although the machines were only used for a fraction of the day they were still cost effective, if not efficient, because they were available when needed.

At the same time, the process of converting Abbey National to a public limited company and de-mutualizing from a building society meant that there was an even greater need for training to be delivered in a fast, efficient and consistent manner. Commercial confidentiality meant that the company was reluctant to bring in external trainers to handle the extra load. Distance learning techniques were seen as an inescapable part of the solution and the CBT Group stopped virtually all other work to work on plc matters for six months. CBT was used for the training along with other media including workbooks, videos, cue cards, overheads etc.

Despite the additional impetus this gave to distance learning, the issues of access and usage rates remained the subjects of great concern. However there was another key driver on the horizon. There were indications that in future, legislation could be enacted that would force financial companies to validate and monitor staff training on a variety of competencies, creating a huge demand for learner management and assessment programs.

By 1990 the size and number of programs being distributed into the branch system had grown enormously. In fact, in that year alone, Abbey National distributed some 43,000 floppy diskettes, not counting additional orders or damage replacements. This had required the formation of a substantial distribution and logistics operation that in turn needed to be 'fed'. At the time it was not possible to use the branch network for distributing courseware, as it was designed to communicate small packets of account details and had not been set up for the transfer of large data files. Sending large executable and graphics files would have slowed the network too much. Instead, the potential of CD-ROM (compact disc, read only memory) to store large amounts of code was investigated. From late 1989 through to 1991 Abbey National reviewed all the then available CD-ROM formats, culminating in a pilot study in late 1991. The purpose of this was to:

- enable larger programs to be sent on a single disk instead of using multiple floppy disks;
- enable better quality graphics, which took up more space, to be used;
- reduce the demand made by the installed programs for hard disk space (though some of the programs ran from the floppy disks);
- remove almost completely the danger from viruses by moving to a non-writable format;
- enable updates to existing programs to be implemented easily and quickly throughout the network without having to be concerned about existing versions already in the system;
- allow encryption of the data so as to protect the training contents during transit.

Despite the obvious advantages of CD-ROM distribution it was interesting to note that, once the innovation of implementing CBT on floppy disks had been proved and the business was reaping the rewards of the work, it was very difficult to persuade the business to move ahead again, and take another risk. Abbey National made a bold step in embracing CBT in such a wide scale implementation as it did. It was then reluctant to migrate to a CD-ROM base when the existing system seemed to work well and was not broken. Once CD-ROM had been adopted, the next innovation, ie broadband multimedia, would need a step change in the business model that was, in 1993 not within the remit of the training discipline. At that point it was realized that multimedia was a business tool with company-wide applications and that training and development were just one, though important, element in this picture. Funding for future technical innovation in training would be made available only on the back of company wide initiatives where multimedia was a business imperative.

During the period covered by this case study the way in which distance learning was implemented in Abbey National changed significantly. In 1986 the mode of operation was completely pioneering, but by 1990 this had shifted to only about 20% pioneering work (the CD-ROM research). The rest of the work was either routine development of new packages, about a third of which were developed by external contractors anyway, and maintenance of existing materials. This created a staffing problem. Individuals who had been recruited because they were excited about joining an innovative group that was developing new programs and techniques were increasingly being asked to undertake maintenance or mundane development of routine mainstream CBT materials.

On the other hand, as user expectations rose, there was a requirement to produce more exciting material with greater levels of interactivity. This meant migrating away from the DOS authoring tools we had been using (TenCORE) towards more fundamental programming languages, (eg 'C') that required much more technical programming skills. The original premise of hybrid designers, project managers and (TenCORE) coders was rapidly disappearing and being replaced by several distinct groups of specialists.

There were learning package designers who dealt in overall concepts, programmers who concentrated on the details of coding and in the middle, another group had emerged concerned with graphic design and production. This third group was highly influential regarding the look and feel of the packaging and overall content of the distance learning 'presence' in Abbey National. As this group were using Macintosh equipment, while everyone else was on PCs, Abbey National tended from 1990 onwards to be at the forefront of technical issues that no one else in training or IT could comprehend. Mixed Mac and PC networks, dual graphic file formats, CD-ROM mastering equipment and 3D rendering software as well as colour printing meant the CBT Group's capital spend requirements as well as non adherence to corporate IT standards in hardware and software caused considerable friction and resentment with other trainers and with the IT function.

1991–93: consolidation and the way forward

By 1991, we had proved the concept of CD-ROM as a distribution channel, but the process had required a complete re-design of large elements of the management system as well as the way the programs themselves were built. This had created a gap between the maintainers and the developers of routine products and the 'ground breakers' who were working on the CD-ROM design and programming. At the same time, the use of CD-ROM opened up the possibility of adding sound via sound cards for the PCs. From 1992 onwards multimedia delivery was possible on live systems in the business. In an attempt to find some new way of providing group cohesion, everyone in the group was involved in projects relating to the development of CD-ROMs. Some were looking after the management system, others the creation of a demonstration disk and a section on the first CD. Others worked on the over-all design of the CD and associated documentation. The greatest difficulty was finding people in the outside world who were doing similar things. Most of the other companies with CD-ROM experience had experimented with small-scale pilots, involving a small number of systems. The intention in Ab-bey National was to transfer all courseware off floppy disks to CD-ROM sys-tems on business machines; at least one per sales office and two per administration centre, some 1,200 systems in all.

It was during this period that legislation to accredit life assurance practi-tioners came into force. This had several effects on the use of CBT and got the systems used again in earnest. First it increased the amount and the range of training required. It caused individuals to revisit their training plans and get themselves up to speed on life assurance and taxation topics, plus they had to study product knowledge materials as well as the more ge-neric aspects of the life assurance business. Secondly, assessment via a com-petency examination became important. This was built in at the end of each formalized training session and administered by CBT. In some respects this had the effect of changing the perception of CBT in the eyes of the stu-dents. Up until that point CBT had been viewed as an interesting and excit-ing method of learning something about the company as well as getting training on topics too short to be covered on a more formal course. As soon as the licensing examinations became 'live', students realized that there was something that might have an effect on their job and future ca-reer prospects. They ceased at that point to view the training system as a 'friendly helper' and began to look on the CBT element as a monitor. This forced a redesign of the appearance of the CBT materials to try to delineate between help and testing, to allow the same system to be two different things. At all stages before the assessments were introduced it was always made clear that any of the tests in the programs were only there in order to enable the individual to check their progress and would only grant a certifi-cate of completion, not competence in the event that they secured a pass mark in the final module test.

By the mid-point of 1993, the CBT Group (by that point renamed the Dis-tance Learning Group, or DLG) established a dedicated resource to review the maintenance requirements of all existing material. This individual was located in a business site so that they could gather information about the use of the material in a live environment, something that until then had been undertaken by regular visits and linking with regional representatives. This move proved very successful. In the sphere of procedural and technical training that was the primary focus of attention for the group, such currency and accuracy was vitally important, in order to maintain a relevance to the business.

An unforeseen consequence of making training programs more accessible and available on people's desktops via their business machines was that people started to use the courseware as reference material, rather than rely on the company documentation and manuals. This caused some difficulties for the DLG as well as the documentation section who saw that there was a need to work more closely with the group. By 1996, Abbey National was in a position to implement a common document reference system through Interleaf WorldView. Prior to this it was very much a matter of trying to ensure harmonization between manuals and the training material.

However, back in the middle of 1993, the work the group had been originally set up to undertake was completed. Access to all training programs, including some management development reference material, assessment and documentation as well as the original remit of technical, procedural and systems training had been put in place in all locations, including on CD-ROM in one of the largest CD implementations in Europe at that time. At that point the author moved on, leaving Abbey National for an external multimedia consultancy. Not long afterwards, a large percentage of the original team moved into freelance consultancy or other areas of the business, leaving a large amount of the ground breaking work in multimedia to the marketing and IT functions of the business.

Conclusions

Abbey National achieved what it did through local champions and central championing of the CBT cause. It was also successful because it was new: a new use of technology and a new way of learning. It is not so certain that such an approach would work in an organization today, but it is likely that the following learning points are still relevant to anyone considering implementing multimedia-based training now.

1. Don't try to be too clever with the technology. The CBT group were lucky first time round that the rest of the company caught up with the idea of PCs as a delivery platform for business applications. Later on, the leap to CD-ROM was much more difficult to implement.
2. An error made early on was not to involve the IT department as fully in the trial as we could have done. Longer term this proved difficult, as their buy-in was not cemented at an early enough stage. The IT department were concerned that an area outside their organization had PCs and were deploying them throughout the business.
3. The initial focus was on production of content, to make an impact. Not enough emphasis was placed on issues such as software distribution, learner management and centralized control. These emerged as problems in later years as the enterprise grew, a victim of its own success.
4. Not enough consideration was given at the beginning about whether or not to have an internal development team or what its composition should be. With hindsight, Abbey National should perhaps not have

established an internal development team, concentrated instead on professional project management skills and contracted out a large percentage of their development efforts, with perhaps only the research and development (R&D) elements being retained internally. This would have had the effect of increasing the overall per hour cost of the CBT material (from perhaps £4,000 per delivered hour in 1991 to £12,000 per hour) but would have enabled the group to concentrate on getting the usage of the courseware up, and creating the right environment for the learners. This was something that was in some respects overlooked, and that is now seen as essential to the successful adoption of distance learning within companies and educational establishments. The team grew in response to needs as they emerged rather than according to a strategic plan.

This had implications in the longer term for:
- the types of people needed at various stages of the development of the organization and the system;
- the impact on the rest of the organization of the remuneration levels expected by specialists;
- the integration of a 'special' team into the training mainstream in the business.

5. If you are using external companies, try to work out if their staff work for them, or whether they are freelancers. You need to know who is 'minding the store' so to speak when you come to work out who is undertaking the programming, design, etc and who, therefore is carrying the risks. And be wary of consultancies who may know even less than you do and want to learn at your expense.

6. Finally, focus on the business priorities. Pick your topics wisely, perhaps something that has a fundamental impact on the business, and where using distance learning can make a difference, and you can prove it.

Whereas creative visionaries, 'architects', were needed at the beginning to get the innovation underway, within five years the requirement had changed to a team of 'maintenance engineers' who could keep it running efficiently and who would not want to keep changing it when it was not 'broken'. Making the change within a tightly knit development team from one type of personality to the other was difficult and would have been easier if people's expectations had been clarified from the start.

Creativity and multimedia require some quite diverse and eclectic skills, some not tied to any one 'profession' and it is therefore sometimes difficult to place a value on that in terms of a salary, easier in terms of a day rate. Also, the corporate environment sometimes finds it difficult to assimilate creative, pioneering, individuals. The CBT team were housed in a different building from the rest of training from the start, began to attract media attention fairly quickly because of their innovative work and went on to have a significant impact on the training identity and to absorb technical training *en route*. Integration of such a group into the mainstream later was not easy because of the attitudes that had developed on both sides.

References

Coopers & Lybrand (1989) 'Relative costs of open and distance learning', report published by the Department of Education and Science, November.

Chapter 5

Implementing distance learning in Barclays Bank

Judith Christian-Carter

Why distance learning?

In 1989/90 the central training function of Barclays Bank plc introduced distance learning as its second main mode of delivering training. Up to this point nearly all the training delivered by Central Training and the regions used various methods of face-to-face learning, with lectures and small group work predominating. The Barclays' policy at the time was that specialist technical training was a devolved responsibility of divisions and departments (of which Central Training was one), with the regions providing training that was specific to them; the training provided centrally was seen in terms of net zero budgeting, whereby Central Training's budget would be recouped by the regions paying for the training provided. Although several areas and departments of Barclays had begun to experiment with distance learning in the form of self study from books and computer-based training (CBT) during the 1980s, this work was more of an exploratory nature to see what distance learning could offer the Bank and for what types of training it could be used.

In 1984 the vice-chairman of Barclays reported on training in the *UK Bank* concluding, *inter alia*, that whilst there was scope for improving its cost-effectiveness, the bank's investment in training was not excessive. A task force report that followed the vice-chairman's report, produced recommendations that combined to place more emphasis on the way the bank managed its investment in resources, including training. In 1988 a project team was formed, sponsored by a member of the bank's executive, and consisting of a project director (who was then head of banking training) and consultants in general projects, management training and development, retail markets, and training methodologies. The project team was tasked with conducting a detailed review of training within Barclays and reported to a steering committee of business users of training. The project team's approach was both extensive and rigorous and undertook the following:

- conducted interviews with over 100 executives and managers within the bank (including a complete range of training management, both central and divisional);
- conducted extensive questionnaire-based surveys of UK regions, divisions and departments and overseas territories, followed up by visits and interviews within a wide cross-section of regions and all major divisions (as it was assumed that the existing policy of devolving responsibility for specialist technical training to divisions and departments was to continue);
- distributed and analysed over 200 questionnaire surveys amongst managers within the UK;
- reviewed, in depth, the content and methodologies of current central training programmes and major divisional programmes;
- researched the extensive literature available on current training and development thinking and practice outside the Bank, including the complete range of existing and emerging methodologies;
- analysed the historical costs of centralized and decentralized training and examined the forecasts and preliminary budgets for 1989 for central training;
- visited, and discussed with, ten other major organizations, which provided for substantial investments in training to review the benefits of alternative approaches to training.

Amongst the *Training Review Project*'s (1988) recommendations was the following:

> 'There is further scope for improving the cost effectiveness of the delivery of training. We recommend that there should be an increased use of properly supported distance learning and technology-based training.
> - Establish a network of managed learning centres (separate locations providing space and materials for self-study) in the UK.
> - Adopt the general approach of using distance learning methodologies to teach knowledge and formal courses to teach skills.
> - Establish through the interactive video project the extent to which distance learning can teach skills in addition to knowledge.
> - Increased use of testing pre-course to ensure participants are properly screened and post-course to measure training effectiveness.
> - Encourage greater use of self-managed learning at all levels and particularly for high fliers.' (p.2)

The recommendations of the *Training Review Project* met with widespread support from both business users and those responsible for training, although the initial reaction from those delivering training was muted; this was probably because the majority felt that they would be unaffected by the recommendations in relation to the subject matter and type of training they were delivering, eg management training.

In order to support the above recommendation, some reorganization of the training function was required. Training was structured into four main areas related to personal banking, business banking, banking operations, and management training and in order to provide the professional training expertise, and apply quality standards and rigour to the design, development, and delivery of training, a Training Development Group (TDG) was established to interface with the four main training areas. In particular, the TDG was required to develop group standards of professionalism in:

- training needs analysis;
- systematic training programme production;
- evaluation of the effectiveness of training.

Both recommendations concerning distance learning and the TDG were accepted by Barclays and the director responsible for Central Training, and work commenced in 1989 to put the two, mutually inclusive, developments in place in order to improve the cost-effectiveness of the delivery of training. The interdependence between the two recommendations was an important feature from the outset. Prior to 1989 the training function, by and large, lacked design and development rigour, although this was not accepted by all those involved in delivering existing programmes and it took a number of years before this acceptance became widespread, due, in the main, to strong leadership from the head of training and a directive that all training had to be business-led, and designed and developed according to set procedures. In order to increase, in a cost-effective manner, the use of properly supported distance learning and technology-based training (TBT) through a network of learning centres, it was vital to establish standards, conventions, and procedures for the design, development, and delivery of all training events or programmes. The TDG was pivotal in ensuring that:

- distance learning was used in appropriate circumstances;
- distance learning was designed and developed as a quality product;
- the learning centre network was set-up and operated correctly.

The *Training Review Project* had also identified three training courses, along with a priority list of further courses, that, at the time, were delivered face-to-face and that, if transferred to distance learning would produce substantial cost savings for the bank; the business case indicated a pay back of 15 months with annualized direct savings of £1.1 million (or £2.5 million if trainee time was included). Evidence within the Bank, which was cited in the report of the *Training Review Project*, indicated that the study of existing distance learning packages was taking 40% longer than needed; this was also related to the experience of other organizations that suggested that distance learning would not work unless there was the appropriate degree of support in terms of attitudes and environment. A general delivery strategy was therefore required to ensure that a mix of methodologies was used to provide a more responsive training service.

Putting the infrastructure in place

In order to test the viability of the business case supporting the use of distance learning, a pilot of 15 learning centres commenced in 1989. The pilot was the responsibility of Central Training and TDG, and the learning centres were intended to be used only to deliver distance learning using a variety of existing methodologies. The TDG had started to convert some of the existing face-to-face courses, which covered mainly procedural and operational knowledge and skills, involving the existing deliverers of the training as much as possible, often in the role of subject matter experts. The idea was to compare the time taken for study of the new packages with their face-to-face counterparts and to measure the trainees' reactions to studying them via distance learning. At the same time the TDG was busy in establishing the standards and procedures required for designing, developing, and delivering training in a systematic manner. Over the course of the next few years the TDG and its successor, Training Services, put into practice, refined and developed further all the standards and procedures before they were, over a period of time, gradually extended to and used by other areas of central training.

The pilot, therefore, concentrated not so much on the quality of the distance learning but more on the environment in which it was delivered, ie learning centres. To this end, considerable thought and attention was given to what constituted a learning centre. The learning centres were set up specifically for the pilot, as none had existed before; each had its own administrator in the form of a learning centre supervisor, and all were established on a common set of criteria. The criteria used to set up the learning centres, and to guide the evaluation of the outcomes of the pilot, were as follows:

- premises (located no more than 45 minutes travel distance from the branch);
- lay-out (discrete work stations to allow for a variety of media to be used: CBT, IV, audio, linear video, paper-based training (PBT), furniture – desks, chairs);
- equipment (computers, video recorders, cassette machines, IV);
- ambience (lighting, decor, space, plants, music);
- trainee support (eg learning centre supervisors, help desks).

Table 5.1   Learning centre supervisor main duties and tasks.

1. Formulate branch training plans in conjunction with line managers as required. Liaise with line managers on the selection of staff and time of attendance in conjunction with the availability of computers and PBT material at the learning centre.
2. Provide one-to-one support to all levels of students with any aspect of the training packages.
3. Act as a point of reference for students by providing technical answers either through self-knowledge or with reference to a help desk.
4. Ensure that the learning centre resources are used in the most cost effective way.
5. Manage and undertake the administration of the learning centre (using the computerized administration system if applicable):
    (a) take bookings via telephone/visits/meetings/letters;
    (b) complete and send out confirmation of bookings and joining instructions;
    (c) prepare the training facility equipping it with all necessary stationery, manuals, practicals;
    (d) raise and maintain trainee records.
6. Carry out an induction programme for each student on arrival:
    (a) administration details of learning centre;
    (b) health and safety details;
    (c) food/drink;
    (d) ensure each student has been pre-briefed (and if not carry out pre-briefing);
    (e) ensure each student will be de-briefed (setting the date if applicable).
7. Provide the Regional Office with information:
    (a) on course codes;
    (b) feedback from branches/students on the learning centre facilities and effectiveness.
8. Negotiate a target with the region for the usage level of the centre and provide monthly statistics to show progress.
9. Provide Central Training and other areas of the bank responsible for distance learning with statistics and information as required.
10. Devise and operate a stock control system for stationery and order when necessary.
11. Mark exercises and tests (with the aid of an answer book). Discuss results with students. If any problem areas are highlighted ensure students are aware of the correct procedures. Record results for feedback to the branch and regional office.
12. Deal with the day-to-day maintenance of equipment, updating CBT and IV packages with streamer tapes/disks upon receipt from Central Training.
13. Prior to the receipt of an official update for a training package, ensure the students are advised of any amendment to the packages they are working through as a matter of utmost importance.
14. Update or amend various training and support manuals as necessary.
15. Liaise with line managers to discuss student performance during a course.
16. Give presentations to branch staff by attending their seminars or during open days given at the learning centre.
17. Validate new packages for the learning centres before 'live date'.
18. Deal with enquiries (administrative or technical) from other learning centres, regional training staff, and branches.
19. Keep up-to-date with new systems and services.

The main method of measuring the outcomes of the pilot was to compare the cost of setting-up and running learning centres, in conjunction with the study time required for, and the staff's reaction to, training delivered by distance learning, against the costs of providing the same training by more traditional, face-to-face, delivery methods.

The pilot was deemed to be a success by both Central Training, the TDG, and Barclays' executive, and proved to the business that substantial cost savings, well above those originally indicated, were perfectly feasible. It also provided a valuable learning experience that allowed the TDG to refine many of its initial concepts and to fine-tune further a number of its future requirements for distance learning.

For example, it soon became apparent that the role of the learning centre supervisor was key to the successful running of learning centres and providing support to trainees. From the experiences gained a job description and profile was produced for recruiting learning centre supervisors and a training programme was devised for their induction. The main duties and tasks for learning centre supervisors are shown in Table 5.1.

It also became clear that central support was required to coordinate and support the activities of the various learning centres and, so, the post of a learning centre coordinator within the TDG was devised. The coordinators main duties are shown in Table 5.2. Criteria relating to premises, general equipment, and the ambience of learning centres were defined fairly easily because they were based on a considerable deal of 'common sense' and knowledge of learning away from the workplace or 'classroom'. However, those that proved to be more problematic, particularly in the long run, were

Table 5.2 Learning centre coordinator main duties.

---

1. Provide details to users of future training packages/updates (giving anticipated dates, audience, medium, administrative time) on a quarterly basis.
2. Gather information re lack of quality/problems concerning the delivery of materials; advising sponsors and users as appropriate.
3. Ensuring (and assisting) the training delivery teams/sponsors to develop and maintain operating procedures regarding packages by collating best practices from different areas and providing these in the form of guidelines (*A Guide to Launching New Distance Learning to Learning Centres* was published in early 1993 by the learning centre coordinator).
4. Gathering management information for sponsors and for the head of training and distributing as appropriate.
5. Identify best working practices and recommend for across the board use to sponsors and users.
6. Organize briefings for new training initiatives liaising with sponsors.
7. Manage and undertake collection and processing of central records relating to learning centres. Undertaking the control of CBT equipment in learning centres.
8. Assist with and provide best practice guidelines re the setting up of new learning centres.
9. Act as the point of reference/help desk to assist learning centre supervisors/ sponsors to carry out their duties.

---

the criteria relating to CBT, both from a hardware and software point of view. Perhaps it is axiomatic to say that both hardware and software had to relate to what was available at the time, but the lesson learned, at a later date, was the need to think ahead and to plan for future developments. The pilot was based on 286 PCs, complete with 1Mb RAM, VGA monitors, tape streamer, 16MHz clock speed, 40Mb hard disk, DOS 3.0, and Mentor as the authoring software.

The results of the evaluation were submitted to Barclays' senior executives in late 1989. Final sanction for a network of learning centres within regions serving the UK bank was obtained early in 1990; by mid-1991 over 60 learning centres had been set up and were operating. By early 1992, some 80 hours of CBT courseware (as opposed to interactive video) was being delivered in learning centres supported by more than 250 workstations. The hardware at this stage was a combination of the pilot 286 PCs and newer 386 machines, the latter being essentially the same specification as the 286 machines except for 120Mb hard disks and the capability of being upgraded to 4Mb of RAM.

Designing and developing distance learning

Whilst the initial decision to provide training in the form of distance learning was justified on the basis of achieving substantial cost savings in relation to existing face-to-face courses, it was realized that in the long term the infrastructure supporting this means of delivery needed to be embedded fully in the quality standards, conventions, and procedures being developed and used by the TDG. Distance learning was regarded as one delivery option that had its strengths and weaknesses and that could be used in whole, or in part, when providing a solution to an identified training problem.

Accordingly, from 1990 onwards the design and development of distance learning took place within a systematic approach that was applied to all training solutions. No training was provided in the absence of a business sponsor and appropriate business sanction. All training was based on clearly identified training needs as a result of conducting a thorough training needs analysis (TNA). All training was designed to:

- address the knowledge and skills that job holders were required by the business to demonstrate in the workplace;
- ensure that the knowledge and skills required were structured in a manner that facilitated learning;
- be delivered using the highest quality and cost-effective means available.

The first key stage in the design of a training event was to produce an instructional strategy. This document formed the 'blue-print' for the training and detailed:

- the competencies (knowledge and skills) required;
- the training objectives (derived from the competencies);
- the training content (knowledge and skills);
- the structure and sequence of the training (modules, units, course map);
- the assessment and evaluation methodology;
- the options for delivering the training with their associated strengths and weaknesses, risks, time-lines, resources, and budget requirements.

The advantage of distance learning was seen to be that it enabled large numbers of staff to undergo training cheaply, easily, and effectively. People could learn at their own pace and could do so in a relatively flexible, participative, and interactive manner, while receiving feedback of their achievements on a regular basis.

The decision, therefore, to use distance learning was part of the instructional strategy, which was required to be agreed and signed-off by the business sponsor. In this context distance learning formed but one option and delivery process within a systematic approach. From the instructional strategy a detailed briefing and specification document for the instructional design of the training event was produced; this document ensured consistency of approach and interpretation across the development and delivery teams.

Using distance learning in learning centres

Although the original intention was to use distance learning to teach knowledge and formal courses to teach skills, it soon became clear that the potential of both paper-based training (PBT) and CBT offered Barclays and its staff far more as a delivery medium when their design and development were set within a systematic approach that was executed by skilled and experienced training professionals. This was particularly noticeable in the case of CBT as the available hardware and software were becoming more powerful, allowing for a considerable degree of trainee interaction and creative instructional design. The IV project had been disbanded in 1992, largely as a result of high equipment costs and unacceptable development ratios, and this exposed the weaknesses of existing CBT equipment. In addition to which, in the same year Barclays had started a major IT initiative in the branch network in order to streamline many of its manual operations and, therefore, the need to use CBT to train staff effectively was starting to become an issue for the training function. In particular, although learning centres had been used predominantly by clerical staff, there was now a growing need for managers to undertake some of their training in this environment.

Experience thus far had shown that through the use of appropriate authoring software, designers and developers could produce high quality, cost-effective training that was far more interactive than other forms of distance learning currently available at a comparative cost. However, rising equipment

performance standards and enhanced user expectations regarding the sophistication of CBT materials prompted the need to review the authoring tools
used. A business case was made to replace Mentor with Authorware and to
upgrade the existing delivery platforms to Windows. The business case was
based on producing 45 hours of CBT over the following 18 months at a maximum development ratio of 200:1 (compared with 450:1 for Mentor), effect-
ing a saving of £450,000 over the period.

In mid-1992 the business case was accepted and within three and a half
months the return on Barclays' investment had been realized! However, this
success needs to be set against the not inconsiderable amount of work and disruption experienced in terms of:

- upgrading heterogeneous equipment;
- installing software;
- training in-house staff;
- writing new menu software to allow learning centre supervisors to load
  quickly and easily both Mentor and Authorware packages from more
  than one streamer tape.

The experience, whilst bringing obvious benefits to both the Bank and to
staff, was quite a painful one for central training staff and the learning centre
supervisors. This experience was exacerbated further when, six months down
the line, the lack of a 256 colour card proved to be a major omission in the
earlier upgrading process necessitating further disruption to the learning centres and additional cost to Barclays.

Organizational change

In 1992 Central Training was restructured to ensure that its organizational
structure and function would meet the changing needs of the business. As
part of the restructuring process, Training Services was formed out of the
TDG with the remit to design and develop, on behalf of Central Training, high
quality, cost-effective training events and to continue the work of the TDG in
laying down training standards, conventions, and procedures. The other
Central Training teams supported the various business lines of the Bank and,
whilst these teams were responsible for delivering face-to-face training, they
also began to develop strong and focused business-line support and sponsor-
ship, which enabled them to act as an interface between the business lines and
Training Services. In addition to which, the means by which training was
financed also changed from net zero budgeting to the provision of: a core
budget for Central Training to provide 'business as usual' training; and, funding from the business lines for new, business-led 'implementation' training.
This change not only simplified and streamlined administrative procedures
but, more importantly, led to training being seen as an integral part of the way

in which Barclays functioned, ie if people needed training then they should have access to it without being constrained by a lack of funding. In all probability, because the regions no longer had to pay for training, any major barriers there may have been to adopting distance learning were avoided.

During the course of 1992 the Training Services team was expanded to ensure the adequate provision of internal staff who could act, on behalf of the business sponsor, as project managers and course designers. Before 1992 virtually all of the development of distance learning was done in-house but with the thrust towards greater cost-effectiveness, along with the increasing use of CBT (in the form of text, graphics, and animation), it proved to be very difficult to provide an adequate base of suitably skilled and experienced developers 1 in-house. At this stage the decision was taken to buy-in the development skills required by using external suppliers and to use in-house staff, where possible, to maintain any distance learning produced; the result of which was the increased production of high quality, cost-effective distance learning.

From such a position of strength it was tempting to hope that a period of stability would ensue. However, for a large organization that had just commenced a major and widespread change programme this was not to be and between 1994 and 1995 the following occurred:

- branches were merged and clustered, which allowed for a wider provision of learning centres by basing these in branches and thereby reducing travel time and permitting greater access to distance learning when it was required;
- growing opinion amongst non-training professionals that most TBT could be delivered more cost-effectively in the workplace as a direct result of increased IT provision in branches;
- Training Services was disbanded in order to devolve those staff with specialist knowledge and skills in the design and development of training to the various business-led training areas; a move that led to a further increase in the use of distance learning, particularly in non-technical and other skill areas, such as customer service and the use of new, sophisticated, computer software;
- a considerable increase in the requirement for computer systems and applications training across all business sectors;
- technical issues in relation to the existing CBT equipment as a result of:
  - improved versions of Authorware with greater instructional design potential;
  - the need to increase the speed at which the CBT ran;
  - the inability of the internal storage capacity of the equipment to cope with increasingly more sophisticated and memory-hungry programming;
  - the increased use of high quality graphics and animation;
  - the greater difficulty of accessing and loading courseware from different streamer tapes.

As a result of the many changes that were taking place, a study of the use and management of learning centres commenced in 1995 that led to improving their accessibility and to the introduction of 486 multimedia PCs with CD-ROM distribution, with the intention that these would gradually replace the existing 386 PCs. Towards the end of 1995 the first multimedia technology-based training (TBT) was produced incorporating audio and quarter screen motion video. TBT was now a practical reality, underpinned by comprehensive design standards and sound procedures, and requiring a conducive learning environment for its use. Although it again required an upgrade of the delivery workstations, resulting in three different specifications of PCs in learning centres.

Evaluating distance learning training

From 1991 all distance learning packages were evaluated in terms of their effectiveness. A variation of Kirkpatrick's four level model (1983) was used to measure:

- Level 1: what the trainees thought about the training;
- Level 2: whether the trainees had mastered the training objectives;
- Level 3: whether the training had transferred into the workplace.

Level 4, the cost-effectiveness of training was rarely undertaken due to the difficulties of controlling non-training related variables and, therefore, being unable to prove cause and effect.

Level 1 data were regarded as formative evaluation and were used to improve the training as and when required. Levels 2 and 3 proved whether or not the training had been effective. Level 2 was based on a sample of the trainees' assessment data and therefore was easy and inexpensive to obtain as it did not require additional measurement tools to be designed. Data at Levels 1 and 2 were required by Central Training but it was left to the business to request data at Level 3, as this level required the construction of custom-made measurement tools and the cooperation of staff, and their line managers, to use the tools in the workplace. All the data obtained were processed and subjected to statistical analysis and the findings were reported back to Central Training and to the business sponsor.

As a result of the standards and procedures used to design and develop distance learning, all the packages produced were proved to be effective at Level 2. In a few instances where transfer into the workplace had not been successful the TNA was able to pinpoint possible reasons owing to non-training related issues being identified as part of the research process. In short, evaluating the effectiveness of distance learning was relatively easy to set up and to implement.

Lessons learned

During the last seven years that saw distance learning, supported by a network of learning centres, become a key medium for the delivery of training within the UK Bank, a number of lessons have been learned:

Why distance learning?

- It is essential to be quite clear from the outset why any organization wishes to introduce distance learning and to identify possible cost-benefits. Distance learning is only one means of delivering training and it is only effective if it is used properly. It is also important to be aware of the knock-on effect that such an introduction will have in terms of people, premises, equipment, and operating structures.
- Establishing distance learning as the main mode of delivering training can lead to the need to reorganize and expand the training function, as well as requiring the use of common standards, conventions, and procedures if the design, development, and delivery of the training is to be both effective and efficient; an absence of such standards is likely to lead to poorly designed distance learning and varying degrees of chaos.
- As not everyone will be convinced about the benefits in terms of costs and effectiveness, it is essential to obtain top management buy-in for distance learning, and a well-planned and executed pilot can go a long way to ensuring this.

Putting the infrastructure in place

- For distance learning to be effective, a conducive learning environment needs to be created and maintained. Considerable thought and effort went into the criteria required for setting-up learning centres and how these criteria would be put into practice and monitored.
- Experience also indicates that unless learning centres are readily accessible to staff, there is a danger that this will lead to inappropriate workplace learning taking place in the guise of distance learning.
- Because any distance learning used for training purposes is rarely totally capable of standing on its own, in order to achieve a greater degree of self-managed learning, adequate human support must be provided both within the learning centre and from outside (eg help desks to help learners with the more technical aspects of the training, for example, explaining new policies, procedures, and practices, by acting as a subject matter expert to the learner).
- The performance of those providing the human support, eg the learning centre supervisors, needs to be monitored and appropriate training and

development opportunities provided to meet their changing and additional needs. Over the period of four years the role of the learning centre supervisor developed from that of administrator to tutor and with this their training needs changed. Failure to identify and address changing training needs would have diminished, considerably, the effectiveness of distance learning.

- Delivering training through the medium of distance learning requires a high level of coordination from the centre in terms of providing adequate support for both users and suppliers; this is particularly the case when launching new, or revised, distance learning packages.

- Any organization wishing to use distance learning in a cost-effective manner must always be responsive to new technology and its capabilities. As it is impossible to control the rapid rate of technological advancement, it is important to accept that whatever the starting level is today, it will be out-of-date in two or three years' time. To offset reactive, and often costly measures, a long-term and flexible replacement strategy needs to be put in place from the outset.

Designing and developing distance learning

- Designing and developing distance learning uses the same systems and processes as any other type of high quality, cost-effective training. It is important to ensure that distance learning does not drive the training solution, and that it is used when the identified training needs can be met best via this medium and where the advantages of distance learning can be realized. The use of a systematic approach across the training function will ensure that distance learning is used appropriately but this will require adequate resourcing in terms of knowledge, skills, and experiences from either/or inside and outside the organization.

- Irrespective of the size of the organization, there is considerable short- and long-term value in using a blend of internal and external resources to produce high quality, cost-effective distance learning. However, the overall control and management should always come from within the organization.

Using distance learning in learning centres

- CBT can serve two useful roles: training staff on a wide range of knowledge and skills related to non-computer-based workplace performance; and, training staff to use new computer systems and software.

- The software used to develop CBT must be capable of meeting the requirements of the designers. It is therefore important to ensure that whatever software is used it is upwardly extendible to cope with the developing sophistication of the hardware and the need to maintain distance learning packages when business objectives, competencies, systems, and procedures change.

- To be clear about when any distance learning package needs to be undertaken in the environment provided by a learning centre. Most distance learning will need to be undertaken away from the workplace and it is important to resist the temptation to reduce both the time and costs involved in learning, by going for what might appear to be, on the face of it, an efficient solution by asking staff to undertake their distance learning in the workplace.
- To promote, from the outset the use of learning centres for all staff, irrespective of their grade. Failure to do so will lead to problems of a cultural nature that, although they are perfectly capable of resolution, will require attitudes to change and, in the meantime, will inhibit the use of distance learning in those circumstances where it is eminently desirable.

Assessing trainees and evaluating distance learning training

Assessing trainees undertaking distance learning is relatively straightforward and, in particular, the use of CBT allows for assessment to be conducted both efficiently and effectively.

In order to ensure that the benefits to both staff and the organization are measured and fed back to both the training function and to the business lines, it is essential to evaluate distance learning packages in terms of the pay-back to be gained and as a matter of policy.

The Barclays' 'experiment' has been a great success and the use of both distance learning and learning centres are now firmly established as part of training delivery policy and practice. Irrefutable proof exists that distance learning can enrich and enhance the cost-effectiveness of more traditional training delivery methods. The initial recommendation made by the *Training Review Project* has not only been achieved, it has been surpassed, with distance learning being extended to other business areas and departments of the UK Bank to teach a range of both knowledge and skills.

References

Barclays Bank (1988) *The Training Review Project*, Internal Report, Barclays Bank plc, September 1988.

Kirkpatrick, D L (1983) 'Four steps to measuring training effectiveness', *Personnel Administrator*, November, 19–25.

Chapter 6

Open learning in Reuters

David Cook

Background

Reuters is one of the world's leading electronic publishers. It serves the financial and business community in all the world's major markets and supplies news services for newspapers, magazines, broadcasters and news agencies. Reuters range of products includes financial data, trading systems, historical databases, news, news pictures and television, which are distributed to clients throughout the world over the world's most extensive international private satellite and cable communications network.

There are 14,637 employees globally including 1,936 journalists, photographers and cameramen in 53 bureaux around the world. Information is also obtained from 267 financial markets and from around 4,100 subscribers who contribute data directly to Reuters.

Reuters is split into three geographical areas, each responsible for the marketing, sales and support of Reuters products in their own area. The corporate core based in London handles product development and overall marketing and personnel functions. Reuters, being essentially a knowledge-based organization, has a flat management structure and relatively few clerical or support staff. It consists predominantly of highly skilled and specialized staff, with a large amount of distributed power, enabling them to innovate, cooperate, and respond rapidly to changing market conditions and technological developments. This group are also young – with a median age of 32. Being used to relatively high levels of responsibility, and the need for flexibility and initiative in their work, it is perhaps hardly surprising that they are also eager to take responsibility for their own learning, and to take up any available learning opportunities.

The UKI (United Kingdom and Ireland) Training Department supports 2,500 employees who are specialists in a variety of areas eg technical, information systems, personnel, sales, administration, finance, editorial, marketing, television. Before 1993 the department had a global brief and its staff had grown to 56, with trainers specializing in sales, management, technical and product training. During 1993 the company was divisionalized and there was a drive to reduce staff numbers. The training department was reconfigured to serve the UK and Ireland only, and staff numbers were cut by 50%. At that time, training usually took the form of face-to-face classroom events, with additionally a small number of bespoke CBT packages for product training, some off-the-shelf CBT for training in the financial markets, and technical training on operating systems and networks. The training department also had its own in-house video facility, which mainly produced videos that were used as classroom support materials. Some workbooks had been developed, which were also mainly used for classroom support.

The department had become set in its ways, and took a reactive approach to meeting the needs of the business, using a prescriptive repertoire of classroom-based training solutions. No systematic performance analysis was undertaken. This situation was self-perpetuating, as it encouraged sponsors, who believed that classroom training was the training department's stock in trade, to 'solutioneer', by approaching with requests for 'a training course on product X' without any further consideration of performance outcomes, learner needs, or learning media.

Many in the business and UKI Training saw the need for a way to break out of this cycle; a means of enabling the training department to respond more flexibly to the rapidly changing needs of the business. The new strategy for UKI Training was to focus its in-house training activities on the key area of business need, ie training on the rapidly developing range of Reuters products for information delivery and analysis, and electronic trading systems. Management training, personal development, generic selling skills, applications training and most of the non-Reuters technical training was to be outsourced.

The introduction of open learning – from trainees to learners

Training management had recognized that there was a need to gear up the output of the department to enable it to meet the demands of the business with its reduced numbers, and that to do this meant a significant increase in the use of other forms of training than classroom delivery. Following closely behind the 1993 cuts, UKI Training made its case for open learning as a means of delivering more with less.

Reuters management was supportive of the idea of a new, leaner, fitter, department that could deliver positive business benefits. As a rapidly growing, successful company, funding for staff development was not a major obstacle to the introduction of open learning in Reuters.

The established trainers, who could have been a barrier to the introduction of open learning, either supported it, or at worst ignored it. As most of the remaining trainers were product or technical specialists, they felt that open learning would not be likely to impinge to a great extent on their activities, as most of the technical and product training required hands-on skills development and practice with software and hardware, for which open learning could not provide a substitute.

However, despite the support open learning enjoyed from management and UKI Training, the stereotype of training as a number of days away from the workplace, often taking place in a comfortable hotel by the sea, is one that, until recently, largely prevailed within Reuters. Staff had to be weaned from the concept of training as a largely passive activity that was 'delivered' by trainers and 'received' by trainees. This model has endured despite research indicating that the traditional didactic model of learning is inappropriate for adult learning (Freire, 1974; Revans, 1981). Adults tend to learn faster and more effectively with a learner-centred approach where the learner is in control of the speed of learning and can choose what to learn, using an experiential, activity-based learning model, particularly where the experience relates closely to the desired job performance.

A significant culture change was also needed to shift this prevailing view to one that viewed learning as an integral ingredient of working life, was a continuing process in a changing environment, and focused directly on individual performance needs and those of the business. Increasing the relevance and 'openness' of training and moving it closer to the workplace helped staff to take more responsibility for their own learning. A major milestone was achieved in the Chief Executive's statement of corporate values of June 1995, which stated that, as a part of Reuters' commitment to being open and accountable, 'We encourage everyone to take responsibility and develop the skills needed to keep pace with the fast advance of the business.'

The strategy for achieving the necessary culture change had two main strands, aimed at managers and potential users respectively.

The 'top-down' approach

The 'top-down' approach aimed at selling the use of open learning to managers using the following approaches.

Targeting open learning at priority areas of business need

To ensure training was focused on and driven by the needs of the business, in 1994 UKI Training adopted a systematic approach to training that has since been agreed as a common approach across all Reuters Training Departments worldwide. The Training Methodology version of the 'training cycle' is shown in Figure 6.1.

One of the key purposes of the Training Methodology is to ensure that the

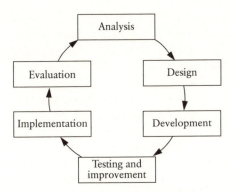

Figure 6.1   *Reuters Training Methodology training cycle*

business impact of any proposed training is clearly visible at an early stage in the analysis, enabling training requests to be prioritized based on objective business criteria. Until the adoption of the Training Methodology, needs analysis had been somewhat neglected. Trainers tended to react to customers requests for training instead of looking for the underlying 'performance gap'. The result was that although the training was what the customer had asked for, it did not always meet the needs of the business. The Training Methodology has been so successful in improving the performance and relevance of training to the business that UKI Training has now been reorganized around the new methodology.

The initial area identified for open learning was financial markets training to meet the needs of customer-facing staff for an improved knowledge of their customers' businesses and relevant Reuters products. Before the open learning solution was available, markets training was done by classroom-based courses run by a mixture of internal and external specialist markets trainers.

UKI Training developed a series of workbooks, which used an activity-based approach to combine markets knowledge with an understanding of relevant Reuters information services, by giving users activities using the Reuters terminal to collect and analyse information from the relevant markets. The roll-out of the workbooks coincided with a major push within the UKI divisions on improving the markets knowledge of sales and support staff.

An integrated approach
In the past, in Reuters and elsewhere, there has been a tendency to adopt open learning as an 'all or nothing' solution with little regard as to its suitability. This is often driven by training sponsors who 'solutioneer', with preconceptions of the kind of training solution they want, before any analysis has taken place. This often happens with sponsors who see a high profile training package (which usually means multimedia) as a political lever, and has resulted in more than one disappointed sponsor and failed or poor quality

multimedia project. Overcoming these preconceptions requires a combination of thorough analysis and justification of the choice of training media, together with highly developed consultancy skills on the part of the training staff, to educate sponsors to understand the issues involved in selecting appropriate learning media.

Open learning is not considered to be a 'cure-all'. We have not attempted to replace classroom-based training, but to expand our repertoire of learning solutions to enable us to provide fit-for-purpose training. This approach has usually meant integrating open learning and face-to-face elements into a training solution that combines the best of both. Increasing numbers of courses have open learning elements as prerequisites for classroom events. The general pattern is to provide much of the knowledge element as open learning, giving trainers more time for hands-on skills development in the classroom.

Integration of the financial markets training involved using open learning workbooks supplemented by CBT and video material to cover the basic knowledge of the markets, and an introduction to using Reuters information systems in those markets. Further workbooks are now being developed for more advanced concepts such as technical analysis, but for in-depth operational knowledge of the more complex Reuters analytical products, people need the support, practice, and hands-on experience that classroom training can offer.

Cost-effective learning
In the currently fashionable organizational climate of cost cutting and shedding of non-core business activities, it is difficult to convince sceptics that open learning is anything other than a cost cutting exercise, and as a result its value is perceived as significantly lower than that of conventional training. The other side of the cost-effectiveness equation, the fact that open learning can be not only less costly but also more effective as a learning tool, is seldom taken into account.

The 'front loading' of open learning development and delivery costs is a barrier to the development rather than the delivery of Open Learning. Because sponsors not unnaturally compare open learning development costs with those of conventional training, open learning looks comparatively expensive. The significantly lower subsequent costs of open learning delivery compared with classroom-based delivery tend to be ignored.

Although this was not a major obstacle within Reuters UKI division, as the Training Department is centrally funded, it becomes more of an issue when UKI Training is dealing either with the corporate centre, or with other Reuters areas, as the department is not resourced to meet their requirements. UKI Training avoided the need to confront these groups with heavy, up-front development costs by changing the pattern of costs to one that was more like conventional training, by using its central development budget to fund the up-front development and replication costs of materials, and recovering these costs later by charging for learning materials where appropriate.

The 'bottom-up' approach

The 'bottom up' element of the strategy for introducing open learning involved getting staff to take on the responsibility and commitment needed to make use of open learning in the following ways.

Relating learning to the job

The materials related as closely as possible to people's jobs. Financial markets theory in isolation was not enough, users needed to see how it related to Reuters customers and information products, and how they could use this in their own sales or support roles. There was a large amount of generic CBT material available covering the financial markets that was seldom used, mainly because it was perceived as unrelated to people's jobs as it lacked a Reuters context, and partly due to the accessibility issues discussed below.

The design of the workbooks reflected this requirement, consisting of 'bite sized chunks' of markets knowledge closely integrated with activities to be undertaken using Reuters information products. Also included were sections on the market players, with descriptions of the various roles, and a 'day in the life' written by people active in the markets. These sections proved to be the most popular in the books.

Part of the rationale for the 'bite sized' structure of the workbooks was to ensure that the workbooks could be used not only as a complete primer in a given financial market sector, but also that people could use them as just-in-time performance support tools, to enable sales and support staff preparing for a client visit to quickly remind themselves about, for example, the role of money brokers, the range of financial instruments they trade, and the relevant Reuters information displays.

Involving staff in the development of products

We involved staff from the business in helping to develop and review packages. This ensured that their existence quickly became known throughout the business, and avoided the 'not invented here' syndrome.

Making learning materials attractive to users

The materials we produced were attractive, and people were keen to acquire and use them. The financial markets workbooks were designed and printed to a high quality in attractive presentation packs, which also contained information from the relevant exchanges and markets. Staff found the packs both attractive and easy to use, and demand for them was high, both in the UK and later worldwide. The payback in terms of increased levels of acceptance and usage of packages that are well presented and packaged outweighed the higher production costs.

Choosing appropriate media

Staff wanted just-in-time learning that could be used anywhere – on client sites, at the workplace, on the train or at home. Despite Reuters being such a technology-oriented environment, print-based materials met this requirement more effectively than computer-based learning for financial markets training. The Training Methodology includes in its design phase a justification of the training media chosen. This provides an assurance that the training solution has been designed to be cost-effective. The same cost-effectiveness argument can be used on training users as well as sponsors. They will also respond to the justification for the chosen training media, although perhaps the effectiveness argument is more compelling for users than that of cost.

No parallel running with courses

After an initial 'running in' period to check the effectiveness of the materials, the classroom courses run by an external agency covering the same content areas were withdrawn. This was mainly as a result of feedback on the popularity of the learning materials, and the inadequacy of the courses, which did not present a Reuters-focused approach to markets. People were finding it difficult to digest context-free markets theory, and to relate the material to their jobs. The workbooks became the main learning resource, supported by discussion workshops with markets experts.

Withdrawing the classroom course was also important to cost justify the open learning solution, which would not have been possible had Reuters not saved the costs of the classroom events, and demonstrated that the open learning alternative was both more popular and more effective.

Conflict management

It was important to avoid encroaching on specialist areas that the trainers saw as their preserve, thus side stepping a problem that could have resulted in battle lines being drawn up within the training department. In corporates with in-house training departments, the introduction of open learning has usually had to overcome the barriers set up by trainers, concerned about the future of their own jobs in an increasingly unstable environment. With downsizing and outsourcing still very much the fashion, in-house training departments have often borne a disproportionately high number of head count reductions. In this climate it is hardly surprising that trainers often view the introduction of open learning as a potential threat.

By focusing its activities on areas that were peripheral to the interests of the established trainers, we avoided creating a polarized situation where open learning was seen as eroding their areas of responsibility. The initial training topic that was undertaken using open learning was partly chosen for this reason, and consequentially was not seen by trainers as a threat. Wherever possible, we made efforts to involve them in the development of open learning materials, both to make use of their expertise, and to give them an element of ownership in the finished products. The cooperation worked in both directions, in that open learning skills and techniques were made available to support classroom activities. Typically open learning was used for cognitive learning prior to a classroom event, because trainers could spend more time on skills development and practice. This resulted in trainers being able to use open learning to leverage both the quality and quantity of their output, thus making their own impact and that of open learning more visible to the business.

The integrated approach, using the appropriate combination of open learning and conventional training, helped to avoid conflict with classroom trainers, and opposition from prospective learners, many of whom initially saw open learning as a low-cost half measure that did not offer a substitute for 'proper' training in the classroom.

Access to learning materials

As mentioned previously, a key element in the strategy for gaining acceptance of open learning methods has been to ensure maximum accessibility of learning materials for the users. Although the technical infrastructure to deliver multimedia training is rapidly becoming available at the workplace, CBT multimedia training is unlikely to be as extensively used as print. One of the reasons for the emphasis on print-based learning within Reuters is that the cultural climate in the workplace is not conducive to learning. As a result people prefer either to use a learning centre, or to have materials in a form that enables them to use them at home, or while travelling, without being hampered by the constraints of delivery technology.

Distant learning centres?

Within the UK and Ireland, around 90% of the staff (around 2,900) are based in 18 buildings in and around the City of London. With such a high concentration of staff, the conditions seemed ideal for a learning centre. However, although UKI's learning centre is now well used, it has taken two years to achieve this level of use. People still tend to use the learning centre mainly for CBT and multimedia packages. They prefer to do workbook-based training in the relative privacy of home, or on the train.

Most users are from within the building that houses the learning centre. Staff from other London buildings often find the time taken to get to the learning centre makes it difficult for them to use. Clearly if this is a problem within the square mile of the City, it will be magnified many times over elsewhere in the world, where staff are much more widely dispersed.

It is somewhat of a contradiction for people to have to travel to undertake distance learning. Our experience indicates that for learning centres to be successful, they need to be as close to the workplace as possible, and consequently as small as possible. Instead of having one learning centre with six work-stations serving six sites, one workstation in each of those sites would be more effective in terms of providing convenient and rapid access for larger numbers of people. This brings its own problems, of access to software, and organizing bookings and management of multiple centres.

Reuters is fortunate in having a well-developed corporate network, which is increasingly used for handling courseware delivery and learning centre bookings. When fully developed, this will enable people to book access to any courseware package or training course from any PC, and to run the learning package from any PC with the necessary hardware. This offers the flexibility of learning at the workplace if required, together with ease of management of courseware, and the ability to set up small, localized learning workstations in every building. This will require control systems to be in place to ensure com-pliance with software licences, and upgrades to the bandwidth of WAN links and server capacity to be able to access multimedia across the LAN. As our learning needs are increasingly being met by generic courseware, particularly in the area of management, personal development, and software training, the issue of license control is increasingly important, and is changing the way we book use of learning packages. Whereas with a small number of centralized learning centres running stand alone bespoke courseware it was only neces-sary to ensure that a workstation was available with a copy of the courseware loaded, now it is more important to book the courseware package.

The Reuters Intranet

A new solution to the provision of flexible, on-demand training has now arrived in the form of the corporate Intranet. This has grown rapidly in less than ten months to a network of over 100 sites worldwide. The Intranet is rapidly becoming Reuters primary electronic internal information source.

The UKI Training Web site gives users access to a database containing details of the complete range of learning materials and events on offer, whether they are face-to-face training events, workbooks, video, audio, CBT or multimedia. Users can also see when courses are scheduled, and the number of available places. Future developments will enable them to book course places, learning packages, and use of the learning centre over the Web.

The user interface is currently being redesigned using interactive 'learning maps' that allow users to identify a specific area of job performance. The learning map shows the skill and knowledge components required, struc-tured according to levels and dependencies, and allows users to select those most relevant to their needs.

Users can also download CBT and multimedia packages as well as work-book files that they can print locally. By making available a centralized set of files for on-demand printing, the traditional problems of high cost and time to update print-based learning materials have effectively been removed.

There are no problems with stockpiles of out of date materials, and the cost of replication has shifted from the distributor to the user of the materials.

Electronic distribution of print has inevitably brought with it a number of new problems. Monitoring and controlling distribution is currently not possible, which makes the job of evaluation difficult, and also makes it impossible to charge for materials, UKI Training generally does for users in areas outside of UKI. These issues will be addressed as the technology matures.

A more intractable problem is the production quality of locally printed material. This is limited by printing facilities, which are unlikely to be better than black and white laser printing. Materials printed in this way lose much of their impact and appeal to learners. Reuters is also unable to include externally produced material as part of the learning package, such as the markets publications included in the financial markets packages.

For these reasons, we are now adopting a two-level strategy for print distribution. Centralized commercial colour printing will be used for high volume, high-level 'overview' materials aimed at large audiences. Materials produced in this way will contain relatively stable content that will not date quickly, such as technical product details subject to rapid change. More specialized modules for smaller, specialist audience groups will be available over the internal Web.

In this way the business can benefit from the economies of scale and high production values of commercially produced materials to attract the initial audience for the product, and meet the needs of smaller, more specialized audiences with on-demand material distributed over the Web, which can be easily updated as circumstances demand.

Conclusion

Open learning, as part of an integrated approach to training, is the outcome of a systems approach to addressing performance issues that ensures that training interventions are fit for purpose, and focused on areas of maximum business impact, ensuring that they are valued both by users and by the business.

There are many similarities between introducing open learning and the market positioning of any new product or service. The four Ps of marketing apply equally well to open learning, although perhaps with a slightly different interpretation.

Product
Is the product designed for its target audience? Is the solution and the media used fit for purpose? Does it have the right image and appeal, and can they learn from it? Is there any competition, and if so what is the competitive advantage of the open learning solution? Is it something that managers and learners will value?

Price
Does the business benefit justify its development cost? The return on the investment needs to be made visible by identifying the business impact of the training at the analysis stage, and checking that the planned performance change has taken place at the evaluation stage.

Place
Is the material easily available, and can learners study it wherever they need to? If study at the workplace is not acceptable, can the materials be studied at home/on the train/in a hotel room? Is there a learning centre within easy distance?

Promotion
Are the audience aware of the material, and of its benefits? In addition to roadshows and management presentations, there are usually many corporate communication channels that can be used – e-mail, Intranets, internal publications.

To these four Ps, for any new initiative in a corporate environment a fifth should be added.

Politics
Political considerations are as important as operational ones in ensuring the success of open learning. It is vital that the needs of *all* stakeholders are met, not just those of learners. This may in the case of in-house training departments involve treading a thin line between encroaching on areas sacrosanct to trainers, while still ensuring that learning materials are focused on areas where there is a demand and a business need. Both classroom training and open learning are necessary and of value when integrated into a coherent programme driven by business needs.

References

Revans, R W (1981) 'Action learning and development of self' in *Management Self-Development: Concepts and Practices*, T Boydell and M Pedler (eds), Gower Press, Westmead, England.
Freire, P (1974) *Pedagogy of the Oppressed*, Seabury Press, New York.

Part 2

Education case studies

Chapter 7

Integrated courseware in language learning

Mike Harland, Erica McAteer, and Niall Sclater

Background

A second year course in Basic Portuguese has been a requirement for the Hispanic Studies Honours degree at the University of Glasgow for over 16 years. It has to bring second year university students to a level of language ability sufficient to continue into Honours, where they are expected to handle a whole range of literary texts. This is deemed possible by the historical situation that obtains at Glasgow – most of the students are assumed to have already learned Spanish. It is also necessary to combine the communicative teaching methods of native language assistants concentrating on functions and notions (eg asking, warning, promising as well as routines relating to time, place, currency etc) with the need for a rapid acquisition of grammatical structures that are often quite different from Spanish. Pronunciation in turn provokes orthographic changes in the language, which, unlike Spanish, make the written and spoken language elements quite separate hurdles to be negotiated and much more attention must be given to it.

Traditionally the course had been taught through language classes and lectures, in part by the resident lecturer, but mainly by the *leitora*, a native language teacher supplied on a two to three year contract from Portugal. The temporary nature of the post and the fact that leitores each had their own methods meant that there was little consistency in the teaching content or approach. This was generally rather outdated, since the assistant was conventionally a qualified secondary teacher in his or her late 30s/early 40s. Attempts to get the Portuguese Institute to send younger postgraduates with up-to-date training and flexible methods were to no avail.

There was also a steady growth in the student population with no corresponding increase in staff. Original numbers of 15–20 were now over 30, which made it necessary to do a double shift at 1pm and 4pm each day.

What was really required was a more modern approach with an emphasis on creative language production through the exploitation of student centred resources. A new environment afforded by a modern languages centre with computing, video and satellite facilities eventually came on stream, and the communicative methods of active language production were feeding up from the secondary level with students expecting a greater emphasis on spoken and listening skills.

A complete rethink on the Portuguese course therefore seemed essential. It was decided that the situation should in many ways be reversed – instead of the *leitora* deciding the content and method, the textbook and the CAL software should lay down what had to be learned within the given curriculum structure and timescale, leaving enough freedom for the teacher to provide 'added-value' with personal materials and individual styles of interaction with students.

At this point the technology was improving rapidly, it was felt that the correct environment was at last available. When the course lecturer and a colleague then won a University New Initiatives grant providing them with funds for an assistant programmer, the necessary resources also became available.

The two lecturers became part of an Information Technologies in Teaching Initiative (ITTI) team, dealing with multimedia design in higher education, and their experience here took their ideas a stage further. They wondered whether goal-based learning, with students producing a 'portfolio' or record of their answers, voice recordings and other tasks achieved, might not give added incentives to the learning process. After observation with some prototype trials, they were confident that students could and would work this way.

Finally, two years ago, the Higher Education Funding Councils' Teaching and Learning Technology Programme (TLTP), within its wide aim of introducing computer-based learning into the university curriculum, accepted a bid from Glasgow for an institutional initiative called TILT (Teaching with Independent Learning Technologies). TILT's function was to support the widespread and effective introduction of IT into the present curriculum and evaluate the implementation of courseware designed and developed 'in-house' or brought in from elsewhere, within courses in various disciplines. This provided a timely opportunity, and essential resources, to implement a complete redesign of the Basic Portuguese course.

A new course book, based on the perceived needs of Glasgow students, was already projected and current open and self-teaching Portuguese language courses were surveyed. The idea of a wholly integrated development project, designing both course book and computer courseware as ongoing, editable resources that would be iteratively revised and evaluated with TILT support, was realized.

Year 1

In 1994–95 the traditional lecture-based course was replaced by an open learning oriented approach integrating:

- Weekly timetabled classes in the computer lab with a thematically struc-tured multimedia drill and practice package, designed and produced in-house. The material is organized into separate episodes in the history of a group of students in Portugal, each addressing one or two weeks' coursework. Following the class, the episodes remain accessible as open access resources.
- A course text book, also produced in-house, with exercises on functions and notions connected to the theme of each computer episode, backed up with grammatical structures and vocabulary.
- Three communicative language classes each week with a *leitora*. These classes are framed by the CAL + book structure, extending and enlarging upon material provided by the thematic episodes.

The class also attended weekly lectures on Portuguese culture and litera-ture throughout the course, in accordance with the requirements for all mod-ern languages degrees at the University.

The current version of the learning software was produced in Macromedia Director on the Macintosh platform, for the delivery machines provided in the Hispanic Studies computer lab. A PC version is presently being produced (Harland, 1995; Sclater, 1995).

Eight thematic episodes, with two introductory sessions to familiarize the student with the pronunciation, the computer interface (sound input and replay, animation and replay, with 'point and click', 'drag and drop' and text input exercises) and ways of working through the material, make up the basic ten week computer course.

Each episode includes a log-on screen, a scenario with a set of cartoon characters (one of which represents the student), a task list of activities to be accomplished by the student within that scenario and an initial spoken (Portuguese) dialogue (passive for the student) that sets the context and introduces some of the activities and concepts to be covered in that session. Playback buttons allow the student to stop, start or repeat the dialogue at will. Online translation resources are also available (see Figures 7.1 and 7.2).

The idea is to prepare the student for the next active task, while affording a self-paced reinforcement of vocabulary and formulaic phrases learned in class. They are then invited to join in a similar conversation by recording their own voices, which can be repeated and rerecorded at will before being saved. When they have finished this active dialogue they can replay it to hear how their responses sound within the constructed conversation.

Each episode also provides drill and practice exercises that reinforce aural

Figure 7.1   Sample screen

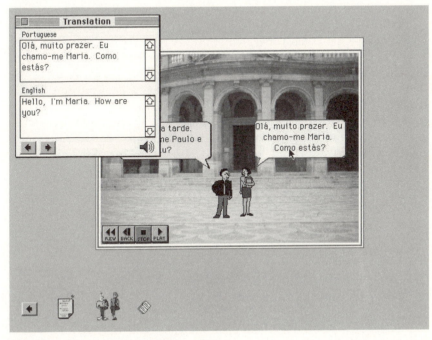

Figure 7.2   Sample screen showing translation

comprehension, pronunciation, spelling and grammar knowledge already covered in the week's natural language classes.

The departmental computer lab provides 21 Apple Macintosh machines, with headphones and microphones. Students can easily interact with side, facing and rear neighbours. The room was booked for two one-hourly periods each week for the exclusive use of the class, who were also free to use it on open access (between 9am and 9pm) when space was available. During timetabled sessions both teacher and developer were present for the two introductory sessions, after which the developer was accessible via online link – or by any student walking up a short flight of stairs. The students were divided into two groups to ensure sufficient availability of machines at each of the timetabled sessions, though this grouping was not rigorously enforced.

The course textbook has the same thematic structure as the computer modules, with two introductory units to familiarize students with the problems of pronunciation. It offers information on vocabulary, grammar and structure with a central focus on interactive exercises dealing with functions and notions connected to the theme of each episode. It can be used by the students when working alone or together, away from the formal classroom or lab context, and by the *leitora* to frame and support the weekly natural language classes.

Three natural language speaking classes were held each week. They ran for an hour covering conversation sessions, a question-and-answer time, exercises and homework assignments. So far as was reasonable they were conducted in Portuguese. Effectively, these were the only 'taught' sessions, with use of the two other main learning components (after initial introductory sessions in the computer labs) being left to the discretion of individual students.

The integrated course is truly multimedia and truly interactive: the natural language classes are interactive in the full sense of the word, using the medium of human face-to-face communication and the book medium, which provides exercises enabling further language feedback and support; the computer element, timetabled to follow this process, then reinforces all these interactions with images, animation, text and sound with a fairly basic level of input and manipulation from the learner and the ability to reflect on the input and feedback provided. It was felt that this order of events is the correct one, placing the more limited interactivity of the computer as a subsidiary resource and one of final consolidation, not prime instruction.

Evaluation

Our experience of evaluating the TILT material in courses across the university confirms a common-sense understanding that CAL never operates as an independent factor but always interacts with characteristics of students, teachers, the course the material supports and its role in that course, as well as the physical and social environment within which the computer mediated learning occurs. Ideally, a close study of each individual case would take student, teacher, course and environmental variables, acknowledge those that cannot be controlled but must be accepted as 'givens' within the study situation, and identify those that might be modified so as to optimize learning. With over 20 sites ranging in discipline from accountancy to zoology, and only 2.5 evaluating staff, the ideal was never realized and a more pragmatic approach used a complementary set of methods to capture some quantitative and qualitative data on critical issues, illuminated by 'sampling' techniques.

Figure 7.3 lists the procedures used, fuller details of these and discussion of the development of TILT evaluation methods is given elsewhere (McAteer *et al.*, 1996; Draper *et al.*, 1996).

Topic experience questionnaires

Computer experience questionnaires

Post-lab session questionnaires

Learning confidence 'logs'

Interviews – students, teachers, developer

Observation of labs

CAL-user logs

Course resource questionnaires

(Exam outcomes were also studied)

Figure 7.3   Evaluation methods

Course progress during Year 1

So far as previous experience with computers was concerned, two thirds of the students had received no training at all in computer use. The rest had, in the main, received word processing training but little else. Most students said that they used computers less than once a month. (This is in marked contrast to some other groups with whom we worked that year, notably a class of first year BTechEd students taking a computer-based maths course, whose responses to the same questionnaire provided an almost completely reversed pattern.) It is not necessarily true that computer experience in itself is a predictor of student behaviour when using computer-assisted learning resources – nor indeed whether existing study strategies (if any!) will be transferred.

For what it is worth, these students were low on declared computer skills, middling on knowledge about computers and 'dubious' rather than negative in general attitude, with low confidence about managing technology. Although using headphones was no new experience for them, most were uncertain and some embarrassed about using a microphone.

All had studied languages before coming to university and for most this study included Spanish, usually at school. Many were continuing their study 'for enjoyment' though two said simply that they were 'no good at science'!

There were few human–computer interface (HCI) type problems even so far as using the microphone and replaying recordings were concerned – a lot of piloting had been done with developing versions of the prototype and it would have been surprising if many bugs had survived through to the actual classroom. By the third episode, calls for help with the equipment or interface had dwindled and most students reported spending all their time concentrating on subject related problems.

Generally speaking students would start up the package, go straight into the appropriate episode, listen to the scene-setting dialogue and proceed through the 'story', participating where prompted by speaking their text. As a general rule they played back what they had said, listening through the headphones and re-recording if not satisfied. From observation and from self-report they enjoyed this activity, as well as finding it useful for developing their pronunciation skills. The familiarization sessions had obviously worked, and the students used the equipment and carried out the exercises with both confidence and competence, so far as the technology was concerned.

A few students made consistent use of the online resources that fronted each episode, such as the 'Task List' or 'Meet the Cast' options that were set up to orientate them. Others did not access these, beyond the first couple of episodes. Nor did those whose logs we studied make much use of the online dictionary – either during comprehension or when prompted to speak themselves. On the other hand, we observed that many students used their own dictionaries, which they would be accustomed to doing throughout their classes. As well as being a familiar action, this could be preferable to interrupting an exercise by on-screen activity. They did tend to access the sound dialogues that were provided to set context for each episode.

When they got to the exercises – which included gap filling, word search, obeying (Portuguese) spoken instructions to move objects, select options etc, they worked right through each, sometimes repeating. The exercises seemed to present about the right level of difficulty – the logs showed that students got half to two thirds wrong first time. Although occasionally a student would pass headphones to a neighbour for a listen, this was not a collaborative exercise – unlike the conversation classes. The students worked with the online material and, effectively, with themselves via the feedback presented by the system.

Responses from the course questionnaires were generally positive for the software, with well expressed reservations ('there should be more and harder exercises!', 'the word search tests are boring'). Students liked the novelty and seemed to appreciate the pedagogy behind it. They liked the graphics and animation, hearing themselves speak and testing their comprehension of spoken text. They went through the exercises until they got enough right to satisfy themselves – from this activity and from other measures it was clear that they wanted to be challenged by the tasks set but also that these had to be interesting to do.

There was a very high level of spontaneous approval, both spoken and in the 'open ended' sections of the questionnaires, for the natural language classes. The students considered these crucial for their learning.

The grammar and language structure teaching was approved by the students, who were able to find very little to supplement this among available library and language lab resources. The addition of an index and dictionary was requested

Overall the students approved the content and integrated structure of the course, though criticisms about points when the information got out of sequence between the language classes and the computer episodes, or did not seem to relate to material currently being covered by the book, were severe.

In general, students' ratings of confidence about the course learning objectives rose slightly through time but was not marked, and for several students confidence on certain objectives (noticeably, grammar) did not increase at all. Talking of this with both students and with teachers it seems plausible to count language acquisition among those skills that seem harder the more you know of them – as one student said, 'learning a language never stops'.

Implementation problems

Before looking at the outcomes of their learning – at least as far as standard assessment procedures measure these – we should describe some of the problems that beset this course during the year.

Beyond the introductory and familiarization period the computer classes, though timetabled, were not compulsory. That is, students could be sure of priority of machine use at that time, but could also come in at their own convenience to go through exercises or to repeat them. Problems here should not have required hindsight – some opted for 'leaving them till the end of term' – a policy we often find adopted in other courses, resulting in mad scrambles before the exams when there is probably a lot to panic about in other directions as well. Also the whole point of sequencing the labs, the conversation classes and the recommended use of the book is lost and the students soon realized this.

Information sequencing became seriously jumbled during the first term because of problems with the *leitora* – one became ill, a replacement couldn't get her leaving papers from the Portuguese authorities... in the end a substitute was found 'at home' and things proceeded in a more orderly fashion.

Toward the end of the second half of the year the episodes ran out. The eight episodes with two familiarization sessions that made up the basic course, and the corresponding book sections had been completed. These had extended beyond the anticipated period as a result of extra revision sessions needed to supplement teaching that would have been given during missed language classes, so that two weeks would be devoted to one episode. There had been clashes of production priority (the development team had taken on further heavy commitments) that for some time had meant that production had lagged to the point of only just preceding demand. A decision was taken to limit the material, for this year, to the basic course only and some bundles of exercises were provided for the rest of term two and for open access use during term three, when timetabled classes stopped for the general exam revision period.

We could 'see' the disturbance waves from all this in the ongoing survey and interview data, and also saw it settle down once the language speaking classes were properly under way.

Exam outcomes

Although the teaching method had completely changed, the course was examined in the traditional way – the degree exam question content changes from year to year, but nothing else (and that not much). We checked student entry qualifications and language background across the 1993–94 and 1994–95 cohorts and found them more or less equal. Tables 7.1 and 7.2 show the course degree outcomes and breakdown by paper.

First, the grades were much improved over the previous year. Secondly, breaking down the overall marks to show those for individual papers, we found that the improvement is consistent across all topics, with the exception of the one component whose teaching did not change from the previous year – the Literature paper.

Students' lack of confidence over the course learning objectives was not reflected in their production fluency. The examiners said that it took just over

Table 7.1 Degree grades (1994, traditional course; 1995, integrated course).

Grade	A	B	C	D	F	G
1994	–	12	5	5	1	4
1995	15	14	3	3	–	1

Table 7.2 Class average exam paper marks (1994, traditional course; 1995, integrated course).

	Average mark (%)	
Exam paper	1994	1995
Oral	62	74
Comprehension	51	57
Translation	59	73
Literature	67	66
Grammar	43	64
Essay	55	71

twice the usual time to mark the papers, which showed whole paragraphs of self-generated text given in response to reading comprehension questions, rather than the usual 'one line reprocessed question text'.

Interim conclusions

Taking exam outcomes as a measure, we have to count this new, integrated course as a success despite its serious problems and occasional glitches. For this we also have to thank the students, who certainly seemed highly motivated, and give a large bouquet to the supply teacher who filled the *leitora* role.

Nevertheless course planning for the second year had to take account of the experience gained in year one, including:

- the need for the new *leitora* to understand the structure and relationship between all the components of the course and base her teaching within this from the start;
- the need for the students to be encouraged – perhaps required – to stick to the timetabled sessions at least for the main part of the course;
- the provision of an extra menu of exercises with each episode that task the skills of the students further, for use in self assessment and revision;
- the evaluation of changes made to the course text book.

Liaison was made with the new *leitora* as soon as she arrived in September to explain the course and its intentions.

It was envisaged that assessment procedures in 1996 would remain the same, ie the traditional exam form. Degree grades and individual paper marks would be examined against previous years' course outcomes, taking account of student variables and teacher changes.

Year 2

When the term started for the new cohort of beginners, it was found that numbers matriculating had increased dramatically and without explanation. With over fifty students, it became physically impossible to have just the two weekly lab sessions and our only option was to form four groups, attending fortnightly.

Networking problems in the first few weeks of term one disrupted classes during this initial familiarization period and to circumvent them it was decided to allow students free access outside timetabled slots. Some students lost faith in the value of the software and the usefulness of the class confirming our belief that initial confidence is a major factor in winning acceptance of computer-aided learning and that CAL must be seen and felt to be an authoritative and essential part of the learner strategy.

However, a look at the logs after the first term indicated that although some students had stopped using the computers at a time coinciding with the network problems, they came back towards the end of term, just before their class exams, to do 2 or 3 modules in one session.

It is interesting to bear in mind here an important point made by several students from the previous year, indicating that they saw the computer as a revision aid rather than a learning aid, contrary to our intentions but certainly in keeping with more traditional views on the purpose and usefulness of CAL (eg an optional tool for drilling and testing). We can therefore see that an open-access approach might presently be 'hostile' to an integrated course where a disciplined use of the software is essential to its aims.

Tables 7.3 and 7.4 show that, despite the problems with the computer class, the results at the end of the year were, with two rather important exceptions, almost as good as those from the 1994–95 session and generally up from the last year of the traditional course. Performance on the oral exam was considerably down, as was that for the translation paper. Although we will certainly watch this situation, we do not feel able to attribute direct causes from any particular change in resource use. Focus meetings and staff debriefings indicated that the general atmosphere was similar and the enthusiasm of the students was maintained.

Table 7.3 Degree grades in first and second years of integrated course implementation.

Grade	A	B	C	D	F	G
1995	15	14	3	3	–	1
1996	11	14	7	5	1	1

Table 7.4 Class average exam paper marks during first and second years of integrated course implementation.

	Average mark (%)	
Exam paper	1995	1996
Oral	74	57
Comprehension	57	66
Translation	73	61
Literature	66	62
Grammar	64	61
Essay	71	66

Conclusions

If the use of computers as an open learning tool is to be successful, then (a) it has to be relevant; (b) it has to be entertaining/engaging; and (c) we still believe it needs to be integrated with the other learning resources supporting a course. Designing for integration is hard. Tying in a computer course with a text course is a much more difficult design exercise than would at first appear and the need to sequence events properly is crucial. The idea of a fully integrated course is nice in theory but rather different in practice. The indications are that the traditional view of computers as primarily a revision or reference tool still holds sway. The need to 'police' classes is an inefficient use of human resources, but if one is willing to include these methods in one's teaching then this study seems to indicate that it can be beneficial for second year students who need to be encouraged into new practices to see their benefits.

The advent of the World Wide Web promises some solutions to the problems faced. The ready accommodation of students to the Internet as an 'accepted' cultural activity and the rapid take up of its Hypertext interface means that students may be more willing to interact with the courseware, especially now that the book can be integrated with the software by embedding the interactive exercises into the reference side of the material. Students can print out any part of the information, the dictionary and the grammar can be consulted while studying the whole text, not only the brief dialogues; in short, the course can be turned into interactive study material in parallel with the classes rather than just tasks and exercises that repeat the revision/reference syndrome.

The key lessons to emerge from our experience have been:

- Timetable CAL elements formally, to signify their importance as an integral part of the course.
- Encourage and support the regular use of the courseware within timetabled sessions, to ensure that careful sequencing and pacing is not lost by students trying to catch up on all the CAL sessions at the end of the course.
- Avoid delivery strategies that depend on a single node or link that might fail. Staff involved in the course should be multiskilled so that they can take over from each other if need be. Try to adopt a 'belt and braces' approach so that in the event of a technical hitch you have some kind of back up.
- Schedule production well ahead of delivery and stick to your schedule.
- Maintain some flexibility in the use of resources by ensuring that you do not integrate open learning components too rigidly with face-to-face methods.
- Remember, success can breed problems. Achievement of learning goals may result in more and higher quality assignment content, imposing greater work loads on assessors.
- Evaluation is an essential and even motivating part of course development. Things seldom come right the first time and at many stages it is typical for a teacher/designer to give up the whole idea because results are not what he or she expected.

The existence of the De Tudo um Pouco course has had a knock-on effect on other subjects within the Department of Hispanic Studies at Glasgow. The courseware outline has been transferred to Spanish and is being used as rein-forcement material, but not as part of any integrated course. It will therefore be possible at a later stage to see the comparative success level of this more traditional non-integrated approach. Perhaps more interesting, will be the effects on beginners who have done this first year Spanish version and then see it as an integrated course for their Portuguese. The danger is that the use of familiar templates may breed contempt(!), as they will know some of the solutions to the tasks, but it could equally smooth the problems of computer familiarity we have already encountered. Meanwhile, plans are in place to adapt the Portuguese templates to a Catalan course where there is an existing course book and a similar integrated method can be implemented.

Acknowledgements

The work described in this chapter was funded by the UK Higher Education Funding Councils' Teaching and Learning Technology Programme. The authors would also like to thank: Paul Donnelly, Chair of TILT Group D (Multimedia), who collaborated on prototype versions of the courseware; Cristina Sousa, who worked hard on the graphic design and animation, in the department of Hispanic Studies; Margaret Brown, Steve Draper and Fiona Henderson, fellow members of the TILT Group E (Evaluation) in the Department of Psychology at the University of Glasgow.

References

Draper, S W, Brown, M I, Henderson F and McAteer, E (1996) 'Integrative evalua-tion: an emerging role for classroom studies of CAL', *Computers in Education*, 26(1–3), 17–32.

Harland, M (1995) 'De Tudo Um Pouco... "A Little Bit of Everything...": A year piloting integrated textbook and computer courseware for Portuguese', Proceedings of *EUROCALL'95, Technology Enhanced Language Learning: Focus on Integration* (1996), 163–71, Universidad Politécnica de Valencia, Spain.

McAteer, E, Harland, M and Sclater, N (1996) 'De Tudo um Pouco – a little bit of eve-rything', *Journal of Active Learning*, 3, December, 10–15.

Sclater, N (1995) 'Strategies for distributing and running multimedia courseware over networked machines', Proceedings of *EUROCALL'95, Technology Enhanced Language Learning: Focus on Integration* (1996), 405–14, Universidad Politécnica de Valencia, Spain.

Chapter 8

Conversion of a mathematics course to tutor-supported computer-assisted flexible learning

Gordon Doughty, Maggie Pollock, Erica McAteer and Ian Turner

Introduction

Teachers at the University of Glasgow overcame a range of impediments to convert a two-year mathematics course from traditional lectures to student-centred, tutor-supported computer-assisted flexible learning. Formative evaluation of the course in 1994–95 resulted in some adaptation during that year, and further adaptation in 1995–96. The course now provides better learning at lower cost. This case study illustrates many conclusions on how to make social and technological changes towards the use of Information Technology (IT) in teaching and learning.

Change is usually sought when at least one stakeholder feels a mismatch between their values and current practice, or becomes aware of strengths, weaknesses, opportunities or threats, particularly economic and other social pressures. They usually try to move in at least one of three directions: better quality, cheaper provision (lower cost), or quicker delivery (less time). Improving in any one of these directions results in one or both of the other two deteriorating, unless more resources can be employed, or greater efficiency found.

Considerations of power, politics and social equity may prevent transfer of existing resources. More resources, such as extra lecturers, are seldom obtainable. Resources available to universities from government have been declining, but performance expectations continue to rise for increased access, excellence in research and better teaching.

Efficiency gains can be obtained through the use of technology, IT seeming particularly promising. However, technological opportunities cannot always be grasped easily. Surveys carried out in 1993 and 1996 showed that many

Glasgow University teachers used computers for some aspects of teaching, and more were interested. Those reporting difficulties in adopting IT cited lack of time, support staff, information and suitable materials.

Demonstrating ways to overcome these difficulties was a key output of the University of Glasgow's Teaching with Independent Learning Technologies (TILT) project, in which the authors were participating (Doughty *et al.*, 1994). TILT was established with grants from the UK higher education funding bodies, the Higher Education Funding Councils of England and Wales, the Scottish Higher Education Funding Council and the Department of Education, Northern Ireland (HEFCE, HEFCW, SHEFC and DENI), under their Teaching and Learning Technology Programme (TLTP), and from the University of Glasgow's New Initiatives Fund. TILT was one of a few TLTP projects funded to show how teaching and learning can be made more productive and efficient throughout a single higher education institution.

Although the initial emphasis of TILT was on using IT, the main focus of the project became more about attending to the quality of the entire teaching and learning situation rather than particular pieces of courseware:

> 'What performs more or less well is not some material or medium (a lecture, a book, a computer program) but the whole teaching and learning episode managed by the teacher who employs [the educational innovation] as one element.' (Draper *et al.*, 1994)

Problems with an existing maths course

The Bachelor of Technological Education (BTechEd) concurrent initial teacher education degree is taught from the Robert Clark Centre for Technological Education, in the Faculty of Engineering, in collaboration with St Andrew's College, Glasgow. It produces school teachers of Technological Studies, Craft and Design and Graphic Communication. In 1993–94 problems arose in the maths course for first year students.

The students vary widely in age and past experience, and in maths background. Most qualifications were recent, but some were years old. Students came with different sets of maths skills, which often did not include the normal prerequisites to a first year maths course.

These students need to acquire manipulative skills, rather than high theoretical understanding. The target level approximates that of first year engineers. Before 1992, the small class was taught separately, with close cooperation between maths teachers and technology teachers. Then timetabling and partnership changes severed our connection with the maths teachers, and led to the students joining a lecture-based maths class of 200 first year engineers, spreading the course over two years. The BTechEd students struggled, neglected other subjects and 29% (6/21) failed the course and dropped out.

Part of the problem was in linking the students' two active learning modes: practising basic maths manipulation skills until automatic, and applying maths to engineering problems of concern to them. The time delay in linking these modes may range from a few minutes in a class to several months before an application emerges in a technology course.

Although the joint class of 200 did cycle between theory, engineering example and practice within the lecture period, our target students were not able to keep up with the manipulative skills. The degree course organizers (the first two authors) would have preferred to teach all maths inside the Technology courses, as and when needed, but could not get agreement from all course teachers: some were unwilling to sacrifice course content and others were unwilling to teach what they considered to be prerequisite skills. We lacked control over staff in other departments, and we were reluctant to weaken their enthusiasm for their teaching. An efficient and manageable alternative was needed urgently.

A computer-assisted flexible learning solution

The problem had been recognized during the 1993–94 session by the staff delivering the maths lectures and the staff responsible for the whole degree course. The latter, being involved in the TILT project, were keen to invest time and resources in looking for computer-based solutions to maths teaching problems. During the 1994 summer vacation several possible maths packages were identified through the Computers in Teaching Initiative (CTI) Centre for Mathematics and other sources, and a package called CALMAT (Computer-Aided Learning in Mathematics) was selected.

CALMAT, developed at Glasgow Caledonian University (Cook 1994, Cook and Hornby 1995), provides 50 modules of teaching, and drill and practice tutorial exercises, with self assessment tests and an associated diagnostic exam. Handouts with paper exercises are provided as a supplement (or even alternative) to each module. Although DOS-based (a Windows version is under development), it has a clear and easy to use interface, has evolved over many years use in higher education institutions with students much like our own (Tabor 1993), and is supported by a maths teaching team.

We felt that its instructional design suited our objectives: to provide practical maths knowledge and skills, applicable in engineering and technology project work and beyond, when students are themselves teaching in secondary school classrooms. It caters for the wide variety of student skills by providing student-centred flexible learning with independent study resources whilst being able to access diagnostic information to promote appropriate teacher support. Although it was anticipated that most students would take advantage of timetabled tutor support, students would be encouraged to take an independent learning approach if it suited them. They could also use CALMAT on home computers if available.

Gaining acceptance

Objections were expected from some members of the faculty who have taught maths before. Some, with experience of unsatisfactory primitive computer packages, were sceptical about using any CAL for maths. Others felt that a large rapid change of an entire course could be disastrous. But being involved in the wider TILT project made it easier to overcome objections from the stakeholders of the degree course. A wider group of stakeholders in the TILT project and its outcomes (including senate committees, management group, faculties, planning units, departments, other course teaching teams, teachers, students) were expected to support an IT solution. The proposal to use CALMAT stressed the use of adaptive strategies – action research and evaluation using the resources of the TILT project.

The problem became widely recognized through the quality assurance system when the results were reported for the main and resit examination, and students dropped out. Politically, the decision to adopt a new approach was influenced strongly by a powerful group who were completing the validation procedure for the degree (the degree had originally been started as an interim measure with no time to pass through all normal procedures). In September 1994, alerted by this problem, and also appraised of possible solutions, the BTechEd Validation Panel noted:

> 'that concerns had been raised regarding the teaching of Mathematics on the course, with particular reference to loading and style of teaching, and sought an assurance that this was being addressed as a matter of urgency. The team referred to a proposal to purchase a teaching package, 'Mathematics', and to run it with tutorials.'

and recommended to the (then) Joint Council of the University of Glasgow and St Andrew's College that approval be given (to the degree course) subject to the condition

> 'that a move towards a different method of teaching Mathematics in the course be implemented immediately.'

Negotiation was needed to persuade the operators of an engineering computer cluster to mount the software on their machines. They did not know, and had not evaluated the software, especially for compatibility with their ways of operating. They had not previously served the needs of this group of students with so many machines over so long a period of time. They felt hard pressed for desk spaces and computer memory. Our timetabling took their loading into account. A promise to fund more server memory seemed to help, although this has not yet been claimed.

IT skill training is part of the first year BTechEd degree course, introducing several CAL packages. No general resistance to the use of a package for learning maths was expected, if it provided a flexible course of study tailored specifically to each student's need. This turned out to be the case.

Course procedure

All students sat an initial diagnostic test of multiple-choice questions. This allowed individual programmes of work to be scheduled for the first term. A weekly three hour (non compulsory) class was timetabled for the year's teaching period in the computer room, which had at least one tutor present. Students were free to use the computer room at other times during term or vacation, with teaching assistance available by appointment, and often on demand. The use of CALMAT extends into the second year of study, and students from both years are now timetabled together.

Copies of the software could be purchased for home use. No formal lectures (or tutorials in 1994–95) were run, except to go over class exam outcomes. Two text books were recommended to complement coursework. Initial problems in understanding how to use CALMAT, mainly in navigation and entering numerical answers, were overcome by intensive tutor and technician support during the first few weeks.

During term two all students followed the same work programme (rather than individualized programmes), but at their own pace. 'Poor achievers' falling behind schedule received extra tutor support. In 1995–96 effort was made to identify earlier those students having difficulty. Fortnightly tutorial classes were provided, led by 'demand issues' and supported by some peer tutoring. Students' progress was also monitored more closely through the modules, though interfering as little as possible with the 'student-centred, own pace independent learning' model.

The diagnostic test was repeated at the end of term one, embedded in the first class exam. The second class exam took place at the beginning of the third term. The course was assessed by a degree exam halfway through the third term. Exemption could be gained through results of the two class exams.

Students' and teachers' perspectives and changing roles

In the 1994–95 session a TILT evaluator (McAteer) surveyed students and staff (Pollock *et al.*, 1996). In questionnaires and interviews students rated themselves generally more confident about maths principles and practice as they went through the course and most students actively liked the working environment, which they felt included plenty of peer support. Teaching staff were interviewed by the evaluator during the course and afterwards and were even more positive than the students.

Changing to this method of teaching has affected the ways in which academics manage their jobs. Pollock took most responsibility for the work, and spent a great deal of time at intervals during the year in ensuring that each student had access to appropriate resources, and in discussing progress through their pre-negotiated course of study. She welcomed the saving of time needed to prepare and deliver lectures, and preferred operating in a less stressful, flexible way, responding to student's needs rather than pursuing a rigid timetable of pre-planned events. The tutoring time was shared with Doughty and Turner, permitting other activities to take place in the time-tabled periods. One of the tutors (Doughty) was pleased that his (rather dormant) maths skills were seldom exercised, most of the students' problems being easily solved by jointly exploring the package. A course team approach, with lecturers, tutors, technician and evaluator, has superseded the lone lecturer approach.

Importing established and supported software, in this case, has been very cost effective. Costs encountered were only £300 per year for the site licence and £2.50 per student per year for photocopying supporting material. Timetabling two years of students together with CALMAT has saved 75 teacher hours each year, as well as lecture preparation time.

Our evaluation of these new approaches to maths teaching has had an impact on ways in which other courses are being developed and delivered. Others teaching maths to engineers have adopted CALMAT to support weaker students, and the Mathematics Department is actively considering adopting it. Doughty has changed a large proportion of teaching electronics and electrical engineering to a similar kind of tutor-supported flexible learning, using very low cost CAL. Pollock is using available packages for teaching a mechanics course, much of which is now student-centred learning. Debate on these kinds of teaching methods with colleagues in other disciplines has assisted their preparations for change.

Assessment results

Detailed analysis of assessment results in the first year of using CALMAT is presented by Pollock et al. (1996). In 1994–95 the first year degree exam mark average was 40% (the better students had been exempt from this exam). The outcomes were acceptable in that they were on a par with the previous year. Although the assessment procedures, of necessity, differed from those for previous years, the same external examiner's criteria had been satisfied. It is not, however, possible to make any direct comparisons between the exam outcomes of 1994–95 and the previous year, apart from being encouraged that the number of failures after resits fell from six (after normative scaling was applied to the raw marks) to four (out of 21) with no normative scaling.

Unlike findings elsewhere (Noss, 1995), entry qualifications were not direct predictors of grades. However, the best predictor was the diagnostic scores at the end of term one – those who came out best on this got the best degree grades, those at the bottom end stayed there. This major issue was tackled with the next cohort of students through the new course. In 1995–96 there were no failures and the exam average score increased to 59%. This time the scoring after the first class exam was not a predictor of the final result. Those who produced the best scores still received exemptions, but the worst scores moved up dramatically for the final exam result – in fact one had an exemption and another the best exam score! The extra tutorials for the students with difficulty had paid off. A better predictor of the degree exam result was the result of the second class exam, which took place about three weeks before the main exam. Those who did badly in that exam also did badly in the main exam.

The improvement in maths may have contributed to improved degree exam results for first year electronics and mechanics in 1995/6.

Reflections on changing to IT in teaching methods

Reviewing the introduction of CALMAT, and its continuing activities, we have interpreted how we were able to make this change successfully. There is much literature on organizational change, some of which specifically identifies variables and processes that affect technological change. Some points of view have been particularly helpful to us in introducing IT into higher education teaching and learning:

- a systems-based methodology for real-world problem-solving (Checkland and Scholes, 1990);
- an action research approach to organizational change and the role of change agents (Elliot, 1991);
- research on *Leading Academics* (Middlehurst, 1992);
- *Rethinking University Teaching* (Laurillard, 1993);
- a taxonomy of skills, knowledge and strategies needed for successful educational innovation (Fullan, 1991; Scott and Robinson, 1995).
- methods of assessing IT investments (Farby *et al.*, 1993).

Our experience of applying these points of view suggests that, in order to make a satisfactory technological change, many interrelated factors need to be identified and understood. Each of them is discussed to show how they were found to be in a beneficial state, or were made so.

Issues

There must be a perception of dissatisfaction or a problem to be solved, eg quality, access, accountability, efficiency, economy, government policy, uncertainty, stress, conflict, strengths, weaknesses, opportunities, threats or failures. We identified a weakness, a quality problem in the teaching of maths to a particular group of students. Our strengths and opportunities resulted from the TILT project and the organizational structure of the degree course. We also intended to improve efficiency in response to government policy that has resulted in more students per available teacher.

Systems and subsystems

It is necessary to identify and understand the systems and subsystems involved and their inputs, outputs, processes, assessment, evaluation, feedback, control, culture, organizational structure, hierarchies and networks. Although teaching of the degree course is shared between institutions and departments, it has a clear identity, with a cohort of students progressing together through all four years, and a base where staff and students meet regularly. A strong sense of ownership pervades. There were many benefits of using a course team approach, with lecturers, tutors, technician and evaluator.

Management, policy and support

Is there top-down command and control, using rewards and sanctions, or are some policies very firm but others and their details in the hands of those who apply them? Can changes be radical, or only small? Do teachers have enough power, resource allocation, room to move, training, staff development and support? Do staff feel that their efforts will be rewarded? The University of Glasgow has clear policies on IT and on IT in teaching and learning. The use of IT for teaching is a bottom up movement driven by individual teachers who have found a use for it and who are spread widely across the institution. Management has not been the driving force. The teachers on this course had made much use of the Staff Development Service and the Teaching and Learning Service.

Leadership, change agents and action

There should be agents of change, leaders in the broad sense, who create a climate for change, and carry out a project to solve 'the problem', modify goals, or reach a better understanding that leads to less dissatisfaction in the lives of those in the system. We were empowered, by faculty practice, and through the TILT project, to be agents of change, and carry out a project to solve 'the problem'. We were prepared, if necessary, to change staff, student activities and organizational structures. So far there has been little modification of goals.

Compare ideal tasks with reality

Associated with any problem will be a mission, aims, objectives and specific tasks. It was clear that the task of delivering a more effective maths course was a necessary prerequisite to achieving the mission, aims and objectives of the degree.

It is helpful to compare the tasks that occur in the problem situation with the necessary activities that would occur if it were solved. Then there is scope for comprehensive investigation of alternatives, and imaginative visions of how they may work. Our most compelling comparison was that students were not getting enough practice in maths skills to enable them to automatically recognize and apply appropriate routines to new problems. Also the lecture course had not taken into account the wide variety of previous maths experience.

Courseware evaluation

If a learning resource such as courseware can be identified, it should be evaluated for content, pedagogy and usability. Only if no courseware can be found, or adapted, should teachers consider producing their own. Several possible maths packages were investigated through the CTI Centre for Mathematics and other sources. CALMAT was judged to be the most suitable, and, with its author being in the same city, was easily investigated by the teaching team and seen in use by a typical class.

Methodology

The process of changing passes through stages of analysis/planning, action, evaluation/appraisal, reflection and revision, proceeding in a spiral fashion over extended periods of time, as in the critically reflexive action research form of social inquiry, the systems-based approach to solving human activity problems, and the design process that permeates current technology teaching. There was much consultation and engagement of those who would be affected by change. The project did pass through these stages, so far in two twists in a spiral fashion over two years. This has been assisted by a study of institutional change through the wider 'action research-like' process of TILT.

Integrative evaluation

Evaluation techniques should be used to integrate IT into the course (Draper *et al.*, 1996). During the first year we applied questionnaires on students' experience of and attitudes to computers and the course, confidence logs, focus groups, and studied assessment results. Teachers were interviewed and debriefed. As a result, many adjustments were made during each year of presenting the course, one being the introduction of special face-to-face tutorials for those students that the assessment revealed as weaker.

Know-how

The agents of change must be able to apply appropriate technology, pedagogy, organizational and project management, and have the ability to learn. We formed a project group as part of TILT's activities. Our previous experience included instructional design and many uses of IT. We were skilled in pedagogy (especially of maths teaching) which is also a major part of the BTechEd degree course. Through projects such as TILT, and earlier industrial employment, some of us have much experience of organizational and project management. We have used and taught a range of design processes. In a very short time – September 1994 – we obtained the courseware, had it mounted on two computer clusters, printed handouts, specified textbooks, designed students' study and assessment schemes, and planned our integrative evaluation.

Resources and investment

A change to using more IT in teaching and learning cannot be made without some investment, either directly in a course, or in the infrastructure of the institution. There will be competing claims on resources, that must be resolved politically or by economic arguments. The agents of change need time, resources, cooperation, support, goodwill and priority to carry out a project. Although resources could be acquired with funds from TLTP and elsewhere, in this project we required no additional hardware or network provision, and only used a small amount of the teachers' time. Priority for us to spend time to carry out the project was justified mainly by the previous loss of students rather than by the need to find a case study for TILT.

People and interpretations

Those making changes need to identify the people involved who may be mediators, leaders, subversives, sponsors or in other roles, and understand their attitudes, values, beliefs and personalities. People will base their actions, or inaction, on their own interpretations of all the factors discussed here. A great deal of dialogue is needed on the meanings of the concepts involved, the nature of the problem and the consequences of its possible solutions.

Throughout TILT we did not advocate culture change for our colleagues.

We adapted our language of presentation to relate to many philosophical/ sociological points of view, often simply at a common-sense practical level. We were interested in how IT is used or required by teachers whose views tend to be formed by adherence to one or more paradigms. The authors tend to adopt an eclectic, mixed methods, pragmatic set of theories and paradigms of designing learning processes, and in this case we chose to use a package and approach that is more behaviourist than constructivist.

Associated university teachers and administrators did require convincing that it was worthwhile to invest in IT for this teaching. The kinds of evidence demanded varied considerably, but, as we have found throughout the TILT project, staff found the most compelling to be:

- peer acceptance, favourable reactions from academic colleagues;
- enthusiastic response from students;
- favourable reports in accreditation and quality assurance procedures;
- results from properly conducted, analysed and reported evaluation;
- learning from the teacher's own experience, including action research;
- theory of its use fits an ideology, paradigm or strong belief about education.

One aspect of the use of an imported CAL package was how to overcome the 'not invented here' problem, where teachers reject whole packages (although less often rejecting a whole text book). In this case we were helped by its widespread use elsewhere, the modular, adaptable nature of the package, contact with its author, and annual improvements based on user feedback.

Conclusions

Changing a maths course to tutor-supported, student-centred, resource-based learning was initially no worse than if the course were delivered using traditional lectures, and was preferred by both the students and lecturers. Staff could devote more time to those students who were slow and struggling with the work, and found it less stressful to support CAL than to prepare and deliver lectures. Overall there were large savings of staff time for little cost.

In response to evaluation results, changes were made during the second year of operation and the students' assessed performance was considerably better. Applying formative evaluation of these changes, in an action-research mode, has substantially assisted the integration of IT into teaching and learning in this and many other parts of the university, and our understanding of how to tackle similar problems.

References

Checkland, P B and Scholes, J (1990) *Soft Systems Methodology in Action*, Wiley, London.

Cook, J (1994) 'Bridge the gap with CALMAT', *Proceedings of the International Conference on Technology in Collegiate Mathematics*, Addison Wesley, Reading, MA.

Cook, J and Hornby, J (1995) 'CALMAT mathematics courseware for access to higher education', *Proceedings of the SMC Conference, Stirling*, in press.

Doughty, G, *et al.* (1994) *Using Learning Technologies: Interim Conclusions from the* TILT *Project*, TILT, University of Glasgow.

Draper, S W, *et al.* (1994) *Observing and Measuring the Performance of Educational Technology*, TILT, University of Glasgow.

Draper, S, *et al.* (1996) 'Integrative evaluation: an emerging role for classroom studies of CAL', *Computers in Education*, **26**, 17–32.

Elliot, J (1991) *Action Research for Educational Change*, Open University, Milton Keynes.

Farby, B, Land, F and Target, D (1993) *How to Assess your IT Investment*, Butterworth Heinemann, Oxford.

Fullan, M (1991) *The New Meaning of Educational Change*, Cassell, London.

Laurillard, D (1993) *Rethinking University Teaching: A Framework for the Effective Use of Educational Technology*, Routledge, London.

Middlehurst, R (1992) *Leading Academics*, SRHE and Open University Press, London.

Noss, R (1995) *Reading the Sines*, Final report of the mid-term evaluation of the Transitional Mathematics/Transmath Project, Institute of Education, University of London.

Pollock, M, *et al.* (1996) 'Rapid conversion of a mathematics course to CAL: a case study of a large-scale rapid change of resources and organization', *ALT-J*, **4**, 28–34.

Scott, R and Robinson, B (1995), 'Managing technological change in education – what lessons can we learn?', *Computers in Education*, **26**, 131–4.

Tabor, J H (1993), 'Using CALMAT in "levelling up" teaching', *CTI Quarterly Newsletter*, **4**.

Chapter 9

Champion for change: learning development at the University of Sunderland

Suzanne Robertson

Introduction

There are many different and apparently equally valid definitions of the term 'open learning' all of which encompass the qualities of flexibility of time, pace and place. Thus distance learning is one form of open learning. The next discussion derives from the question 'what is distance learning?' The University of Sunderland has examples of a variety of delivery and support strategies amongst the open and distance learning opportunities it offers.

Student-centred learning was the intermediary term that bridged the gap between the distance courses that were organized and running before the use of open learning materials was embedded into the normal delivery strategies for full-time students. The culture change was unevenly paced and is still ongoing but there are some key lessons to be learned from the way the University of Sunderland decided to address the issues.

Staff experience

Many staff have extensive experience of being Open University (OU) tutors and many more have used OU materials as texts for their courses. Unfortunately the cost of OU materials still precludes us from using them as they were intended to be used.

Some staff became involved in writing materials for agencies other than the OU and nearly ten years ago organizations such as the National Pharmaceutical Association, which runs courses for dispensing technicians, and ACOL (Analytical Chemistry by Open Learning) were two examples of this. Training

111

courses for potential authors were either not available or not widely publicized so the learning curve at the hands of editors who must have been frustrated by early attempts were steep. However, authors learned quickly and materials were produced that were user-friendly and applied to the learner's needs.

A brief history of distance learning at Sunderland

Early experiences in the School of Chemical and Pharmaceutical Sciences, later to become part of the School of Health Sciences, involved courses that were run as part-time day or block release courses. Employers could no longer afford or were not prepared to release staff because costs of replacements, travel and accommodation, for example, were too restrictive with increasingly tight budgets or profit margins. The requests to convert these courses to distance learning came therefore from the employers and, in the case of the pharmaceutical company Glaxo, financial support for early development work. Two specific cases were the Post Graduate Diploma in Quality Assurance (PGDQA), which addressed quality assurance in the pharmaceutical industry and the BSc Honours in Podiatric Medicine, a conversion course, run jointly with the then School of Chiropody at New College, Durham, for state registered chiropodists holding a diploma, which was popular with both private practitioners and NHS employees. An HNC in Science (Pharmaceutical) was added at a later date but production on the first two programmes began in 1988. Programmes for delivery to students geographically separated from the university are now offered by the Schools of Computing and Information Systems, Health Sciences and the Business School with opportunities from the other schools to be added later this year.

Institutional decision

Within the School of Pharmaceutical and Chemical Sciences there was no intention on the part of the staff involved to use the materials prepared for distance students in delivery to full- or part-time students. However, at about the same time as DES attention began to turn from the assessment of quality of teaching through HMI inspection to identifying quality in learning, an institutional decision was taken to introduce the first Teaching and Learning Strategy.

This decision resulted from an institutional consideration of early documents from HEQC and even earlier statements from its Scottish counterpart, which overtly identified quality in higher education with active learning. Up until this point, HMIs had paid regular visits to institutions but had based assessments, not so much on what the students did, but on how the staff performed.

The first institutional strategy outlined several action points among which were to:

- hold awareness raising events;
- set up teaching and learning groups in each School;
- promote student-centred learning;
- set up an Open Learning Development Unit (OLDU) with a specific remit to introduce open learning into the core provision of the University;
- offer pump priming funding for projects leading to the production of resources promoting flexible learning;
- set up a learning resources task group.

In the short term the awareness raising events probably had the greatest effect on the culture of the organization. At one particular event presentations to about 200 staff, including some from students, were followed by group discussions on topics designed to stimulate thinking towards involving students in active learning. The receptiveness to the new ideas was mixed but the debate was underway and the scene for future developments was set. One challenge issued at that event was 'try to teach only ten per cent of the current content of your course'. This was a step too far so the outcomes of the event were less uniformly positive than they might otherwise have been.

Many schools set up teaching and learning groups that at this time were for enthusiasts but again they provided a forum for discussions that had never taken place before. Some school groups held their own events, inviting recognized experts to contribute. Bitter lessons were learned about the use of external facilitators when some who had national reputations as experts in key topics turned out to be disastrous when it came to running activity-based events. Over the years we have built up a small group of consultants who have been well received and influential in helping us to change to the extent that some of our staff now offer similar services to other institutions.

The pump-priming projects that were instigated at the time were largely audiotape and text-based. Materials were produced in microbiology for dispensing technicians, chemistry (a course for beginners resulting from a series of five minute radio broadcasts), psychology and health and cancer and anti-cancer drugs. These projects were facilitated by a former BBC educational producer with recordings being made in the BBC studios in Newcastle. Some of the materials were used in existing distance courses, some for new courses and others were embedded into full- and part-time provision. Each set demonstrated a specific benefit of using audio technology. The microbiology tapes provided a solution to the problem of pronunciation of complex Latin names for distance students and the chemistry was partly recorded in a kitchen, making what might be thought of as a very theoretical subject, a highly attainable practical experience. The psychology and health tapes contained interviews with the elderly about their perceptions of growing old and the cancer and anti-cancer drugs tapes included interviews with specialist clinicians regarding current therapies. None of these materials would have been as effective using print alone.

The learning resources task group was chaired by the then head of the School of Computing and Information Systems, later to become the Pro Vice-Chancellor with responsibility for teaching, learning and learning support. Members of the task group included the chief librarian, the head of academic computing, and the head of Management Information Services (MIS), bringing for the first time all potential physical learning resources into the same discussion forum. Audiovisual and broadcasting media had been distributed within the schools, which had led to an unstructured increase in resources and a much more difficult task if rationalization of usage was to succeed. Apart from auditing what was available in physical terms this group also looked for examples of innovative uses of equipment to support active learning. Funding was provided under a bidding system for Broadcasting Development Awards (BDAs), which were for projects to develop materials for use in a flexible way to improve the quality and effectiveness of existing courses. Projects included videos of practical techniques in science, tapes of radio production, and the first cable video project. This practice of providing funding for which staff can bid, has proved to be very effective and has been adapted in many ways throughout the teaching and learning initiatives at the university.

OLDU, the Open Learning Development Unit, was established as a result of this first T&L strategy and was centrally funded. Initially it comprised three staff. The manager of the unit had extensive experience in open learning and publishing and was well matched with the assistant manager of the unit, whose experiences in educational technology have continued to benefit the university with respect to the current trends in media for delivery of open and distance learning and learning support. An administrator completed the team.

Progress

OLDU began by initiating four projects, each with the aim of producing high quality print-based learning materials in generic subjects, namely: the Effective Learning Programme (study skills), Micro-Computing Skills, Basic Statistics and Maths for Engineers. Euroform funding was successfully sought for the Micro-Computing Skills programme and provided for the development of the materials and piloting with groups of non-traditional learners, in the 'Gateway to Learning' project. Job-sharing project managers were appointed to the project. The Euroform funding was matched with a BT Higher Education Development Award which provided VC 7000 video conferencing facilities and computer conferencing (audio graphics), using Fujitsu application sharing software. This telematic support was available for learners who were distant from the university. Groups who took part included women returners, unemployed men and employees of small businesses. A group of prisoners took part in the project but were not permitted to access the online communication facilities.

A cable TV project with teletext campus information was initiated at the same time and a multimedia developer was added to the staff of OLDU. These events heralded the introduction of learning technology into the provision and support of open learning but at this stage we could not have forecast the impact it would have in the near future.

OLDU also set about organising staff development events to promote the production of good interactive materials and as a result of some excellent sessions run by external consultants many staff were able to begin developing or improve their writing and editing skills. The pattern was set for staff development in open learning techniques and has continued successfully to date.

The School of Health Sciences, in conjunction with Glaxo, who had sponsored the PGDQA programme mentioned earlier, initiated a project to produce a whole HNC in Science (Pharmaceutical) to be delivered as a work-based programme. Writers and editors gained expertise through the staff development programme and although initially students were from Glaxo at Barnard Castle, which tutors could visit easily, telematic support, primarily in the form of video conferencing has allowed participants from other parts of the country to join with students on site for tutorial sessions.

The School of·Computing and Information Systems also became involved in devising their Masters programme in Computer-Based Information Systems for delivery at a distance. The staff in this instance decided that video was their preferred medium so that students in the remote sites, with local tutors, would have as near as possible an identical experience with those on campus. A potential description of this model might be 'franchising learner support' since materials and assessment are the responsibility of the University of Sunderland.

Another contribution that OLDU made to progress was an internal publication called 'A guide to writing open learning for validation'. These guidelines were written such that they offered check lists for open learning to be used in a variety of situations from part of an existing module to whole delivery at a distance and because they concentrated on support, they forced authors to think of materials as only one part of the process. The guidelines seem cumbersome now that much of the thinking has become embedded, but they were invaluable to inexperienced authors, editors and validation panel members and have helped enormously in shaping the way the institution perceives the integration of open learning.

The mix of open and distance learning was definitely under way and although the production systems have been modified in the light of financial constraints and technological advances, the patterns that were established have proved to be extremely robust.

One very important aspect of the approach was that all initiatives should be encouraged. Many staff were already thinking along student-centred lines, a good example being one of the biology staff who had produced genetics problem-solving tutorials at a very early stage. The central provision was not intended to take over any individual initiatives but rather to act in partnership with staff to support their endeavours and promote school and team-based activities. This message was not always delivered effectively in earlier years but confidence has built steadily with time and effort.

Now that there was central support for open learning activities added to the initiatives being pursued by individuals and teams within the eight schools, the time had come for a revision of the teaching and learning strategy and the formulation of an institutional vision.

The second teaching and learning strategy

The chair of the learning resource task group conducted a series of consultations at all levels within schools and services and reported to the directorate concerning the physical resources available, their use in teaching and learning and the ideas currently circulating regarding departures from classical delivery methods. The result was the second teaching and learning strategy, which was much wider in vision and more focused in terms of deliverables than the first, calling for changes to the institutional structure and financial investment.

Some of the specific actions identified were:

- An IT strategy to be produced.
- A broadcasting strategy to be devised.
- An information services strategy to be introduced.
- Teaching and learning coordinators to be appointed in each school. These were principal lecturer posts and were to go to staff who were recognized for their ability and innovation in teaching and learning.
- A learning resource centre to be established in each school. Some schools had already established such a facility but the aim here was to have open access computing facilities and other services for students in their school base. It was not intended to duplicate library facilities or services.
- A staff development policy for teaching and learning was to be developed.
- Learning Development Services was to be created from the merger of OLDU and the Reprographics Unit

Outcomes

The intended outcomes of the strategy included:

- empowerment of students to take responsibility for their own learning,

understanding why and knowing how;
- experience of a range of teaching, learning and assessment methods by all students;
- promotion of transferable skills;
- introduction of quality performance measures;
- introduction of a teaching and learning strategy by each school.

Implementation

Learning Development Services was to have a wider remit than OLDU and should:

- work with schools to produce learning materials in print, audio and video;
- produce and develop computer-based learning materials, especially multimedia;
- introduce telematics as tools for learning and learning support;
- collaborate in projects to broaden access to our courses;
- investigate models for obtaining learning materials including buying in, swapping, employing external writers and working with internal module teams;
- work with staff on the induction and support of learners, specifically to help staff to let go, have less but more effective contact with the emphasis on learning management with workshops to complement materials;
- work with staff to support students by producing materials and introducing an induction workshop for all first year students, ensuring a continuation of support by promoting timetabled tutorials and drop in surgeries.

The university's provision for staff development has subsequently aided our achievement of Investors in People status. Provision has been both central and school-based and included:

- Over 300 courses provided centrally for all university staff to choose from. These were organized into themes, two of which were, IT training at all levels and open and flexible learning.
- Each School to hold it's own teaching and learning conference.
- Academic staff attendance at teaching and learning conferences to be promoted and other specific school-based events to be promoted.

The original version of the broadcasting strategy was couched in very general terms using broad definitions for production, use and transmission with reference to video, audio, multimedia, TV, radio, satellite, cable and video-conferencing. A Broadcasting Action Group (BAG) was established and took on responsibility for the Broadcasting Development Award projects mentioned earlier.

The Information Services strategy had the following strategic objectives:

- to unleash the potential of electronic databases;
- to focus on access not holdings;
- to engage with staff development for information services staff and for users;
- to collaborate in establishing the eight school resource centres and two university libraries (in the event four libraries were needed) using the model for learning resources; if all students must have it then staff should provide, if a few need it then it should be available in a resource room and if the need is unpredictable then a library should provide.

The IT strategy was dependent upon support for academic computing being devolved to the Schools and Information Technology and Communications Services (ITACS) taking responsibility for the infrastructure. Some of the objectives were to:

- introduce an IT for all programme (currently six half modules at various levels to support the development of IT skills for all staff and students);
- involve IT in as many aspects of the curriculum as possible;
- establish and continuously upgrade a campus network;
- promote the appropriate use of the OMR (optical mark reader) facility for assessment;
- take care that learning models were not impoverished by the expense of production;
- promote the use of desktop conferencing as an interactive medium;
- engage with staff development to allow staff to keep pace with IT developments;
- consider only those developments that affect our core activities. (If we cannot deliver we don't want to know!)

Three years on

At the time of writing it is very rewarding to look back at how much of the vision has been achieved during a time of financial constraint and change in response to external factors. We now have four established libraries and are leading developments with electronic access and self-issue. Our communications infrastructure is developing on a rolling programme and its stability is the envy of others and much taken for granted by our own staff.

Central and local production of interactive print-based learning materials has led to considerable external sales, publishing contracts and licensing of our materials to other institutions. We discovered unexpected benefits to some of our investments in print-based production. One very strong point in favour of investing the considerable time necessary to produce good open learning materials is that once they have been produced for one purpose, they can be adapted for others – either a different delivery mode or for a different course.

Thinking through the issues can result in solutions that kill more than one bird with one stone. When our social geographers decided to embark on a project to produce materials for their two level 1 half modules, not all of the members of the team were committed to the idea. They were also faced with the problem of wanting the materials to have as long a 'shelf life' as possible. During their team discussions with an external facilitator they became united as a team with all members fully committed, and decided on a 'process, issues and resources model' that has proved able to address several ideals. For example, Regional Issues is a learning package about the issues facing a particular locality and requires the students to investigate for themselves. The process pack deals with the process of conducting investigations of this type and would be expected to change little over a five year span. The Issues pack could easily be adapted to include new issues, or issues from different localities as the need arises and the resources pack starts the student off on the collection of materials to support their investigations and helps them to identify potential sources of information.

Quality with respect to learning materials is often misunderstood. They can be very attractive to look at and yet poor in quality. Open learning is all about active learning, engaging the learner in the process instead of allowing them to read, listen or even watch passively. We define quality in materials as being about the level of interactivity the materials engender in the learner. In order to maintain our standards we try to have all materials reviewed by external experts to ensure that their quality is appropriate for their purpose. Obviously presentation is important and we have found attractively produced materials motivate students who appreciate the investment in their learning.

Support is crucial

You can have good learning with bad materials and ineffective learning with good materials. I have heard several people quote this adage in different guises and it is absolutely true. But we are back to how do you define 'good support'. I would contend that good support is not necessarily elaborate, but it is reliable. For distance students a telephone helpline or e-mail system that produces a fast service to the learner is much better than a workshop session that not all students can attend. Students need feedback on the problems and progress while it is fresh in their minds and not some time in the future. Very often just knowing that help is at hand means that it will not be called upon. For full- and part-time students workshops and drop in surgeries are commonly used but best results for these students are still attained with timetabled workshop sessions with specified outcomes particularly if assessment is involved. The difference is the motivation of the students. If you have plenty of time it is difficult to manage, whereas if time is tight it is used effectively and distance students tend to have other commitments and so work to tight time schedules.

With the range of media available for synchronous as well as asynchronous support these days, effective systems are much easier to devise with computer conferencing and video conferencing joining the telephone, fax and face-to-face varieties.

We were the first institution (1994) to appoint a Telematics Development Officer to work with ISDN video and computer conferencing and the World Wide Web to enhance interactive learning for our students.

Lessons learned

We are now in the process of finalizing our third strategy, now a Learning Development Strategy, and have learned much ourselves as we have implemented each of the previous two. Probably the most significant contribution to our progress has been the level of support from the top. Much of the initial work was undertaken by the Director of the School of Computing who was subsequently appointed as a Pro Vice-Chancellor with responsibility for teaching, learning and learning support.

Recognition of achievement is also very important. Vision is necessary as well as commitment and our experience has demonstrated that having leaders in teaching and learning who are appointed because of their recognized ability has had two effects. First our Teaching and Learning Coordinators have credibility when promoting changes and secondly because it has provided a recognized promotion route for teaching ability. When we followed up the appointment of Teaching and Learning Coordinators two years later with Teaching Fellowships of two years' duration and carrying salary enhancements for projects to introduce an innovation over at least two schools, rewards for teaching began to be appreciated as real commitment by the institution when compared with the traditional expected rewards for research.

Where staff development is to be facilitated by external consultants, it is very important to choose carefully. Our experience showed that a mistake here is not just ineffective, but actually very detrimental. Wherever possible, home grown champions of change are best because everyone knows that the achievement has been under the same working conditions and it goes some way to prevent staff from claiming that 'it's all right for them, they don't have to...' because they do!

Another important incentive is to actively promote and disseminate success. We have several mechanisms by which we achieve this. All new open learning materials are publicized in our Learning Development Services newsletter, which is published twice a year. Articles about staff innovations and successes make headline news. But the greatest success has been our internal University Teaching and Learning Conference.

This year we held our third and 272 academic and learning support staff attended this voluntary one day event complete with conference dinner. Over 50 staff ran workshops or gave presentations on the innovations they had introduced. Presentations covered topics such as computer-based learning, flexible learning, WWW and teaching and learning, distance learning, and international issues in teaching and learning. Workshops entitled; Making students more active, Open/resource-based learning, The friendly text: writing accessible distance learning material, Using the WWW for delivery and marking of tutorials and tests and Using games and simulations in teaching and learning, were very well attended. The very titles are a measure of how much we have achieved.

Conclusions

We now have a range of distance learning courses available with plans for more in various stages of development. Open learning or resource-based learning is now well embedded within our core provision. We have established materials production procedures in all media and the recent addition of a Resource-Based Learning module as an option within our CertEdHE, which is compulsory for all new staff with less than two years' teaching experience at the appropriate level, has proved to be popular.

The use of multimedia and telematic communications in teaching and learning is also well established with students gaining IT skills from their curriculum studies in many instances. Optical scanning technology is established as a mechanism for assessment and survey work because we have paid attention not only to the technology but also the appropriateness of its use. We have provided staff development in objective testing strategies to test high level learning outcomes and not just factual recall.

Following a review of the current initiatives and resources we are in the process of refining our new Learning Development Strategy, which will take us towards the 21st century.

Chapter 10

Innovation in a traditional setting at Sheffield University

Ruth Sharratt

There are always pressures in any organization to change, and adapt to new pressures. On the whole, these pressures are ignored or contained, and the organization continues as before. Sometimes changes take hold and the organization itself adapts to these new pressures. In the work on technological innovation, innovation is described as a 'two-sided or coupling activity'. The two sides are the recognition of a need and the technical knowledge or know-how. In considering the success or failure of innovation, both aspects need to be considered (Freeman, 1974). The question has to be why does innovation succeed in some situations and not in others. In order to begin to explore this issue, I want to look at an example of where innovation has been incorporated into the structure of the institution, and not left as marginal activity.

The development of distance learning courses and the establishment of the Distance Learning Unit is an example of a successful innovation. It is worth determining the factors that enabled this development to be embedded in the institution, and analysing which of those factors were specific to Sheffield, and which could possibly apply generally. No organization exists in a vacuum.

Like many universities, Sheffield is facing the problems of a reduced unit of resource and a change in the sort of student coming to the Institution. This led to two main problems: that of maintaining and increasing income to the Institution when traditional sources were reducing and at the same time maintaining a quality service. These were the institutional imperatives. However at a departmental level, there were other, but related, pressures.

There were changes going on in the social and political environment in which universities find themselves (Schuller, 1995). The decision to increase the proportion of young people attending higher education (up to 30%) had an enormous impact. It put great pressure on the services that the universities were providing. Not only did they struggle to teach the large numbers in the lecture theatres and seminar rooms, but services such as sports facilities, libraries, computer services, and student accommodation were all put under severe pressure. There has also been a change in the type of student attending university, although at Sheffield this is probably less than in other universities, as many are still the traditional post A-level student, but, these changes together increase the pressure on staff.

In addition, like many universities, Sheffield was facing the problems of a reduced unit of resource. That is, the income associated with each student was steadily being reduced. This led to two main problems: that of maintaining and increasing income to the institution when traditional sources were reducing and at the same time maintaining a quality service. These factors, while affecting the environment, were not the main impetus for change.

Much of the work of a university is at post-graduate level. Given the funding regime that universities found themselves in, there were two major areas for increasing income: research and post-graduate courses. For the purposes of this discussion, I only want to look at the latter. Post-graduate provision was seen as an area where the university could expand its provision and thus its income. There was though, a problem. The traditional post-graduate student who attended full-time for a year, was disappearing as employers were no longer prepared to release staff for a year, and people were reluctant to leave work in order to take a course, even if they could afford the fees plus loss of income. The demand was increasingly for part-time, flexible provision, but part-time attendance creates its own problems. The potential recruitment area is limited. Students who are likely to be in full-time employment, found getting time off work difficult. In many cases the time and cost involved in travelling, what were often long distances, for a half day session prevented students from taking the course. The obvious solution was to go to distance learning modes of delivery.

Obvious it may have been, but there was considerable debate as to whether this was the way forward. From a department's point of view, was it worth putting effort into distance learning course development. Although faced with reducing student numbers and the associated loss of income, was converting their programmes to distance learning and developing more the best way of solving the problem? Perhaps they could market their courses better, perhaps do more research, put on short courses or provide consultancy; all viable alternatives. There were also more profound arguments. Was distance learning something a traditional, face-to-face university ought to be involved in? Would it contribute income to the university or would it be a drain on resources? There were good theoretical reasons to be concerned, as the consensus was that distance learning was cost effective because of economies of scale, and there was no way that the university could manage a distance learning enterprise on the scale of the UK Open University (Moore and Kearsley, 1996; Rumble, 1993).

I want to look at this view in a little more detail. Otto Peters (Keegan, 1993) in his analysis of what differentiates distance learning from face-to-face delivery of courses, put forward the hypothesis that distance learning was an industrialized approach. By dividing the process of production and delivery into its component stages, as has happened in most industrial processes, the craft of teaching has been turned into a more efficient process. Just as the industrialization of manufacturing was necessary for mass production whereas craft methods were more appropriate for small production runs, distance learning is best suited, he puts it stronger than that, 'only suited', for mass education. Thus the development of OUs with course numbers of 1,000 plus. While I have some sympathy with his analysis, and the conclusion that distance learning is appropriate for mass higher education, experience has shown that distance learning is not only appropriate for large numbers (Rumble, 1993). Perhaps the model we ought to be looking at is that of batch production rather than mass production, where small runs provide a flexibility of response that is difficult with mass systems of production.

Background – the story

However, whatever the reservations, the imperative was to maintain and where possible increase student numbers. In some of the departments, the fall in post-graduate numbers was threatening the viability if not of the departments, then several courses that they were running. In others, there was a need to increase the portfolio on offer in order to stay a thriving department. In others, there was a strong request from outside to put on a distance learning course. A request that they did not want to refuse! For all these reasons, the decision was taken to develop distance learning courses. As a result, here at Sheffield we have a number of very successful distance learning courses with numbers from ten to more than 100. To understand the innovation it has to be put into context of the institution, the needs of students and the people involved.

Much of the work on innovation has stressed that it occurs at the edges of organizations, not in the mainstream. The first courses were in the Division of Adult and Continuing Education (DACE) and the Department of Automatic Control and Systems Engineering, quickly followed by the Division of Education. DACE used to be the Extra-Mural Department and by its very nature is not mainstream. Its position is always somewhat precarious, its students and courses are on the whole non-traditional and different. As a department it needed to be imaginative and entrepreneurial to survive. It is not surprising that distance learning courses were developed here. But the motivation in the case of the Department of Automatic Control and Engineering Systems and the Education Department is less obvious. We need to look a little more deeply into the reasons for the development and the players involved. Innovation happens because individuals want it to happen, rarely because an organization wants it to happen (Hedge, 1996). It could be argued that organizations never want innovation to take place, but have it forced upon them, but this is probably somewhat unfair.

Changes occur when there is a coincidence of forces. It is rarely enough for one factor on its own to engender change. In the case of the early developments of distance learning at Sheffield, there was one factor in common. They were all in response to a recognized need. They were not developed because someone thought it a good idea, or wouldn't it be interesting if? Nor was it grant led, although funds were made available to help with development costs. The main criterion in pushing them forward was the fact that they were seen to benefit the students, the department and the university. Interestingly, being of personal benefit has not been important in motivating staff to be innovative. In the case of Automatic Control, it was in response to the demands of students in Singapore for the course. Distance learning was obviously the only route. Similarly with the courses in education, the demand was from the students themselves for distance learning courses.

All these developments occurred largely because of the enthusiasm of individuals working to achieve their own goals, working on their own, but with the support of their heads of department. In other words, each distance learning course or programme had its own champion. The reasons for producing distance learning courses varied, but the outcome was the same. The distance learning courses were successful, both in terms of numbers and income, and have flourished. As a result of individual initiative, the institution was able to accommodate them.

What was crucial about those courses was that they showed that distance learning courses were not only possible, they were also successful. As a result of these courses, the University began to look at how it could harness distance learning in its own development plans. Its goals were simple:

1. To increase the numbers of students, in particular overseas students;
2. To increase income;
3. To increase the number of distance learning courses across the university.

Distance learning was and is seen as important, partly as a way of generating income through increased student numbers, but also because of its impact on the teaching and learning strategy of the university. Although it was not clear at the time, as the edges between distance learning and face-to-face teaching have become blurred, the latter reason is of growing importance. It is interesting that the pressures that affected post-graduate provision and those that affect undergraduate provision are causing a convergence of delivery systems towards distance learning methodologies.

However, the university was not sure of the best way to achieve these goals. The decision was taken that pump priming funds would be made available, and that these would be invested through a unit based in the Department of Education as that was where the expertise was primarily based and where the largest number of courses were. The problem with this, was that staff's number one commitment, quite rightly, was to their department. This meant that there was considerable further development of courses, and research in the area of distance learning within the department. Whilst this is important, it did not meet the goal of increasing the amount of distance learning provision across the university. This is not a criticism, it was rather a function of placing responsibility for development in a particular department. This created a problem for the university. It was believed, rightly in my opinion, that development should be firmly practitioner-based, and that a central unit was likely to be ineffective in encouraging distance learning development as it would be isolated from departments. Staff tend not to respond positively to the central organization trying to get them to do yet more work. However, the dangers of putting a unit in a department were clearly showed by previous experience.

This is where the characteristic of much innovation comes from. It is down to a combination of personalities in the right place at the right time. In this case, the leader of the distance learning Masters in Training and Development who was based at DACE was a champion for the further development of distance learning. She also firmly believed that distance learning should be informed by practitioner experience. If it was to grow and flourish, it would be because of the commitment of staff at all levels, and not because of edict. Therefore, development could not come from a central unit. It was believed that there should be a distance learning unit, which needed to be firmly associated with the academic staff, but not attached to any particular department. An almost impossible situation, but because of the people involved, it actually was achieved.

The director, who was not paid separately for her work, was a senior lecturer in DACE. Whilst personal benefit is rarely strong enough to get an innovation off the ground; personal commitment is essential. The unit was set up with a centrally funded budget so that it was neither a financial drain on any one department, nor of immediate financial benefit. The distance learning unit's development officer, whilst physically based at DACE, was not a member of the department. Management responsibility went through the director to the ADC (Academic Development Committee). The balance of 'in', but 'not in', has worked although it has left the unit somewhat in a state of limbo.

The decision was taken very early that the distance learning unit should not be a production unit. It was unlikely to be effective as it would always be under-resourced relative to demand. More importantly, control of development had to be with academic staff, and it was for them to bring in resources as appropriate, and to build up the skills as necessary. Its role was to provide advice and consultancy, and to act as a networker. It also was the mechanism for pump-priming development. It distributed funds across the whole University. This helped reinforce its independence as it was seen as not favouring any particular department. The funds involved were small, but sufficient to get courses off the ground. The aim was that once started, they will generate enough funds to be self sustaining. Having some funds available encouraged staff to think about distance learning as part of their course provision. It was not and is not envisaged as replacing face-to-face provision. It was to supplement and complement provision, increasing what was on offer, rather than diminishing. It has also proved a lifeline in some cases where departments were struggling to get sufficient full- or part-time students.

The current situation

There are fourteen distance learning courses currently running, with sixteen (at least) in development. They are funded in a variety of ways using both internal and external funds. As they develop the university is having to solve a range of problems. These are primarily financial, but there are also issues of student registration and student records. The materials are sent out from the department, whereas funds come in centrally. Coordination is crucial, and new systems are required. New demands are being made on central resources as a result of this development, which are being dealt with; not as rapidly as we would like, but the university is responding to the changing demands made on it.

As the amount of provision has grown, the decision was taken to mainstream distance learning wherever possible. For purposes of HEFCE funding, it is treated the same as part-time courses. However although similar in many ways to standard part-time provision, there are important differences. The initial investment in time and energy and often real money, is significant. If this is to happen, there needs to be a return on the investment both for the department and individuals, as well as the university. Getting the tax regime right is a situation that we are still struggling with. It is not easy to be fair to all concerned whilst maintaining incentives. If distance learning is to grow to the extent wanted, then not only the tax regime needs to be right. Personal reward systems also need to be in place. This is an issue that has not really been addressed, and is a major block to its further development.

Quality control is an important area. The current approach is to use the same mechanism as that used for face-to-face courses. As it happens, because of the public nature of distance learning courses and the people involved, not only has the quality of distance learning courses been high, but it has improved the quality of teaching in other areas. As distance learning provision grows, quality assurance needs to be looked at, without it being onerous. The quality assessment of HEFCE will undoubtedly have an impact.

The issue of sustainability is crucial. Due to the high initial investment, there needs to be a fair degree of confidence that the numbers of potential students are there, and at a fee level that will sustain the course. The market is difficult to assess, and it has been a mixed success. Distance learning high-lights marketing strategies, which means more than simply selling. It means getting into the right market, packaging the courses in the right way and working with and through the right organizations. We have had to learn and are still learning. While much is still done through personal contact, the nature of the scale of distance learning means much greater care is needed in establishing provision.

The university not only wants particular distance learning courses to be self-sustaining, it also wants growth in provision to be self-sustaining. This is a problem as there is a natural reluctance by departments to subsidize other departments. We are not sure how to do this, as it relates to other taxation issues. We also do not have a very clear idea what the 'profits' are. This is not peculiar to distance learning but applies to all courses. While it is extraord-inarily difficult to measure profits absolutely, it should be possible to compare them with face-to-face courses. This is important for a number of reasons. Not least if we are to assess whether the money going into distance learning is a good investment.

One of the major reasons for the University's support, was that distance learning courses are seen as successful in terms of quality, numbers of students and income. However, the data is fuzzy and relative cost effectiveness and cost-benefits are extremely difficult and problematic when looking at courses. At some point we need to analyse the cost effectiveness of our provi-sion, but in the meantime we are using the relatively crude measure of whether the courses generate a surplus using the same measures as applied to other course provision. Most have done so and will continue to do so as long as they are meeting real needs.

Outstanding issues

The initial remit of the unit was to assist the development of distance learning courses. It was envisaged that this would mean working with staff on distance learning programmes, providing advice and information to them. As the development has progressed, it has become clear that the most important function of the unit is in relation to the centre. Accepting that development has to be bottom-up and has to come from the staff involved, means that wherever possible responsibility is delegated to departmental level. This is the case in all other courses, and fits in well with the culture of the institution. However, there are differences with face-to-face courses and fitting distance learning courses into current systems can be difficult.

All the administrative systems in the university are premised on the assumption that students attend the university. As a 'taken for granted' it is neither recognized nor questioned, but it causes all sorts of problems for courses that do not fit into that criterion. The sorts of problems that are faced by distance learning courses are for example, that copyright licences are also site licences. Student records are kept separately from the course leaders so that information such as the financial status of the student is not known to the Department. In a face-to-face course this is not a problem as the course tutor knows immediately if the student is not attending and therefore not taking the course and if the student does not attend the costs of that student are minimal. However, with distance learning, materials will have been sent to the students, they will have been allocated a tutor, perhaps e-mail accounts will have been set up. Costs will have been incurred whether they were taking the course or not. This is clearly a problem where courses are on tight budgets, and are expected to cover all costs from income.

Internal costing criteria are based on attendance with library provision, counselling, student facilities etc, coming out of central funds whereas services such as photocopying are costed at a departmental level. Quality assurance procedures, accreditation, validation, assessment; all assume face-to-face provision.

If distance learning provision is to grow, it is clear that university systems need to change so that there is the right framework for growth. Words of support are fine but are of little use, even if supported by funds, if internal systems work positively against the development. Whilst there were very few distance learning courses, the university was able to accommodate them on an *ad hoc* basis. People were prepared to put themselves out to make the system work. As the numbers have grown, it can no longer continue on this basis. But the system must not stifle the development. It is vital that whatever systems are put in place they, at the very least, accommodate distance learning provision.

For this to happen, there needs to be dialogue between academic staff and central administrative staff. The advantages of being to some extent a 'floating unit' become apparent. The Unit is a conduit for course teachers and course administrators to talk to each other. Documents giving guidelines to everyone involved in distance learning provision are being written. Quality systems that both meet the needs of tutors and satisfy the demands of the central administration are being created. Thus, a major task of the Unit has been and is, to ensure that the institutional infrastructure is appropriate for distance learning development.

The problem is that the solutions we have put, or are putting in place are responses to yesterday's innovations. However, the situation is not fixed, and we have to deal with and encourage today's innovations. Thus, it is important, and it is a criterion for any of the solutions proposed, that they can be reviewed and modified as required. We want to be at the cutting edge, but not so far ahead that we lose the firm basis in practice. It is about turning ideas into reality and improving provision and providing the environment for this to happen.

I guess at this point we are no longer talking about an innovation. It is a development that is well and truly incorporated into the mainstream. Perhaps not completely, but well on the way. Ironically we are now concerned with the loss of the innovative element. The fear is that in incorporating distance learning into mainstream provision we will lose that adaptability, flexibility or whatever, that made it so successful in the first place. Will the entrepreneurial zeal get quashed or directed into something else. This fear is almost certainly valid, and inevitable. If an innovation is to be successful, then it must become mainstream, or as a marginal activity it is always at risk of collapse. The aim is to provide space for innovation to take place wherever it happens. By its very nature, it is impossible to anticipate. Universities ought to be quite good at encouraging creativity even if they are not sure what to do with it when it happens.

Conclusion

In reflecting on what has happened at Sheffield, it can be seen in two ways. At one level it has been an evolutionary process, change gradually being accepted and accommodated by the Institution. It has been a struggle and a lot of negotiation, but change has taken place. Systems have been modified, rules adapted and new procedures drawn up to incorporate distance learning in to mainstream provision (Peters, 1971). That is evolution.

At another level, it has been revolutionary. There has been a change in perception. Calling it a paradigm shift is too strong, but the implication of that change in thinking is as profound (Inglis, 1994). The 'taken for granted' that a course and therefore learning needs attendance for it to take place has been challenged. It is now possible to think of learning as taking place at a distance; away from the institution. If that can happen with 'distance learning' courses, then why not with others. Whilst it has always been known that teaching at a distance works, the OU has shown that, this is merely knowledge. It is the experience that causes the real change. The implication of this is just starting to filter through but is enabling ideas about the use of information technology mediated learning and online delivery, student attendance and student learning, that were previously unthinkable by all, except a few, to become real options. These things have been happening at the margins for a long time and in many institutions. What is now happening, is that they are becoming part of mainstream thinking.

The irony of this whole process is that the difference between distance learning courses and other courses is slowly disappearing. It is more likely to be a matter of where on the spectrum of delivery, from teacher delivery to self-study, a course is, rather than what label it attracts. Which in the end could lead to the demise of the distance learning unit as it has worked its way out of a job!

References

Freeman, C (1974) *The Economics of Industrial Innovation*, Penguin, Harmondsworth.

Hedge, N (1996) 'Balancing the elements: a way of looking at issues in distance education', in *Going the Distance: Teaching, Learning and Researching in Distance Education*, University of Sheffield Division of Education.

Inglis, A (1994) 'A new paradigm for the future' *Unlocking Open Learning*, M Parer (ed.), Monash University, Melbourne, Australia.

Moore, M and Kearsley, G (1996) *Distance Education: A Systems View*, Wadsworth Publishing Company, Belmont, CA.

Peters, O (1971) 'Models of university-level distance education' in *Otto Peters on Distance Education: The industrialisation of Teaching and Learning*, D Keegan (ed.), Routledge, London.

Peters, O (1993) 'Distance education in a postindustrial society' in *Theoretical Principles of Distance Education*, D Keegan (ed.), Routledge, London.

Rumble, G (1992) 'The competitive vulnerability of distance teaching universities', *Open Learning*, 7, 2, June.

Rumble, G (1993) 'The economics of mass distance education' in *Distance Education: New Perspectives*, K Harry, M John and D Keegan (eds), Routledge, London.

Schuller, T (1995) 'Introduction, the changing university' in *The Changing University*, T Schuller (ed.), SRHE and Open University Press, Milton Keynes.

Chapter 11

Computer-based education at Queensland University of Technology

Jenny Winn

The Australian higher education sector

As early as the 1960s, the value of computers as educational tools became apparent through both private and commercial investigation. Funding, operational complexities and the perceived threat computers posed to some sectors of the education system were, however, obstacles to their widespread use. It is interesting to note that these obstacles still exist today.

With the introduction of microcomputers in 1975 and the accompanying reduction in costs, increased power and ease of use during the 1980s, came a recognition of their potential for use in higher education. Funding concerns of tertiary institutions, which had been purchasing and experimenting with microcomputer technology since the early 1980s, were beginning to ease despite internal budgetary constraints and price/performance ratio fluctuations in the microcomputer mass market.

Issues of quality and productivity opened the door for computerized instruction. By relieving teachers from repetitive duties (drill and practice sessions, testing and scoring) and hence freeing them for more interactive involvement and attention to class work, students profited. Quality control could be achieved through storing responses and checking reactions to courses on the computer, thus enabling instructors to determine the appropriateness of course content, and alter it accordingly.

In brief, pressure to reform from internal sources, combined with a vague recognition of the scope of functionality of computers in the education process, provided the platform for the development of computer-based education at Queensland University of Technology in 1985.

The QUT context

Created in January 1989 by redesignation of the Queensland Institute of Technology (QIT), the Queensland University of Technology (QUT) has emerged as a major university in the Australian context with a broad academic profile, encompassing eight faculties: Science, Engineering, Built Environment, Education, Business, Health, Law and Information Technology. Enrolment is now approaching 30,000 students and sustained growth is expected, despite problems of managing increases in attendance and per capita funding. QUT has also become an important university for international students.

The early years (1980s)

The beginnings

Computer-based education (CBE) at QUT first came into existence in 1986 amid uncertainty and indecision at the policy level as to the effects the introduction of microcomputers would have on the Institute. The ramifications of providing subsidized microcomputers to students, stipulating the ownership of microcomputers as a course enrolment prerequisite, and the numerous possible applications of computers to the educational process were priority concerns. Microcomputers had the potential to change the face of tertiary education, and as had all institutions of higher education in the 1980s, QUT recognized this impact.

In response to the dilemma, an informal committee evolved from conversations among interested individuals from both academic and non-academic sectors of the Institute. Membership of the committee included representatives from the Educational Research and Development Unit (ERDU), the Information Technology area, the library and some academics. The task being to consider the effects of, and strategic action most suitable for responding to, developments in information technology. Significantly, one of the committee members, Dr Dan Ellis, a senior lecturer in the Physics department, approached Institute management with the proposal of trialing a Computer Based Education Facility on campus. A two year trial period was stipulated and CBE commenced operation in 1986. At this stage the committee disbanded in the belief that it's task had been completed.

To pave the way for the trial, a survey was prepared and distributed to 600 universities world wide. The aim was to gauge the appropriateness and functional diversity of computers in education. Collation of results revealed that if computers were to be effectively utilized they could only be applied in a simplistic manner, vis-à-vis, computers are educational tools, not dissimilar to blackboards or textbooks, and in that sense, should not be a replacement for educators. The second message was that computer capability must be matched to instructional requirements.

One of the more commonly used strategies for computer-assisted instruction, drill and practice, was of particular interest to QUT. The response of the United States Air Force Academy provided supporting evidence that the drill and practice approach was relatively easy to design and develop and showed the most obvious immediate benefit in classes with large student numbers and constant course content.

In the context of university teaching in the 1980s, this attitude determined that computers were to assume the role of a delivery medium for supplementary tutorial activities and instructional support, but never as a total replacement of lecture programmes.

Satisfied with these findings, the Deputy Vice-Chancellor supported funding of $50,000 from the QUT equipment budget and embarked on the dilemma of locating and regulating a Computer-Based Education Facility. The latter part of 1985 and early 1986 saw the resolution of such issues, with the outcome as follows:

- the facility should be located centrally to provide easy access to all students should the experiment prove to be successful, hence, the QUT library was an appropriate location;
- hardware and software installation should be the responsibility of the initiator;
- issues of security would be met jointly with the library;
- annual reviews of funding would be made;
- CBE was to be organizationally located within ERDU (positioned adjacent to the library in the same building).

The basic approach

Computer-based education at QUT was introduced to enhance students' learning through the acquisition of knowledge or skill by way of repetitive practice (or rote learning techniques) and self-testing, in place of some of the usual tutorial processes. Tutorial and computerized instruction were almost commensurate in the primitive days of CBE.

As with other early tutorials, a frame or more of information is presented on screen, a question is posed, and student responses are the mechanism for the selection of subsequent information, ie incorrectly answered questions prompt resubmission, while the correct response will guide a student to the next question or information frame. Dr Ellis' term for this approach, in which the lecturer leads the student by presenting a series of questions, is 'Socratic dialogue', and provides the framework for interaction between the student and the material.

Such drill and practice routines were recognized as essential to effective learning in the technology-based subjects of QIT in the 1980s. Lecturers did not have the time to assist students in practising basic principles. Programmed instruction allowed students to reinforce the knowledge acquired in lectures, with the advantages of allowing the students to work at their own pace of personal progress, time and location and at varying degrees of difficulty, lesson content being designed to fluctuate with student's responses. A major factor in the establishment of CBE was in the science and business subjects where large amounts of drill and practice for terminology and numerical questions was required. Lecturers found that they did not have the time to mark weekly tutorial questions and CBE was used to facilitate this.

One of the important benefits of this approach was in the chosen authoring package AUTHOR, an Australian DOS-based tool allowing for easy programming of questions but with the added advantage of an in-built course record keeping system for student results. Lecturers are given the option of having results printed after each tutorial as well as having all or the best attempts by the student recorded.

CBE was marketed throughout QUT by its association with a service area for lecturing staff, located in the library. This area was called the Educational Research and Development Unit. Early clients of CBE simply submitted large numbers of multiple-choice questions to the CBE manager or programmer, which would consequently be programmed into AUTHOR and made available for students on the Local Area Network in the CBE laboratory.

'Value-added' services

'Value-added' services encompass the various other utilities available on the network installed to operate the CBE facility. The network was originally established within the constraints of an agreement making it available for purposes other than programmed instruction. One of these purposes was the use of the microcomputers as adjuncts to other PC laboratories on campus.

The appeal of annexation was enhanced due to availability of supervision for extended hours (the library operated 84 hours per week), and availability for issue of software acquired for general student use. Moreover, the library was itself interested in utilizing the network for the dissemination of information to students, including the library catalogue, CD-ROM information services and courseware developed outside of the QUT CBE facility. As application software proliferated so too did requests from lecturers to have various packages available for students to use.

The later years (1990s)

Production methodology

By 1991 there were 16 staff in the section and in 1996, 58 employees in both full- and part-time capacity on the payroll. The CBE facility or lab grew from ten PCs in 1986 to 84 in 1996, while a further 25 PCs with interactive videodisc players are used for language learning. The campus network delivers to over 30 labs with approximately 1000 PCs. Student users grew from 3,200 in 1988 (when first measured) to 13,000 in 1996. This huge growth was funded through some increase in the operating grant, external earnings for production of CBE materials for Queensland Rail and the introduction of grants to fund teaching initiatives both within QUT and Commonwealth funded within Australia.

With sustained growth the need arose for defined procedures for project development and delivery. These assisted production staff to look closely at the requirements of projects at an early stage of development. The introduction of graphic artists and instructional designers in the early 1990s paved the way for role differentiation within project development teams as follows:

- The *graphic designer* produces the graphic and interface design elements, as well as providing advice to the project team on all graphic design issues and ensuring the quality of the graphic design aspects of the courseware.
- The *instructional designer* provides advice to the project team on all instructional design issues and ensures the quality of the instructional design aspects of the courseware. This person usually enters CBE with teaching and/or instructional design expertise but keeps up to date with developments in his/her field through staff development initiatives.
- The *authoring specialist* authors the courseware and provides advice to the project team on all authoring or programming issues and ensures the quality of the authoring aspects of the courseware. The authoring specialist is a qualified programmer or authoring expert and is trained in new languages as required.
- The *project leader* provides leadership and support to the project development team and the review team to ensure a quality product and service is provided to the client. CBE trains all of its production staff in project leadership skills in externally based courses and the production manager keeps tight control of project management.
- The *subject matter expert* provides advice to the project team on all subject matter issues and ensures the quality of the subject matter aspects of the courseware, this person is usually the lecturer in the subject or the main lecturer in a team of lecturers. This is the only team member from outside the CBE Department and is generally given faculty or grant paid release time to concentrate on the project.

Teamwork has become the foundation for production of CBE projects and the key to departmental functionality. Early definition and analysis with the SME, project leader and instructional designer is succeeded by the completion of a 'requirements document'. Following this a more detailed 'specification document' is prepared addressing delivery, interface and design issues. The production phase is finalized by testing and evaluation (see Fig. 11.1).

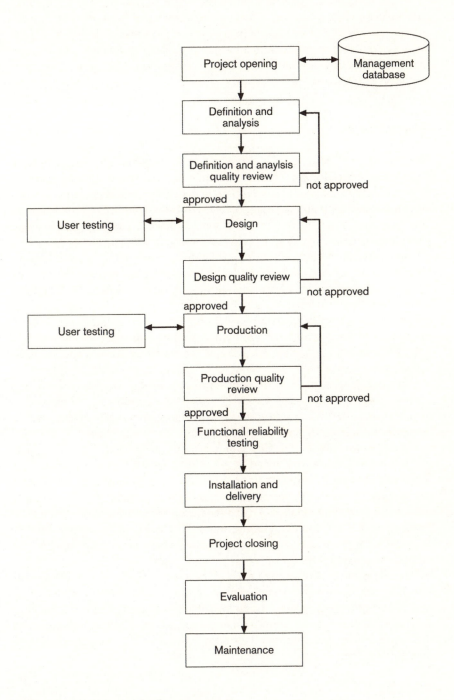

Figure 11.1   Courseware development process

Teaching methodologies and technologies utilized in the development of courseware at CBE have diversified significantly since the early 1980s, elaborating on the typical question/answer routine (multiple-choice, true/false and short answer) through the incorporation of decision-making models, dialogue, guided exploration, multimedia and simulation – the controlled representation of real world phenomena.

Graphic design

The first graphic designer was employed in 1990. Although designers were limited by technological constraints, their contributions in the areas of design, colour theory, layout and illustration added new levels of understanding, communication and meaning to CBE projects. By late 1995 the software and technologies available and the growth and scope of CBE's projects had provided a need for five graphic designers working full time.

The increase in the availability of colours (from 16 to 64,000), combined with improved screen fonts and the ability to incorporate textured or 3D graphics, have widened the possibilities for the user interface. Graphics, used to support learning in the form of diagrams, illustrations, and animation require a range of design skills: digital photo manipulation, 2D and 3D illustration and animation, and video. Greater diversity in the technology available has led to maximization of the potential for visual communication.

With improvements in technology and the growing sophistication of the student, user interface design has become an integral part of each new project. User interface design draws on the cumulative skills of the graphic designer, authoring specialist, and instructional designer. Some projects use a visual metaphor such as an office, which provides the user with a context and means of navigating through the program. Others provide the users with a sense of reality such as the simulation of constructing a building. The design and production of these interface experiences is dependent on the specialist skills of the graphic designer. Recent advances in technology have allowed the production of 3D graphics including animations and in the near future it will be possible for projects to incorporate 3D environments that allow the user to navigate through 3D space.

As with all project team members, graphic designers have also developed skills in other disciplines. Some graphic designers have become multiskilled to the extent where they can assume the role of project manager or authoring specialist. The current technological and educational environment demands that graphic designers continually develop more specialized skills and extend their knowledge.

Instructional design

In 1991 a new phase was incorporated into the development of CBE projects –
Instructional Design. At the time of its introduction, most projects were
databases of multiple-choice questions due to the limitations of the software
and the CBE approach to using computers for teaching and learning was still
quite restricted. The ID (as they are referred to in our teams) was therefore
very limited in scope. As technology changed and hypertext/hypermedia programs, such as ToolBook, were introduced, the CBE approach changed to
include decision-making models, multimedia incorporating video, games and
simulation models. Instructional designers became key figures in working
with SMEs in determining the most appropriate use of the technology for
particular learning outcomes.

It is interesting to note that large private multimedia producers call their
educational designers *interactive designers*. Now that CBE is moving into the
area of developing whole learning environments, the idea of labelling designers *learning environment designers* seems more appropriate. In 1996 CBE has
eight such designers who also assume authoring and project leadership roles.

Academic staff development and marketing of the CBE department has
become a considerable task within QUT. The Academic Staff Development
Unit (ASDU), administered by the Pro Vice-Chancellor Academic, is closely
linked to the CBE department due to popular interest in the use of technology
in teaching. CBE is often invited to attend faculty or school-based 'teaching'
days in conjunction with ASDU and provides academics with information
regarding CBE's services and latest techniques. More recently the Educational
Media Facility (EMF) within the Division of Information Services has provided guidance and information to lecturers wishing to use technology in
teaching and learning. The EMF has been established as a means of addressing
convergence of technologies within the departments and sections of the division (see p.144 for expansion on this).

To assist academics in comprehending the role of design in their teaching
and learning materials, CBE produces a 'client pack', which explains some of
the important issues to be considered when contemplating the use of CBE.
This pack addresses much more than just educational design by addressing
the issues of delivery, acquisition of existing resources, marketing, copyright,
funding sources, time commitment, evaluation, and maintenance, as well as
the project development process involved. The educational questions to be
raised are:

- How is the CBE material going to be used in conjunction with the rest of
  the unit?
- Why use computers to do certain tasks?
- Why are students required to learn the material?
- Clearly describe the desired learning outcomes. What do you want your
  students to be able to do as a result of using the courseware?

- List as many characteristics as you can about your user population (age, professional background, reason for taking this subject, experience with computers etc).
- How much do students already know about this subject?
- How do your students learn most effectively?
- What types of tasks would be most appropriate?
- What options for assessment would be appropriate for your learning outcomes?
- How much control should users have? What sorts of things should they be DOING while using the material? (Think about your learning outcomes.)

Multimedia

The introduction of multimedia in the form of sound, video and animation was gradual at CBE because of the cost in terms of time and technology. In 1992 a substantial project devised to instruct Arts and Business students in four languages was commenced. Due to the timing for release, interactive videodisc was chosen as the delivery medium for cultural video in the target language. In 1996 conversion to CD-ROM commenced, however there remains considerable material on interactive videodisc. Delivery issues, such as the reliability of interactive videodisc players and associated hardware, have been a continuing challenge due to the many possible points of failure in the equipment.

In 1993 two significant projects were commenced applying multimedia. These were Physics for first year subjects over a number of different courses and Law modules in Evidence, Criminal Law, Succession and Civil Procedure. The Physics project used simulations in order for students to manipulate variables and see the physical effects in a diagram. The Law modules used video to translate a three minute incident from which legal implications arose and charges were laid. Short segments of courtroom and other relevant scenes were selected to illustrate points of law throughout the tutorials.

A multimedia specialist was employed in 1994 to optimize and rationalize the use of multimedia in projects. CBE now closely examines all incoming projects to determine whether multimedia is relevant or beneficial to the achievement of the learning objectives of a particular project or if another medium is more appropriate. In short, CBE is at present consciously evaluating the expediency of multimedia as a result of development and delivery issues. The overall cost in terms of production time and technology required can make the use of the medium prohibitive. With changes in technology, particularly delivery hardware, this issue will not remain an important factor, however, instructionally, the project must strive to achieve its learning objectives.

Delivery of multimedia is achieved in one of three ways, depending on the project: by network for projects with audio and animation; by CD-ROM for projects in prototype and with video suitable for take-home delivery; and by a Netware video server, allowing streaming for multiple users. In CBE the issue of compatibility has been addressed adhering to standard delivery machine specifications for faculties and students who wish to use projects at home. The future of multimedia is an exciting one as the Internet, WWW, Java and Virtual Worlds is changing the way information can be transmitted. The use of the Internet will speed the development of cross computer communication technologies, and cable TV will likely offer an answer in the near future.

Template development

The cost of developing computer-based learning is extremely high if each project is produced from scratch. The use of templates is the most effective method of reducing costs and making computer-based learning available to a large range of courses. CBE has decreased the time required for developing question and answer type tutorials by inputting of word processing files into databases. This has been common practice since 1991. The large Language Learning project, commenced in 1992, developed a generic approach to student language learning using interactive videodisc, and templated this for use in four languages. Lecturers input all interactive videodisc and text information into the template. Figure 11.2 is a 'screen dump' of a page of the template.

Figure 11.2   A page of the template

CBE is currently developing template approaches for different learning environments and recycling them in various subject areas. Templates that allow lecturers to input their own subject matter will devolve some of the work directly to the faculties and provide lecturers with the opportunity to maintain their projects over time. Lecturer training for using templates at this stage occurs on a needs basis but it will be addressed in the future as a more general staff development issue.

Delivery issues

One of the major contributing factors of CBE's success at QUT has been the approach taken by management, *viz*, fusing the areas of delivery and development with equal importance attached to each. CBE has addressed delivery issues by employing its own systems staff to manage delivery in CBE labs. These issues include file server set-up, network operations, installation of projects on the file server, delivery input to project teams, and workstation support.

Support for students using CBE Laboratories has become another reason for success. The employment of QUT students as lab advisors who offer 'over-the-shoulder' help to students has proved to be advantageous in many aspects. Students who are unfamiliar with CBE or computers may book into the supervised labs, which open 100 hours per week during semester. The lab advisors are trained by CBE staff twice yearly with new intakes each semester. At present there are 21 technology literate students working four hour shifts as lab advisors on three campuses. These valuable employees often work in the CBE production and systems sections during their university vacations and two full time staff are ex-lab advisors.

'Take-home' CBE is a recent development that allows students to access CBE tutorials on home PCs. The distribution of these has to date been via two publishing houses who market and distribute the disks and CD-ROMs. The lab advisor scheme offers support for these products through a phone-in help service.

Evaluation

During 1991 a federally funded Department of Employment, Education and Training (DEET) grant allowed QUT to undertake an evaluation of the impact of CBE at QUT and educational technologies at other Australian universities. Staff and student perceptions were gathered and investigated by questionnaire, focus group and interview techniques. Results showed surprisingly high levels of satisfaction from both staff and students in their use of CBE projects. Some results are as follows:

Students

- 85% said that CBE helps in their studies a moderate to very large extent;
- 78% said that they approve of the use of CBE in their studies;
- 95% said that question and answer tutorials are moderately to very useful;
- 41% said that they were dissatisfied with the size of the CBE facility (since extended);
- 22% were positive to CBE use before they used it and 52% were positive after use.

Staff

- 70% said that the use of CBE tutorials has affected student learning in a positive way;
- 56% said that the quality of student learning has improved with CBE tutorials;
- 38% said that time marking had decreased with the use of CBE tutorials;
- 55% were enthusiastic to use CBE before they used it and 75% were enthusiastic afterwards.

Other benefits have been indicated by the use of CBE since its inception at QUT. These have been:

- the encouragement for students to work in groups and discuss the material;
- the familiarization with the technology;
- the chance to benefit from peer group help in the form of lab advisors.

In 1996 the Division has funding to undertake further evaluation of the use of CBE. After much discussion and refinement, the evaluation will be in the form of two studies.

1. A close analysis of use of CBE approaches including analysis of reasons for adoption, success in achieving intended outcomes, incidental outcomes, deployment within courses, interactions with academic staff and related issues. Five large projects have been targeted.
2. A formative evaluation of potential directions of use to QUT in the development of CBE projects. This involves the future provision of information to those responsible for resourcing decisions regarding the progress of educational technology at QUT. This will be a concentrated scan and assessment of the increasingly complex field of available techniques.

These studies should be completed by early 1997.

The future

Convergence and changing structures

The Division of Information Services at QUT is currently moving towards restructuring the departments and sections that provide teaching and learning support. This move has arisen as a direct result of a recommendation from a quinquennial review in 1996, which suggests amalgamating the Computer-Based Education Department with Audio Visual Services, the Educational Television Unit (responsible for producing teaching videos) and the Open Learning Unit (responsible for off-campus distance learning by correspondence tuition). Convergence of services in these departments, together with a trend towards the need for flexible delivery of teaching and learning materials in the university of the twenty first century, are motivations for the recommendations. In effect the users in the faculties are driving the change at a time when senior university management and staff in the Division are aware of technological convergence and service issues.

There no longer seems to be the need to justify the use of computer-based learning in education due to widespread affirmation of the benefits to be derived. Some of these can be listed as follows:

* easier access to consistent information;
* learner centred materials catering for different learning styles;
* richer learning materials with feedback;
* availability of more information because of storage ability;
* easier/more simplified teaching of expensive, dangerous, time intensive and complex processes;
* lecturer time liberated for group discussion or project assistance;
* efficient management of student records and progress reports.

Flexible learning

Of current contention is the determination of ways in which to extend the benefits of CBE to other areas of QUT. Policy and resource changes for the new department should put money into gradual development of mixed media learning materials for faculties on a needs basis. At the same time, a policy for flexible learning is under discussion and will provide direction for future use of technology in teaching and learning. A recent model for definition of flexible learning at QUT is as follows: 'Flexible learning and teaching involves using a range of strategies and technologies to meet the diverse needs of students regarding location and time of study, allowing options in relation to learning goals, content, styles and assessment, and providing readily accessed support.'

The use of templates and the amalgamation of four departments or units will expedite and simplify the process for QUT.

Key points

In retrospective assessment of the evolution of CBE at QUT, the following factors manifest themselves as key contributors in the success of the department:

- the continued support for CBE from senior management even when faculties complained that funding could be better spent elsewhere;
- the energy and motivation of Dr Ellis;
- the fact that the initiator was an academic attempting to help other academic staff;
- the decision to have CBE in a central service area of the university, physically and politically;
- the simple approach used in the early years when understanding of the process and technical capabilities were limited;
- recognition of the importance of delivery in the whole process of development and delivery of projects;
- the use of teams in development;
- the commitment to making materials educationally effective;
- the commitment to the lab advisor scheme and service to students;
- the move towards the use of templates in recent years.

Chapter 12

METTNET®

Iain Skelly and Jackie Hargis

What is METTNET®?

For the technical, METTNET® is Wirral Metropolitan College's (WMC) college-wide network covering some six sites, with additional links to a local
school, and incorporating 1,500 PCs, 30 file servers and over 100 networked
CD-ROMs, networked sound and video, local and Internet e-mail, and access
to the Web on any one of its 1500 workstations. It has 'evolved' over the last
six years. This evolution has taken place within certain parameters that have
ensured that the main aim of the network (which is to support the learning of
WMC's students) has been retained.

The technical support consists of a network coordinator, four network
managers and 13 technicians. This team is responsible for maintaining all the
PC hardware, network hardware such as switches, bridges, routers, micro-
wave and megastream links etc, installing and maintaining software, managing the e-mail, and so on. The system is used by both administrative and
academic staff as the college management information system (MIS) uses the
same cabling infrastructure. At present it is all based around Netware 3.12.

At the time of writing (1996), there is a European bid going in to extend
METTNET® to 18 secondary schools and other Local Education Authority
(LEA) centres on Wirral. Funding has already been obtained to expand
METTNET® into additional sites including training centres within industry (eg
Vauxhall Motors), a local business park and other areas. The physical size of
the network will probably double in the next two to three years.

In general, technology has posed few operational problems to the development of METTNET®. The human issues around the role of information technology in learning support, and the need to re-skill a sceptical workforce have

been the most complex. The issues of job security are also critical at a time when technology is 'attempting' to offer more support to the learner. Terms such as distance learning, autonomous learning, open and flexible learning while often being vaguely defined, all add to feelings of uncertainty and confusion, and result in attitudes that develop more from what psychologists might describe as 'cognitive dissonance' than clear statements about educational and learning futures.

Why METTNET®?

In the mid 1980s WMC underwent a general inspection from the Department of Education and Science (DES, as it was then). One of the issues identified in the Inspector's report was the lack on an integrated approach to IT (ie a college policy) – which resulted in duplication of resources in some paralleled by wastage in others. The college responded quickly to take on the issues identified. One of the major outcomes was a learner centred IT policy based on the recognition that:

1. IT would play an increasingly important part in the vocations to which our existing and future learners aspired. WMC had an obligation to all its learners to ensure that their needs were catered for.
2. That IT would play an increasingly important part in supporting learning in all areas whether or not these areas were directly linked to technology. WMC should take this on board when developing strategies to deliver IT to its learners.

In order to ensure that our learners could use IT in such a way that these 'needs' would be satisfied, the first step was to talk to staff and students in order to identify the difficulties faced when using IT within the existing structure. The outcome of these talks indicated that current provision failed in three vital areas. In essence, our users found it difficult to access IT (they could not get at computers or software in a way that was convenient to them). When they did, they found it was difficult to use, (the 'concession demanding' nature of IT was exacerbated by different PCs, operating systems, software packages etc). They often found IT irrelevant to their needs (they were using IT for IT's sake – outmoded software in highly contrived situations). These arrangements also stretched the 'credibility rating' of IT for staff, who, while receiving 'staff development' on BBC micros suddenly found their delivery platform was an Apricot or IBM PC!

In order to combat these problems WMC set out to develop an IT infrastructure that satisfied the needs that we had identified. The initial emphasis was hardware focused, because without the appropriate infrastructure none of the other planned developments would be possible.

Features of METTNET®

The Customized Menu Learning Resource (CMLR)

As the college moves towards more flexible patterns of delivery it has become increasingly important to use IT as a communication device between tutors and learners. The college uses two complementary systems for this function (e-mail and the CMLR).

The CMLR system was designed as a way of enabling staff to have a direct input into managing the IT-based (and traditional) resources used by their students. It was founded on the belief that, as part of any flexible or resource-based/supported learning process, staff needed to be able to identify and bring together appropriate resources. The system enables staff to make links to the huge range of materials already available and to say why and how they should be used within units of study etc. It also features the ability to regularly update students with new resources, links and additional material. It provides a simple point, click and drag interface to allow staff to construct groups or menus of resources and then to deliver these to their students together with appropriate support materials. It is probably obvious to most teachers that there is nothing revolutionary about this approach. It draws on established good practice in teaching and provides a vehicle to expand and develop this using IT. However the use of IT adds some additional dimensions that provide the following benefits for staff and learners:

1. easy and simple access to all IT-based resources;
2. encourages and demands an awareness of appropriate resources by students and staff;
3. provides a simple induction for learners into the college's IT system;
4. provides on line help for every item of material available;
5. allows the user to find appropriate material by item name, topic or subject area searches;
6. allows staff to incorporate links to both IT-based and more traditional learning resources and present this to learners in a compact and easy to use form;
7. allows staff to focus on specific resources appropriate to their programme of study (whether on the local network or Internet), while at the same time allowing students to search for more material;
8. provides a simple mechanism for updating resource and other program information (ie via a standard word processor);
9. allows students to be notified (through METTNET®) of any changes made by program teams to these resources etc, and for these changes to be made immediately available.

CMLRs from all programs are available for any student and staff member to view on METTNET®. How one program team use a particular resource to support learning can be viewed and used by other teams or students on other programs. In addition to students and staff, it can be accessed by college advisors, prospective students etc to obtain up to date information about the programs available within WMC. At the same time it still enables staff to be fully involved in the process of learning support as it simply adds a new and 'evolutionary' dimension to this, one that encourages staff to view new possibilities, developments and share appropriate materials.

This public and shared approach, which is an inevitable consequence of using networked IT in this manner, has the potential to make major productivity gains in education and consequently free up resources to support further developments. The amount of duplication of learning resources in further education is huge and is difficult to cost in terms of time and effort but a managed approach to resources using IT is likely to produce significant savings. It is important to stress the 'managed' aspect of this. Unless organized properly, computer networks can become an even larger labyrinth of 'private' and hidden resources than the traditional filing cabinets that they replace.

An additional benefit is that of quality improvements. The first stage in any attempt to improve the quality of learning support materials distributed to learners is that they should be publicly available. From then on, whatever quality control systems are implemented will produce more effective results compared to their previous operation.

E-mail

A complementary area in relation to the use of the CMLR is that of e-mail. At WMC e-mail is available to all staff and students, however at present the use of e-mail is largely either staff to staff or student to student. Breaking through this barrier is a task assigned to IT curriculum officers (ITCOs). A considerable amount of work needs to be done to encourage the use of e-mail as a means of supporting the learner outside the more traditional patterns of classroom operation. The distribution and receipt of assignments, student tracking, support and guidance etc. are all possible via e-mail systems providing thought is given to their operation.

We have tried to ensure that the focus is very much on staff involving themselves directly in the use of IT to support learning, an approach that is going to remain essential to the successful integration of IT and learning for sometime to come. Big 'systems approaches' where students are assessed, accredited, directed, supported, tracked and awarded may be part of the future, but only if they progress from the developments that are possible in the immediate and medium term. It is perhaps slightly worrying that the administrative convenience offered by such systems might tempt decision makers into their premature adoption with little or no consideration for the consequences for learning.

The Internet

One of the most rapidly expanding areas is interest in the Internet. We provide Internet access at any one of the workstations on the network (except for the local school who provide a single point of access). We limit access to 60 concurrent links at any one time though a small group of users have priority access and will always be able to get a connection. The main issue however is how we and our students use the Internet. We have already mentioned that staff have the facility to integrate direct links to Web pages into the customized resources that they produce for their students. In addition to this we have an Internet librarian who is responsible for maintaining a list of appropriate Web sites and making this available over the system.

Guiding principles

At all times the key issues of access, ease of use and relevance were of paramount importance to the design process and controlled the evolution of the system.

Access

It was decided at an early stage at WMC that IT was not a classroom-based technology. The replacement of a tutor in a room with 20 students, by a system in which 20 PCs are added to the equation has never struck us as the way forward with IT. We decided from the outset that as IT was a 'concession-demanding technology' we would minimize the number of non technology concessions the learner had to make. Being able to access IT at a time, place and pace suitable to individual needs seemed to be a fundamental prerequisite for the successful adoption of IT.

It was also important to ensure that the bulk of the facilities provided by the system were available on any workstation. This was a very ambitious undertaking, but one that was crucial to the concept of access. The only effective way forward was to develop 'open access' facilities that provided the learner with direct access to the materials available on METTNET®. No more having to go to a particular room or the library to use a CD-ROM, these should be available on any workstation.

The vast majority of the PCs available on METTNET® are now utilized on an open access basis. WMC provides access to METTNET® workstations from 8.30 am to 9.00 pm five days a week and from 9.00 am to 5.00 pm on Saturday. All students at WMC are issued with a 'learning pass'. This is simply a folder with a floppy disc (that contains a selection of essential resources), and a small booklet that explains how to get started on METTNET®. It does provide a physical link to the system and one that encourages even the most technophobic of students to try IT.

One key issue that this form of access raises is the system's ability to record student activity. Most students on the system at present do not have an individual ID and password (except for e-mail), although facilities are in place to record PC usage (by room, site etc), and to monitor software access. However, there is increasing demand to record activity and to link IT usage with performance and learning outcomes.

Ease of use

The aim was to remove as many barriers to use as possible. The idea of a single-user access for students (using the guest ID) was based on the problems that learners had with passwords and more complicated access procedures. Likewise, emphasis has been placed on designing a single interface (used from any workstation) that is customizable and easy to use. Any material on the system can be accessed by a single point and click. To enable students to find appropriate items from the thousands available on the system there is a search engine linked to support material for the various applications or databases. Staff can customize both resources and access to specific learning outcomes for their students through a simple mechanism. This also includes the ability to add WWW pages as icons to a student's resources.

To support users, the college has a number of staff designated as study assistants. As well as providing e-mail, telephone support and software documentation, they play a vital role for many of our learners and provide direct feedback on the problems students experience when using METTNET®, which enables refinements to be made to the system and signposts the way for future developments. Because of their expertise in the field of IT they can articulate the problems experienced by users much more effectively, and as such provide an invaluable link into the process of effective provision, and development aimed at ensuring ease of use for all learners. These staff offer a 'one stop shop' for students and can deal with a variety of requests, for example, a jammed printer, explaining how to search a CD-ROM database, or how to save a file in Microsoft Word.

Relevance

The key to ensuring that IT applications are regarded as relevant by users is to involve them in development. We have attempted to ensure that at all stages the college lecturing and support staff are fully involved in the development process, although for a variety of reasons we have not always succeeded.

For example, the college established a multimedia production unit as early as 1991. Academic staff were encouraged to participate in learning materials preparation as subject specialists. However, even with concerted effort in terms of promoting the unit and what multimedia had to offer, the initial take up by staff was minimal. Even if projects were started, they rarely reached completion. Over time a pattern of concerns started to emerge:

1. They felt they were being asked to spend time altering the format of materials that already worked for them.
2. By releasing their learning materials to the unit they were losing owner- ship of them.
3. The college may be looking towards generating income from the fin- ished product with no recompense to themselves.
4. They would be losing control of how their information should be pre- sented.

Faced with this information, a change in our internal strategy was needed. It was felt that rather than look to developing entire courseware, we should prepare a plan that could support staff in developing supportive learning materials as a first step. This would at least address the fear of losing control of 'their' information. It was agreed that a model should be developed that could accommodate staff with a low IT skill base through to the competent IT user who might already have analysis and design experience.

We looked for authoring software that offered two main things: first, as easy to use as possible (in particular no need for knowledge of a programming language), and second, software that would allow a natural progression from the lowest level IT skills to the highest level. In this respect it was important that it would handle the launching of external programs so that the resources (such as video, picture/sound files) could be run in the same way. We settled on Word for Windows 6, Helpmaker and MasterClass.

Workshops were used to promote the new plan. These workshops gave an opportunity to discuss the benefits of multimedia, delivery through METTNET® and how we could offer staff development through action plans to allow for individual needs. Attendance figures were favourable, but few delegates became actively involved in developing materials. Some time later a sample of academic staff was asked to take part in a small evaluation study. It found that barriers to taking up the opportunity were time, ownership and lack of resources.

Management responded to the time issue by offering financial reward. This meant that as long as projects met specified criteria, the author(s) could be recompensed in a number of ways. This could be direct payment for those doing the work outside their normal day or alternatively remission. It worked on a contract being signed at the start of the work with payment upon com- pletion. This resulted in a handful of materials being produced that now reside on METTNET®. However, this scheme has not been continued for several reasons. First, the college has not been able to allocate funding to this area. Second, the set target dates were still proving to be unachievable.

Finally, it was deemed to be an unfair scheme as we still had some individuals who were preparing materials within the framework without requesting payment.

With regard to resources, three laptops were made available. Alongside this, the existing multimedia unit was equipped with multimedia PCs to give authoring staff a well resourced room away from their normal workplace. This room was then replicated on another main site. Within these units trained staff are on hand to give support in both using the software or guidance on how media inclusions might be best introduced and used.

This means that staff can request video, photographs or sound files without needing to understand how this is achieved. The benefit of this service not only works in favour of authoring staff, but it has also meant that we have been able to build a large resource bank of media files. All media clips/files created are catalogued and made available across METTNET®. Any user can then browse the catalogues and include existing media files in their work. Whilst the idea of cataloguing is nothing new, it does mean that careful planning has to take place in order to make effective use of network server space as well as assigning appropriate file names to offer easy retrieval.

We now have more than 40 named staff actively working on materials for distribution via METTNET®. In addition there are more than 500 materials available to its users, all of which have been developed in-house. With most of these materials being generated in Word, it could be argued that these are not multimedia. On the other hand, Word has provided an excellent transition platform in that staff are starting to change delivery styles in a small way. One of the main strengths of this has been the fact that high quality print-outs are still an option whereas in 'true' multimedia this is sometimes restricted.

The staff development work of METTNET®

An outline of the support team

The work of the learning support team in METTNET® is aimed at ensuring that IT is used in a way that is relevant to the needs of the learner. It encourages staff to take on new styles of delivery and to ensure that all staff can feed back into the development of METTNET® in such a way that the integration between IT and learning support becomes more transparent from the learners perspective and an obvious evolutionary path for the teacher.

Today, the team consists of 14 people whose jobs, in varying degrees, feature supporting staff in the use of IT.

Figure 12.1 shows that the team is headed by the IT manager. Coordination of skills training is handled by the IT staff development coordinator, and the learning technology managed by two learning technology development officers (LTDOs). With the exception of the study assistant and METTNET® support assistant roles, the jobs predominantly involve working with staff.

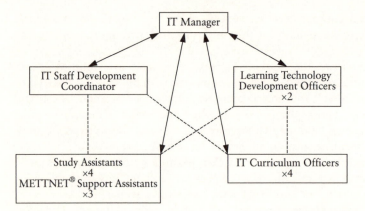

Figure 12.1   Learning support structure.

The latter roles combine offering support to staff as well as all other METTNET® users. Within the context of staff development, these posts are used as a valuable back-up service when quick or additional support is needed.

The two LTDOs have specific responsibility for materials development and organizing the user interface on METTNET® (what we call the CMLR system). They work in project teams with four IT curriculum officers (ITCO's) who have responsibility for supporting staff development in Administration and Business, Arts and Humanities, Science and Technology and Student Services. They work with staff on a one-to-one or group basis and can provide ongoing support on materials development projects, respond to new large scale training needs (eg the introduction of a new e-mail system), solve basic technical problems for staff, help with software evaluation and in general provide a link between METTNET® and the needs of the further education curriculum. The ITCO posts have evolved over the last three years in response to the needs of staff whose experience of IT ranges from highly sophisticated to non existent. Project teams, under the guidance of LTDOs are flexible, responsive and task centred. They are able to identify good practice and bring it to the attention of others. They can ensure that staff problems with IT are quickly identified and where appropriate responded to by others in the METTNET® team.

The IT staff development model

IT skills training is the start point in the IT staff development life cycle. Without at least a working knowledge of e-mail and word processing, staff cannot perform their jobs effectively. All staff have in the past been given an opportunity to attend a short programme spread over four weeks. However, college management has now made the decision that new employees should be able to provide evidence of use of the college's e-mail system and word processing (Word 6) within a six-month probationary period. One of the influencing factors in this decision was, that given a choice, some staff decline the opportunity to attend the programmes and to all intents and purposes ignore METTNET®'s existence. Such resistance can be for a variety of reasons, but in many cases will be linked to a perception that IT can threaten jobs in the long-term. This is especially so in the case of academic staff, and had to be addressed to enable headway to be made in using METTNET® as part of programme delivery.

As METTNET® grows the need to include more within the introductory training programme has become an issue. Over the last three years, the format has changed on an annual basis. This has evolved from being one programme of 12 hours spread over six weeks through to the current situation of 16 hours spread over eight weeks. The programme is now in two parts: part 1 covers the basic introduction and overview of METTNET®, which includes e-mail and word processing. It is seen as the obligatory part of IT training for new employees. Part 2 covers the use of e-mail, information handling skills, materials development, CMLR and concentrates entirely on the use of IT within the curriculum. Planning is underway to re-design the programme on a modular basis whereby staff can study modules in an order of preference. As far as possible, the materials will be made available through METTNET® thus giving an opportunity for flexibility in place, pace and time of study. Mandatory modules will be included to cover the college's policy on IT skills and new employees.

It has also been found that to start to use the system effectively, possession of information handling skills is essential. This is based on the results of a survey that was conducted in 1992–93. The report recommended that this should be included in IT staff development (Hargis and Cunningham, 1993).

Moving on from basic IT skills, the next level of development is concerned with developing skills to effectively evaluate software in terms of content and usability. It is fair to say that in the beginning, most software selection was driven by members of the METTNET® team. It has been necessary to shift this emphasis to user requests so that the true benefit of METTNET® being seen as a 'central shared resource and owned by no one' could be achieved. An evaluation system has been established that operates on the basis that anyone can put a request for software forward. This is then followed through by a member of the learning support team who will start to explore how it will be used within the learning environment. Throughout this process we are looking to correct any deficiency identified in IT skills as well as promoting and comparing the existing resources on METTNET®.

Ultimately, we are looking towards exchanging one method of delivery for another by using IT to develop materials. As a minimum, this would mean that the traditional 'hand-outs' could be word processed. At a more advanced level we are aiming to train staff to produce learning materials that use resources already on METTNET® (information resources, text, images, sound, video) and to organize learning resources and programme delivery via METTNET®.

The success and failure of METTNET®

METTNET® has been developing rapidly over the last six years. In terms of usage, we clocked a total time in excess of 1,300,000 hours of use for the year 1994–95 (students, staff and administrative use) with the vast bulk being for educational support.

E-mail is the single most popular application on the system, followed by Microsoft Word. It must be pointed out that although Word is used as a word processor, it is also utilized as an authoring and viewing package, which helps to explain its popularity and high usage.

The next most popular group of material on the system is CD-ROM databases. METTNET® provides a single point and click access to any CD-ROM on the system and allows the user to have multiple CD-ROMs in use at any one time. The CD-ROMs cover a wide range of material from multimedia encyclo-paedias to newspaper databases, census information, structured training and educational programmes (including NVQs) etc.

By and large METTNET® has been very successful for both staff and learn-ers at WMC. Usage of IT has grown rapidly over the last six years (there has been a 60% increase in staff usage in the last two years) and there is increasing demand for additional resources, access and training. Over 40 programmes of study are now supported by the CMLR system (compared to ten a year ago), and it is hoped to more than double this in the next few months.

The issue of staff acceptance of IT however is still a major concern. Staff training continues to expand. Examples of involvement in the use of IT to support delivery are increasing, but there are still many who either question its relevance (though fewer and fewer do), and also, those who are concerned because of the impact on traditional teaching methods, on staff workloads and the potential impact (real or imagined) on job security.

One area that did not work was the network links with two partner col-leges that were developed during the period 1992–95. The technical issues of linking three college networks together caused few problems. The main issues revolved around the need for each of the three colleges to get their internal IT strategies sorted out before expanding into links with partner institutions ie if staff and learners are not willing or able to make full and productive use of internal facilities then it is unlikely that they will make full and productive use of more remote links. It is a shame that these links are being discontinued at a time when the Higginson Report is stressing the need to expand inter college links, though the expense of maintaining them was high (in terms of BT charges). The message is quite clear. Before expanding into the world of super highways and unlimited access to the information stored on the world's computer systems, colleges need to have a sound and successful strategy for incorporating IT into curriculum support and delivery. IT must be delivered to and used by most of our learners in a focused and structured manner. Allowing learners to flounder around on the Internet or on internal college networks will not work. The relationship they have with IT and the resources it makes available to them must be managed with care or a great opportunity will be lost. Key players in this strategy are the teachers and tutors, who must increasingly see themselves as links between learners and the resources that IT makes available, taking on the roles of assessors, guides and contributors.

Reference

Hargis, J and Cunningham, M (1993) *The use of CD-ROMs in the Library/Open Access Areas*, Wirral Metropolitan College.

Chapter 13

Technologies to extend out-reach

Gerry McAleavy and Gerard Parr

Background

The ACTOR project (Application of ISDN Technologies to Extend Out-Reach) is designed to make use of advanced telecommunications systems and services to address the challenges of extended access to the university's courses, to assist with the transfer of technology to business in Northern Ireland and to improve the competitiveness of local economies by the further development of higher education and vocational training. The project is therefore targeted at client groups such as women in rural areas, post-16 trainers, teachers converting to technology teaching, staff currently in employment in the computer software industry and other training providers. The project employs a PC Videophone (VC8000), which comprises a small video camera that sits on top of a monitor, a video graphics card, a telephone handset and connection unit. Software that runs on Windows can then be used across this extended classroom or office environment.

Rationale for ACTOR

Programmes designed to improve education and training have to be delivered in a flexible manner if equity in educational provision is to be achieved. This is particularly important in the context of the increasing demand for education from mature students and persons who are retraining and the need to raise standards across communities that have experienced disadvantage. For example, researchers (Roper and Hoffman, 1993) have found skill differences to be a key factor in explaining different levels of productivity between

Germany and Northern Ireland, while the Northern Ireland Economic Council (1995) claims that, 'employers have adjusted their production methods to the low supply of skills, reducing incentives for students to acquire qualifications, leading to a low skills equilibrium'. There is, therefore, a clear need to address both the needs of individuals and the requirements of a modern economy by the application of new methodologies of learning and training designed to enhance access and raise standards.

In order to deal with these deep-seated concerns, it was decided that consideration should be given to determining the optimal ways in which new communications technologies could be utilized to assist the development of flexible learning systems and, in particular, to share scarce expertise and resources across the further and higher education sector. Advances in telecommunications have ensured that communications systems have become central to both the transformation of public discourse and the development of the economy (McAleavy and Parr, 1995). Recent telecommunications developments on both sides of the Irish border, assisted by EU initiatives such as the STAR (Special Telecommunications Action for Regional development, 1990) and Telematique programmes have provided the infrastructure for the development of advanced networking facilities across Ireland (McAleavy and Parr, 1995):

> 'The significance of these developments can hardly be underestimated. One result has been the development and provision of the first operational Synchronous Digital Hierarchy network in Europe, with a bandwidth up to 622Mbps. At the entry level an Integrated Services Digital Network (ISDN) is widely available that can provide between 2 and 30 64Kbits per second channels of bandwidth enabling the transmission of compressed video, voice, data and text to destinations in Ireland and abroad. Currently ISDN2 is available from 44 exchanges in Northern Ireland and, in recent months, has become widely available across the Telecom Eireann network.'

It was proposed that the ACTOR project should utilize these advanced communication systems and networking facilities, taking advantage of the new possibilities offered by the ISDN2 service, to address challenges faced by the University of Ulster in providing access to new student populations and assisting with the transfer of technology to businesses in Northern Ireland. It was also intended to provide a testbed for North–South cross-border collaboration in Ireland using ISDN2 and the provision of support to internationally accredited courses through building on the extensive telecommunications and distance lecturing expertise within the University of Ulster. In addition, it was intended to provide entry-level bandwidth into SuperJANET for university-led projects.

The University of Ulster has four campuses – two in the Greater Belfast Area – (at Belfast and Jordanstown), one in the north-west (Magee College)

Figure 13.1   Map of Ireland

and one in the north of the province (Coleraine), see Figure 13.1.

To enhance the University of Ulster ACTOR coverage, selected further education colleges in the province were identified to act as *nodes* on the ACTOR *network*. The project was also designed to have a cross-border dimension involving Letterkenny Information Technology Centre in the Republic of Ireland. In order to initiate the project, a meeting was convened to which representatives of the relevant colleges of further education were invited together with the further education officers from the Education and Library Boards (the Northern Ireland equivalent of local education authorities). The project was presented to the sector representatives in the context of the policies being developed between the university and the college such as the franchising of Higher National Diploma (HND) courses and the creation of 'associate college' status to enhance collaboration between the university and the vocational education sector. The relationship between the university and the colleges is long-standing and is reflected in the commitment in the university mission statement to the continuing provision of vocationally oriented programmes. The project was, then, perceived by college representatives as being a part of the general policy of strengthening cooperation between the sectors rather than a separate focus on technology for a specific purpose. In addition, the project was perceived by college staff as a dynamic way of updating knowledge and developing new skills within the college.

The colleges in Northern Ireland responded positively and the college from the Republic of Ireland was also extremely interested to participate, given the potential for cross-border links. Other colleges in the Republic also registered interest and to date, ACTOR, has extended University of Ulster outreach to many organizations from both Education and Commerce within Northern Ireland and beyond, including the Republic of Ireland, Norway and the USA.

Phase 1 (February 1994 to February 1995)

Initially the project was concerned with the testing of the technology and delivery of programs to client groups. The aims of this phase included: investigation of the technical aspects of delivering programs using the VC8000; examination of the relationships between different modes of conferencing and needs of different client groups; determination of the curricular implications of delivering at a distance using these forms of learning; and assessment of the costs and benefits in both quantitative and qualitative senses in relation to traditional modes of curriculum delivery.

One key aspect of phase one was the identification of staff within colleges who would support and champion new technologies of learning and to establish effective networks with them. It was found that the traditional audiovisual technicians were a crucial source of expertise and initiative. Their backgrounds, though generally not oriented towards computer technology, included experience of using a wide range of equipment to improve teacher–student communication. The technicians rapidly grasped the possibilities of the desktop video systems and were in a strong position to informally network with staff as they were frequently consulted regarding technical aids to teaching. College staff tended to feel comfortable liaising with technicians and were reassured to find that they could participate in the new technology without any great initial investment in training. Having used the system, though, they could, then, be asked to consider the pedagogical changes that might be desirable if the full potential of the technology was to be realized.

With the assistance of college managers and other relevant staff, such as technicians, the VC8000 systems were deployed in the colleges, tested and put into operation. University staff then visited colleges and gave presentations to college managers and schedules for the delivery of programs were drawn up. A research protocol for users, both staff and students was also prepared.

Phase 2 (February 1995 to June 1996)

The second phase extended the programs started in phase one by initiating new developments and services targeted at management groups, community development enterprise and small and medium businesses. The aims of phase two included: to build on the data derived from the evaluation carried out in phase one for the purposes of developing new forms of curricula specifically designed to include new technologies of learning; and to develop structures of delivery that would permit the uses of the system for more effective management of the educational organizations involved including:

- management development programs;
- more effective dissemination of staff development;
- exchange of perspectives on curriculum development;
- management information exchanges;
- testing the functionality of delivering programs on an international basis.

The delivery technology

The ACTOR project is built around the Olivetti Personal Communications Computer (PCC) incorporating the BT integrated desktop videoconferencing product, the VC8000. The VC8000 provides real-time interactive multimedia transactions including videoconferencing, audio telephony, chalkboard interaction, application sharing and high speed file transfer. The PCC also has interfaces for extra cameras and audio equipment, which allowed the ACTOR team to convert it into a fully-fledged group-to-group Computer Supported Collaborative Working (CSCW) system, enabling a large audience to participate in the *lecture* by virtue of enhanced mobile audio links and large screen projection facilities. A high-specification colour camera was linked to the system to enable higher definition images to be captured from the audience, and by virtue of the respective mixers, the audio-visual equipment was interleaved as required from radio microphones, document cameras and video recorders. This configuration (see Fig. 13.2) has proved worthwhile as it renders the PCC accessible to a wide range of users who may have little or no experience of communication systems.

The Personal Communications Computer (PCC) provides direct links to other integrated service digital network (ISDN) users either on a national or a global basis given the international nature of the ISDN service. The conferencing system can also however, be connected by an Ethernet card to university local area networks (LANs) and through to the UK university computing network, SuperJANET, giving access to the Internet and the World Wide Web (WWW).

Because of the LAN configuration on each campus of the University of Ulster, it was possible to interconnect via a Novell LAN to a SuperJANET server

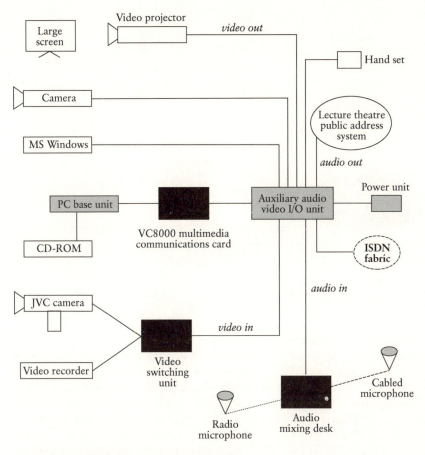

Figure 13.2   ACTOR project reconfiguration

residing on the Coleraine campus using the inter-campus network. This new level of connectivity has enabled the ACTOR coverage to provide a new dimension to access, by facilitating entry to the resources of the UK university system and the Internet. The experience with the roll-out of ACTOR was that the access to information/knowledge bases, such as the World Wide Web, is seen as a very important adjunct in support of any real-time delivery. The ACTOR project enhances the quality of the 'university experience' to remote students by making university online information resources available to supplement lectures and tutorials (see Figure 13.3).

Phase 1 findings

The current experience from the ACTOR project is that a group of up to eight persons can adequately cope with the monitor and handset (on hands-free

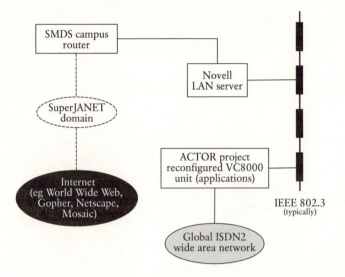

Figure 13.3   *Connectivity of networks and services to ACTOR nodes*

mode) without the need for peripherals. The handset has a capacity for comfortably picking up sound in a room from a speaker at a distance of three metres. Decisions concerning visual projection need to be taken in relation to the size of the group and the nature of the learning that is intended to take place. The team has tested a range of projection equipment and concluded that visual projection is available that can be used in a room that has not been darkened (an important factor in learning) and such a facility can serve a large group, in excess of a hundred persons. Projectors are available that also provide sound amplification. The use of projection, however, has the effect of encouraging the students to focus on the screen and interaction can diminish. This situation may be desirable in contexts where it is required that students carefully study image or video for a period but may not be appropriate where it is necessary for students to also engage in interaction with the tutor. In this case, the use of a 28" monitor display would be more suited to the educational demands of the situation.

In the case of large groups (more than 30) it is possible to chain monitors, an option that is nowadays generally used for conferences as it gives speakers a greater flexibility in varying pace and introducing different kinds of learning inputs. It should also be noted that a monitor that can display both video and computer data would normally cost around half the price of a projector. In addition, it is possible to use existing video monitors, which will adequately display images and sound, in situations where it is not necessary for the students to use the applications sharing facilities. Indeed, it also possible to combine the uses of existing video monitors with existing data tablets to provide separate displays, video on the monitor and computer data on the tablet. While this might not be the most desirable configuration, it will enable cost-effective use of existing equipment. Monitors of industrial quality tend to be of substantial size and are best used in situations where they do not need to be moved from one building to another.

Some students reported, however, that 'there should be a bigger screen' and 'some people may have had problems in seeing the monitors', or 'I feel that it would be more beneficial if there was a larger monitor', or 'I could see the screen quite clearly but it would be more beneficial if it were a larger screen other than the TV screen' or 'I would prefer a large screen like the cinema screen because it would be easier to see if there had been a large crowd'. In fact the preference for a single large screen was the most frequent comment made by students. Since the technical quality of the smaller screens was comparable (if not superior) to that of larger screens, it would appear that the issue, for students, is the need to focus, as a group, on a single source of visual input.

Another alternative that has been explored is the use of a data tablet that can project both video and computer data. This usually also requires the provision of an overhead projector of at least 400 watts capacity. This is suitable for large groups (100 persons plus) though it will require some darkening of the lecture room and, unlike other forms of projection, this solution will require the addition of speakers (the public address system, if existing may be used) to provide sound. Video quality may not be equal to that provided by monitors or other forms of projection.

The research team has conducted tests on radio microphones to enable students, in a large group, to respond to a lecturer and this has proved an effective and flexible tool in enabling students to share opportunities to give feedback. Document projection is available through the use of a document camera; experience has shown that it can be enhanced by the use of the still facility, which enables the video to freeze on an image.

There is considerable scope for the linking of external cameras, which can provide a range of facilities including the ability to focus on a particular speaker who is using the radio microphone to respond to a tutor and also the ability to manually adjust light settings and camera angles. In practice the quality of an external camera, available in a college, is likely to be superior to the relatively small camera that accompanies desktop systems and there are, therefore, considerable advantages in making use of the range of college video equipment. Equally many colleges will have audio-visual staff who have considerable experience of using video cameras and they can bring their expertise to the improvement of the quality of the virtual encounter.

It can, therefore, be seen that there are a range of audio-visual peripherals that need to be considered both in relation to the educational outcomes that the tutor wishes to attain and to the finances available. Factors that should be taken into account by the tutor are:

- the size and nature of the learner group;
- the logistics of the room to be used (lighting, power points, audibility);

- the kinds of interaction desired between tutor and student in the home base and at the distant location;
- the degree to which the learners need to experience application sharing;
- the positioning of students in relation to peripheral devices that are to be used.

Phase 2 findings

After the completion of phase one, schedules were compiled for the roll out of programmes using ACTOR facilities to three Northern Ireland sites. Tutorial sessions with students from the Post Graduate Diploma in Further Education took place between their tutor in Jordanstown and students at their nearest ACTOR location in Newry. Guest lectures from the School of Health Science are currently given via ACTOR from the Jordanstown Campus to students on an HNC Social Care Course at Newry. Computer Supported Collaborative Working has been initiated across a number of sites with information such as a college prospectus between colleges. Students on HND Business Information Technology at Newry are exploring the World Wide Web via SuperJANET under instruction from the ACTOR Team by use of the desktop conferencing facility. Students on Health and Beauty Courses at Newry and Fermanagh have discussed differences in treatments after first observing a recorded practical class that was shared across the system. Staff at all three locations have taken part in virtual meetings to promote working between students at their colleges with students from other ACTOR Sites.

During October and November 1995 the ACTOR team assisted the School of Commerce and International Business at Coleraine by providing a desktop videoconferencing unit to support the supervision of third year placement students on the BSc (Hons) European Business Studies course at their places of work in France, Belgium, Spain and Germany. In total 48 students were contacted in 16 European Locations during this period.

Review of the issues raised by participants in the ACTOR programme

The key participants in the programme are the teachers and learners, though it is clear that managers have an important role in organizing and authorizing access, while technicians have both facilitating and gatekeeping functions in relation to the system. The early indications are that the opportunity to experience an amplification, both literal (through use of radio microphones) and metaphorical, of their responses to the session, enables learners to feel that their contributions are valued. This may be particularly the case for learners who are normally reluctant to venture contributions in a class, learners with special needs and those with a reflective learning style.

For lecturers and teachers, however, it should be noted that there are concerns that participation in virtual engagements may be a risky process. There is a crucial difference, for example, between a prepared, edited, video of a teacher giving a lecture and the live interaction that takes place using the VC8000. In addition teachers may be concerned that problems that may arise during live interactions will be recorded for future scrutiny.

For the teacher, this technology may involve the devolution of authority, formally or otherwise, to a session organizer who will implement a strategy of planned interaction for a particular group. This is an unfamiliar world and the nature of work roles may have to undergo change as teachers begin to experience the impact of more autonomous patterns of interactions from students. Teachers will have to learn to live with, and gain from, the experience of communication with learners who are located in another context, which is not only separate, from a geographical perspective, but that is also differently positioned in relation to expectations regarding the way in which outcomes are to be achieved. This suggests the need for training both for teachers and students in the use of virtual systems. It also clearly indicates, however, the need for the construction of an architecture of educational encounters in virtual contexts, which would enable educational planners to begin to design structures for curriculum that are embedded in the recognition that instruction and interaction will be located in different space–time dimensions. In practice such a task may well mesh with the different educational initiatives, for example Credit Accumulation and Transfer System (CATS), National Vocational Qualifications (NVQs), and Open College credits (the latter now recognized by the Further Education Funding Council (FEFC) for funding purposes, which are concerned with the provision of flexible and individualized learning systems.

From an educational perspective, however, the opportunity for spontaneous participation and interaction for learners is one of the exciting aspects of the system. There is a need, then, to balance the possible educational gains (which may be considerable) against the need to reassure teachers that their participation will not be disadvantageous in terms of career progression.

A related issue emerging is that where lecturers (and learners) have prepared material in a form that is reducible to digital storage, the more versatility is afforded by the system. So, for example, when a student has a query regarding a piece of work, and the work has been produced on a word processor/spreadsheet etc, then the material can be shared on the system and discussed and jointly annotated. This points to the strong continuance of policies across disciplines, which encourage learners to move away from handwritten work when it is possible to do so. Equally a teacher can share a resource in a more flexible manner when it has been prepared in this way.

At this stage it is possible to begin to draw tentative conclusions regarding the management of virtual sessions from an analysis of the data that is emerging and to commence the task of examining what may be the components of successful learning encounters for the wide variety of groups involved. It is clear, however, that there will be radical implications both for management in terms of curriculum design, staff development and the restructuring of physical space in educational institutions.

Corporate implications for university competitiveness

The experience of the project suggests that provision of facilities for shared teaching with further education colleges should be further encouraged in order to:

- assist the process of quality assurance in relation to franchised programmes;
- offer the potential for the provision of additional specialist modules on programmes;
- enable students on parallel programmes at colleges and the university to work collaboratively;
- enable the provision of bridging modules to students based in rural areas to enhance access to degree programmes;
- provide controlled entry-level access to SuperJANET and appropriate LANs that can support the teaching/learning aims of specific programmes.

Furthermore, the flexible range of facilities offered by the current PC Videophone system provides opportunities for a range of additional functions to be carried out remotely:

1. Course committee meetings have been held across campuses and also between university staff and further education staff elsewhere working on franchised programmes.
2. As the area of research and consultancy has become increasingly competitive within the university sector, tenders are often required at very short notice, and it is necessary to have extremely effective protocols for processing proposals in order to ensure that submission dates are met and quality metrics are embedded in the tender responses. During 1995 the Information Technology Centre in Letterkenny, in cooperation with the ACTOR team examined ways in which the technology might support proposals for a cross-border degree programme and commercial training courses and how it could facilitate business meetings specifically in the European Union.

    There are, therefore, opportunities to strengthen the corporate approach to project management so that:
    - joint document processing can be carried out;
    - the nature and quality of responsiveness can be enhanced;
    - collaborative working practices can be extended;
    - the process of identifying industrial needs/problems and providing customized solutions can be sharpened and focused.

3. There are also considerable opportunities for improving the quality and throughput of administrative duties by enhancing the capacity for communication between administrators and academic staff and for supporting group working on documents. The development of group working practices can enrich administration by enlarging the skill mix that contributes to decision-making and ensuring that core policy issues are not ignored in favour of dealing with immediate procedural tasks. Increasing pressures are creating considerable burdens and stresses for administrative staff and the use of virtual administration will prove effective in terms of facilitating time management, improving productivity and reducing cost overheads (eg travel).

4. Course marketing, on a national and international level can also be enhanced. ACTOR was used to provide remote students with the opportunity to receive first hand knowledge of the wide range of courses offered on the university campuses. This is a good example of the use of the University Multiple Conferencing Unit to link various ISDN destinations. The implementation of this activity can be further extended to support the marketing of the university's spectrum of courses to perspective undergraduate and postgraduate students in countries where ISDN is available.

Conclusion

The new forms of virtual interaction used in ACTOR can potentially enrich the curriculum as students become enabled to communicate more widely with others. Opportunities can then be provided for access to additional ranges of content material from online sources. The continuing use of network applications will lead to a paradigm shift in the ways in which students conceptualize computing technology, which will increasingly be perceived as a pervasive tool central to the learning process.

The ACTOR project has demonstrated how it is possible to utilize advanced networking to improve university performance in teaching, administration, research and consultancy. It is hoped these experiences will feed into the continuing debate and, in some way, lead to a more accessible and manageable environment for all concerned

Acknowledgement

This project was funded through the British Telecommunications plc, University Development Award Programme 1994–96. For further information about ACTOR contact the authors or refer to: http://info.ulst.ac.uk/staff/gp.parr where information can be found on ACTOR and related projects.

References

McAleavy, G and Parr, G (1995) 'Telecommunications: routes for the information superhighway' in *Border Crossings: Developing Ireland's Island Economy*, M D'Arcy, and T Dickson (eds), 186–93, Gill & Macmillan, Dublin.

Northern Ireland Economic Council (1995) *Reforming the Education System in Northern Ireland,* NIEC, Belfast.

Roper, S and Hoffman, H (1993) *Training Skills and Company Competitiveness: A Comparison of Matched Plants in Northern Ireland and Germany,* NIEC, Belfast.

Chapter 14

Flexible learning as university policy

Louise Moran

The concept of flexible learning

Distance education has moved, in some jurisdictions, from the political and educational margins into a position where it is viewed by governments and institutions as a mainstream educational process. Distance learning methods and information technologies are converging with classroom strategies to create what will be a substantially different and exciting educational environment. In so doing, they present intriguing challenges to deeply embedded norms and values, to organizational systems and structures, and to university cultures. In Australia, this convergence is termed 'flexible learning'. While rhetoric still outstrips reality, some universities are revolutionizing their approaches to how, where, when and what they teach. For them, 'flexible learning' is mainstream educational strategy, not a marginal experiment. This chapter analyses the experience of one institution – the University of South Australia – in taking a whole-institution approach to flexible learning. In particular, it examines some of the key policy and structural issues that the university has faced in the 1990s.

As it is evolving at the University of South Australia (UniSA), a flexible learning environment is one that is assumed to produce quality outcomes and to be efficient and effective (Nunan, 1994). It is student-centred and recognizes diversity and the importance of equity in access and learning outcomes. For UniSA, the philosophical basis is a constructivist one that asserts that learners are self-directed, and that shifts the emphasis from teaching to learning and the conditions of learning. As Nunan (1996) argues, 'Put bluntly, flexible learning is code for deep learning.' The process and outcomes of students' learning are influenced by teaching, and teaching is affected by the resources, technologies and specialized supports used (Ramsden, 1992). Flexible learning relies partly on a rich array of resource-based learning techniques and information technologies to respond flexibly to the diverse backgrounds that students bring to their study, and to free up the place, time, pace, media and modes of study. Flexible learning is equally concerned with enabling students to learn how to continue learning after this study period is finished – that is, with the skills and aptitudes of lifelong learning. The role of the teacher moves from an emphasis on provision of information and direction of teaching, to facilitator of learning and advisor on information sources – with all that implies for changes in the power relationship between teacher and learner.

Thus far, one could argue that these values and approaches epitomize any high quality distance education operation. The key difference for UniSA is that the University intends that the philosophy and practices of flexible learning will encompass and integrate *all* its educational experiences, thereby abandoning organizational and other distinctions between distance and face-to-face teaching in favour of a spectrum of modes and media appropriate to the circumstance. The university is building on its history as a dual mode institution with a well-established distance education infrastructure to take this whole-of-institution approach to changing teaching and learning. Flexible, student-centred learning is not being treated simply as the use of distance education techniques and information technologies to improve classroom teaching. Rather, it is treated as a key concept underlying the University's codes of good practice, its evolving articulation of the core qualities of a UniSA graduate, its policies and quality assurance processes for teaching/learning, and its goal of equity in access and learning outcomes.

This whole-institution approach involves a lockstep development of policy and practice in multiple dimensions of flexible learning.

- *An emphasis on equity and openness in access arrangements* – e.g. through targeted entry and learning support arrangements for disadvantaged groups; credit transfer and other strategies to articulate passage from school and technical/vocational education to university; and recognition of informal prior learning.
- *Interactions between and among teacher and learners are as adaptable as possible in terms of place, time and medium* – the goals being to increase students' control over where, when and how they learn, and to optimize opportunities for meaningful interaction. This presents challenges to established features of university operation (eg the daytime, weekday, lecture/tutorial format, and two-semester academic year), as well as the traditional locus of teacher authority. On the other hand, it opens up the university's programmes to teaching in workplaces and other environments away from the campus.
- *Study patterns are diverse and adapted to the requirements of lifelong learners* – eg flexible course structures, such as 'nested' certificate,

diploma and degree programs, that enable learners to move easily in and out of credentialled study; custom-tailoring of course content and teaching strategies to suit the needs of particular groups including employer clients; and an emphasis on information literacy as a generic quality of graduates.

- *Curriculum content is flexible and inclusive* – balancing intellectual breadth with the specialist requirements of a professional knowledge/skills base; content is inclusive of multicultural norms and intellectual interests, and sensitive to the needs of overseas students who may or may not ever come to the campus

- *Teaching and learner support systems accommodate diverse student needs and learning styles* – whereas it could once be assumed that students were relatively homogeneous in terms of prior learning experiences, level of knowledge and approaches to learning, it is now necessary to build diversity positively into curriculum content and teaching methods. Study skills and language/literacy supports can no longer be treated as 'Band-Aids' but as integral elements of a course and learning outcomes.

- *Learning resources support the teaching/learning process at every stage* – that is, using self-instructional materials that combine print, electronic and audio-visual media in ways that are appropriate to the subject, the students and the location, place and mode of study. 'Resource-based' learning is equally applicable in classroom and off-campus settings. It is the most obvious aspect of convergence of distance education and face-to-face teaching, but is relatively ineffective if the other dimensions are not also taken into account.

- *Appropriate information technologies underpin inquiry and discourse* – by redesigning curriculum content and teaching strategies to capitalize on the Internet as an information source, enable teachers and learners to interact electronically in ways that suit the subject, students and circumstances of study, and use computer-based technologies to change the nature and construction of knowledge.

- *Organizational structures and policy processes are designed to maximize flexibility and creativity* – eg through resource allocation and management processes that recognize the industrial and other features that distinguish flexible learning from traditional organizational patterns; nested planning processes and quality assurance mechanisms that make explicit what is deemed good practice within a flexible learning environment; encouragement of internal partnerships of academic support groups such as academic and student services, the library and information technology services.

- *Collaboration with others to improve the quality, range and relevance of teaching/learning* – through national and international strategic partnerships with other universities, the vocational education and training system, industry, professional associations, and government. Some of these partnerships are commercial in focus; others emphasize joint effort to achieve cost-benefits and economies of scale as well as expand the range of options open to students in terms of what, where and how they study.

These dimensions, the particular way in which they are being realized, and the barriers that have to be faced, are deeply affected by the history, values and aspirations of the university.

The University of South Australia: the background

The University of South Australia came into being in January 1991 through a merger of the South Australian College of Advanced Education (SACAE), and the South Australian Institute of Technology (SAIT). In 1996, the university enrolled 24,300 students, approximately 3,800 of whom studied in over 600 subjects at a distance (with an additional 2,300 students taking UniSA courses through its partnership in a national open learning consortium, the Open Learning Agency of Australia). It had an academic and general staff of 2,100 based on six campuses and operating revenue of A$200 million.

The partners brought to the merger distinctive cultures, traditions, academic programmes and administrative structures that continue to flavour the style and ambience of the new University. SACAE was itself the product of a series of mergers of smaller colleges during the 1970s and early 1980s, one result of which has been a prolonged re-evaluation of traditional philosophies, values and practice and, like most colleges of the time, it focused on teaching rather than on research. Its culture included a strong tradition of concern (and national reputation) for social justice and equity issues in curriculum and institutional policies that has carried through into the university. Distance education had been a feature in many of SACAE's courses since the 1960s, and the Distance Education Centre was one of eight major federally supported centres. The institute, in contrast, was one of a small, prestigious national group of institutes of technology with a high reputation for its courses and applied research. It relied predominantly on conventional classroom-based pedagogies, and many departments had developed close links with industry and professional associations. There was little reason or incentive to question its teaching/learning arrangements till the 1991 merger brought an urgent need to identify a common set of values and goals in teaching, research and community service for the new university.

The merger was one of equal but different partners. UniSA was one of a number of universities created from the late 1980s following Australia's abandonment of a binary system of colleges and universities, combined with large-scale, government-driven increases in enrolments, and pressures for greater accountability and efficiency in use of public funds. To survive and prosper in a highly competitive environment, the new university needed to distinguish itself not only from the other two South Australian universities, but also from the rest of the national higher education system (and increasingly, of course, to establish a distinctive international profile). While tradition and history were still treasured, an uncritical maintenance of the *status quo* would have been a recipe for disaster and unlikely to serve the university's future community well. These factors have exercised a powerful impetus for choosing a mission that would reach innovatively into the long-term future, with an emphasis on professional education, applied research, and close community links.

The university chose a faculty and school academic model operating across campuses, a structure that has helped reinforce organizational unity and evolution of a shared, new corporate culture. Authority over teaching and research has been decentralized to the faculties, but is balanced centrally by a strong senior management group whose energy, forcefulness and shared educational philosophy have been potent factors in the shaping and management of the new university's goals, and moves to instil a whole-of-institution approach to flexible learning.

The university faced a familiar, complex range of immediate political, social, financial and educational realities and problems – teaching large numbers in a semi-mass system; increasingly heavy workloads (including the pressure for research and publication as well as teaching); the educational and social implications of students' diversity; the effort to find new ways to balance breadth and depth in study, especially for professional qualifications; the need to teach cross-campus as well as on- and off-campus; the impact of new technologies on the nature of knowledge and on institutional resources, and irresistible pressures to integrate technology into teaching/learning; and educational and financial imperatives to find new markets at home and abroad in a highly competitive national and global environment. All in a continuing climate of severe financial constraints and the 'push-pull' of collaboration and competition.

Strategies for change

The change process, of course, has not been smooth or uncontested, and there is a long way to go before the university can confidently assert that flexible learning values and practices are ubiquitous. There are continuing temptations, in the face of financial and other difficulties, to retreat towards the familiar (even when some traditional modes and media of study are demonstrably not educationally or cost effective). The primary driving force countering these temptations and providing a clear sense of direction is largely top down, from the senior management group and faculty deans. However, the change processes typically involve extended collaboration through to school level, and the use of representative and multi-skilled working groups to tackle particular policy problems and solutions across all dimensions of flexible learning. While budgets are devolved to the faculties and units, the senior management group and senior university committees set corporate priorities for resource allocation so as to influence closely the pace and nature of change, and foster rewards and recognition accruing from changes towards more flexible teaching/learning arrangements. In addition, the university has put in place an elaborate planning and review cycle and quality assurance processes for teaching and learning that provide a clear corporate view of the nature and speed of change. It has also created the Flexible Learning Centre (FLC) to provide the specialist services to support these changes and also take a leading change agent role.

Corporate planning

UniSA's corporate planning process is perhaps the most comprehensive and pervasive of any Australian university. It comprises integrated annual plans of faculties and units, 'nested' within a corporate annual plan, within the university's ten-year planning cycle. The plans are framed within objectives cascading from the university's mission statement, sothat explicit expectations about flexible learning are identified under headings ofimproving teaching/learning arrangements, meeting student needs, addressing equity issues, research, efficiency and effectiveness as an organization, and so on. The quality loop is closed through a rigorous annual review by the senior management group of each area's progress against its agreed performance indicators. No planning process is perfect, but this strategy has played a major part in enabling the University rapidly to push through substantial changes in all the dimensions of flexible learning in a reasonably coordinated,mainstream fashion.

Since 1991, the plans have addressed and implemented a (continuing) rationalization and restructuring of courses and curricula; adding breadth to the depth of professional studies; a raft of quality assurance processes in teaching and learning; and strategies for development of more flexible modes of delivery on campus and at a distance through encouragement to individual staff to pursue innovative teaching/learning approaches, and provision of academic staff development, student learning support, and production and delivery services to facilitate flexible learning in all faculties. One of the most significant strategies concerns the setting of university-wide priorities for flexible learning developments, given tight resource limits and the need to improve cycles of development, revision and evaluation.

Historically, the distance education and classroom-based courses were organized and largely funded separately. Systemic moves towards convergence began in late 1994 with the senior management group requiring all faculties to take a more structured approach to implementing student-centred learning by establishing priorities in their 1995 academic plans for developing courses in flexible learning mode, and for the staff development required to accomplish the changes in pedagogy that would be necessary. Initially, most faculties focused on the development of self-instructional learning resources. The first sets of plans revealed great variation in faculty understanding of the concept of flexible learning and of practical aspects of production of resource-based learning materials – largely commensurate with the degree of their previous experience in distance education. Since then, considerable effort has been devoted to refining the planning and resource allocation processes that, from 1996, involve a staged process of faculty planning and priority-setting, assessment of workloads to meet those plans, and university determination of relative priorities across the faculties. Distinctions are no longer made between on campus and distance units. By 1998, the planning, production and maintenance cycles will involve not only preparation of learning materials, but their integration with all aspects of staff development and student support in language and learning.

Quality assurance

A second major thrust towards flexible learning has been created through an interlocked set of quality assurance processes for teaching and learning. Since 1991, codes of good practice in teaching, assessment and research supervision have been articulated through extensive debate at school, faculty and university level. Working parties have argued out hard questions about, for example, lifelong learning and what it means for curriculum, the integration of information technologies into teaching/learning, and internationalization of the curriculum content and teaching methods – and consequently set in train a range of policy development and implementation programmes, all of which are characterized by performance indicators and review mechanisms. The quality feedback loop is closed through mandatory evaluation of all units when they are taught, and cyclical external reviews of faculties and courses. These factors played an important part in the 1994 and 1995 successes of the university in winning recognition in the top band of Australian universities in the national quality review process.

In late 1995, with a raft of quality assurance processes in place, the university embarked on a programme that will have profound consequences for its entire curriculum and pedagogy over the next decade. After extended consultation around the university, a set of seven generic qualities to be expected of every UniSA graduate has been agreed. That was the (relatively) easy part. The next stage, in the context of periodic review and internal re-accreditation of degree programmes, is to define curriculum objectives, teaching/learning strategies and support processes in terms of how (unit by unit) they will contribute to one or more of the generic graduate qualities. The first to start is the Faculty of Engineering and the Environment following a major restructure in late 1995 to revitalize and position itself better in a rapidly changing engineering environment. The restructuring process has been often painful, challenging deeply ingrained assumptions and territory, but agreement was ultimately achieved through a high degree of consultation and widespread recognition of the need for change to suit new conditions. At the time of writing, the process of shaping the new curriculum to meet desired graduate attributes has just begun, but there is widespread acceptance that the complete redesign of the faculty's undergraduate course structure presents an ideal opportunity to redesign its hitherto traditional face-to-face pedagogies as well. Undergraduate students will continue to study primarily full-time on campus, but their courses take problem-based approaches to learning, use self-instructional learning resources, and progressively integrate information technology as a mainstream medium for individual and group learning.

Flexible learning centre

A third major strategy for change to a more flexible learning environment has been creation of the Flexible Learning Centre (FLC) in January 1995 as both a provider of expert services and infrastructure in relation to flexible learning, and as a change agent through institutional policy development and leadership in new developments. The centre – an academic and professional unit comprising 90 staff in three sections – was created through a merger of the Distance Education Centre (which gave curriculum design support to faculty staff, produced distance learning packages, and offered administrative and other delivery support to distance students) the Centre for University Teaching and Learning (which provided a range of academic staff development programmes and learning support to students), and the Visual Productions group of media specialists. The centre's brief is to provide academic leadership in the university in relation to policy development in the many facets of flexible learning; provide specialist services in academic staff development in relation to teaching and learning integrated with language and learning support for students, production and delivery of resource-based learning materials, and administrative support services for distance students; conduct research into aspects of flexible learning; and develop entrepreneurial and collaborative ventures with others in Australia and overseas. The FLC is viewed by the senior management group and faculties as a key tool in the university's teaching/learning arrangements and change processes. Its activities are driven by university and faculty priorities for increasing flexibility in teaching and learning.

Thus, for example, the FLC Staff Development and Support Group works with faculty staff on the design of their curricula and choice of media and teaching strategies, including preparation of learning resources for teaching on-campus or at a distance. This occurs in the context of university and faculty priorities for flexible learning in nominated subjects and other aspects of teaching work – eg academic staff induction, innovative teaching/learning grants, multimedia and computer-mediated communications, higher degree supervision, and design of an inclusive curriculum. The model for staff development blends the classic Australian approaches of distance education (with its emphasis on instructional design) and academic development units (with their emphasis on the personal performance aspects of teaching). This model is a new one for Australia, focusing on learning and the conditions of learning, and the teaching strategies needed to achieve the desired qualities of a graduate lifelong learner. The group's work is intimately linked to the codes of good practice and other quality assurance processes in teaching and learning.

Academic staff development is complemented by, and overlaps with the FLC's other academic group – Student Learning Support (SLS). Traditionally, the study advisors emphasized one-on-one teaching of students to develop language and learning skills in their chosen disciplines. With increasing diversity in students' backgrounds and learning styles, coupled with a university-wide emphasis on equity and inclusiveness in curriculum and pedagogy, and rapid integration of information technologies into teaching/learning, the study advisor's role is not only more complex, but the traditional approach cannot keep up with demand. Moreover, it implied a deficit model of teaching and learning that runs counter to the philosophy of independent student-centred learning inherent in 'flexible learning'. The SLS group is now developing programme clusters for tertiary literacy, language and learning in scientific and electronic contexts, non-English speaking background students, and international students. One-on-one has now become one approach among many. Far greater emphasis is being placed on groupwork in workshops and peer/mentoring approaches, and the production of high quality self-instructional resource materials in print and electronic form. Some activities are generic (eg orientation to study programmes), but most in future will be course or discipline-based, determined by faculty priorities and annual plans, and will include academic staff development as much as direct support to students.

The third, and numerically the largest group in the Flexible learning centre is the Production and Delivery Group. In 1996 it comprised four sections of professional and technical experts concerned with the production of printed, audio-visual and multimedia materials; and administrative services to distance students. The integrated services, expertise and facilities provided by this group are similar to those of any sophisticated distance education operation, and the style of operation was largely based on linear programming of production. In dropping the distinctions between campus-based and distance teaching, the new whole-institution approach to flexible learning has caused dramatic changes in the nature, volume and timing of demand for production services. The centre's university-wide responsibility for coordination of multimedia development and integration of information technologies into teaching and learning has posed major challenges to the entire set of subsystems for production and delivery and for the working relationships among the professional and technical staff. The linear programming approach is being replaced by project management, which will enable a fusion of skills and improvements in quality control and cost efficiencies.

Implications for flexible learning

A whole-institution approach to flexible learning is not easily achieved. The gaps between rhetoric and reality are real, as staff come to grips with what teaching and learning mean in a constantly changing social, political and economic environment. Flexible learning challenges fundamental values and systems of both individuals and institutions. The difficulties are compounded by a large gap between goals and resources.

The first challenge is to replace a view that education is *either* face-to-face on-campus *or* at a distance, with a blended approach. This is neither easy, nor uncontested, since distance education is still disparaged by many as a second rate form of education. As UniSA has found, this blending also presents challenges to institutional structures, systems and management processes. There is a need for production facilities and technology, plus a range of expert supports and processes that not only change the time and place of course design and delivery, but also the number of participants in the processes of teaching and learning. While distance teachers are accustomed to this paraphernalia, traditional institutions are not. They typically have difficulty coming to terms with what Evans and Nation (1992) have aptly labelled 'instructional industrialism' – that is, the complex planning and scheduling processes, long lead-times, divisions of labour, and sophisticated, centralized production and delivery infrastructures required by resource-based teaching/learning.

Secondly, flexible learning requires a shift from a concept of education as teacher-dominated to a learner-centred, constructivist approach based on the assumption that knowledge cannot be taught but only learned or constructed (Candy *et al.*, 1994). This challenges the authority–dependency relationship that has traditionally characterized education from early childhood upwards. A recent UniSA study of staff and students' attitudes to learning (Moore *et al.*, 1996) reaffirms the persistence of assumptions in both communities about education as transmission process from expert to acolyte. It is clear that while the university has moved a long way in the last five years to implement a pervasive learner-centred, constructivist philosophy in its policies and procedures, change in individuals' attitudes and practices is less rapid. As Ramsden argues (1993, p.90), academics' 'vernacular theories' of how teaching and learning best occur in their subject are intrinsically static and resistant to change. Moreover, for academics the shift away from teacher domination to student centredness brings into question the role and power of the teacher at a time when, certainly in Australia, the academic's security of tenure and the nature of academic work are subject to major industrial relations negotiations and financial pressures.

Thirdly, the resources required for flexible learning can be a major barrier for those institutions without pre-existing distance education infrastructures, specialized professional and technical expertise, and appropriate resource allocation mechanisms. The University of South Australia could not move into flexible learning as fast or as comprehensively as it is doing without having this base. For others, the solution is to collaborate with a distance teaching university or to outsource the necessary expertise and facilities. The FLC, for example, provides staff development, materials production and delivery services on contract to several other educational institutions.

The perceived cost-benefits of flexible learning are not straightforward either. There is no doubt that the huge increase in popularity of distance education in Australia from the 1980s has been driven by government's convictions that distance education methods offer much needed flexibility and considerable economies of scale. This conviction is not based on rigorous cost-benefit analyses between flexible learning/distance education programmes and classroom teaching programmes, because such comparisons are extremely difficult to draw, and are limited in their generalizability. There have been several recent Australian attempts to assess costs and benefits of various aspects of flexible learning – eg of electronic networks (Deakin University, 1993); and resource-based learning (Commonwealth of Australia, 1994; Taylor *et al.*, 1993). However, they tend to become outdated very quickly, or the context is institution-specific, or the methodology does not permit effective comparison of flexible learning and face-to-face teaching.

Nevertheless, flexible learning is acquiring orthodoxy in Australian public and institutional policy as a more economically efficient as well as a more educationally effective approach to teaching/learning. The question is becoming, not whether flexible learning can enhance the cost effectiveness of traditional teaching (important though that question is), but whether a university will survive and prosper in the next century without rapidly integrating the various dimensions of flexible learning into its processes, culture and values.

Conclusions

In 1996, Australian higher education is entering a new dark age with draconian cuts in federal funding and a retreat to 1950s style conservative elitism. The temptation to reinstate time-worn teaching/learning strategies, renew emphasis on homogeneity in the student population, and concentrate on local rather than global concerns is barely resistible in the face of the difficulties of innovation and change. Yet unless we grapple with all the dimensions of flexible learning outlined here, our institutions will die. They will become irrelevant, anachronistic and regurgitative, rather than the creative, vibrant and intellectually challenging centres of the information society that universities should be. Merely to address the use of distance education materials in classroom situations – which many assume to be at the heart of convergence – is to skim the surface. The task is a profound and comprehensive transformation of the nature and practice of both teaching and learning – and therefore of the nature of the university.

References

Candy, P, Crebert, G and O'Leary, J (1994) *Developing Lifelong Learners through Undergraduate Education*, Commissioned Report No. 28, National Board of Employment, Education and Training, Canberra.

Commonwealth of Australia (1994) *Costs and Quality in Resource-Based Learning On and Off campus*, Commissioned Report No. 33 (F R Jevons and P Northcott), National Board of Employment, Education and Training, Canberra.

Deakin University (L Moran, J Bottomley, J Hont, J Calvert) (1993) *Electronic Facilities Network to Enhance Tertiary Open Learning Services*, Occasional Papers series, Department of Employment, Education and Training, Canberra.

Evans, T and Nation, D (1992) 'Theorising open and distance education', *Open Learning*, 7(2), 3–13.

Moore, B, Willis, P, and Crotty, M (eds.) (1996) *Getting it Right, Getting it Together,* University of South Australia, Adelaide.

Nunan, T (1994) 'Flexible Delivery – a Discussion of Issues' (unpublished), Flexible Learning Centre, University of South Australia.

Nunan, T (1996) 'Flexible delivery – what is it and why is it a part of current educational debate?' Paper presented at *Annual Conference of Higher Education Research and Development, Society of Australasia,* 8–12 July, Perth, Western Australia.

Ramsden, P (1992) *Learning to Teach in Higher Education*, Routledge, London.

Ramsden, P (1993) 'Theories of learning and teaching and the practice of excellence in higher education', *Higher Education Research. and Development*, 12(1), 87–97.

Taylor, J C, Kemp, J E, and Burgess, J V (1993) *Mixed-Mode Approaches to Industry Training: Staff Attitudes and Cost Effectiveness*, Higher Education Division, Department of Employment, Education and Training, Canberra.

Curriculum or culture change?

The preceding case studies describe a variety of approaches to distance and open learning, using a range of different technologies in various different contexts. So what can we learn from all the hard work and experience that has gone into them? Each author has reflected on the lessons they have extracted from their own experiences and, if you have read through them yourself, you have probably begun to form some general conclusions of your own about what works and why and what pitfalls to avoid. This final chapter attempts to draw these lessons together in a framework that can help to guide the process of planning and implementing changes in teaching and learning methods. As the title of the chapter implies, we can view the issues from the micro or the macro perspective. I am going to argue that even at the micro level there are inescapable issues concerned with culture, roles and values that significantly affect the outcome of innovations depending on how they are addressed. Of course, if the key players in the situation are unaware of these issues they are unlikely to handle them very well. The whole point of using case studies in this book is to enable you, the reader, to learn from the experiences of those who have had to work their way up the learning curve without the benefit of such guidance.

Changes in teaching and learning methods are often dependent on, and regarded as synonymous with, changes in delivery technology. This is particularly the case with open and distance learning, which, by definition, separates the learner from the teacher in space and/or time and that places emphasis on learning resources of one kind or another (workbooks, video cassettes, broadcast programmes, computer-based software, etc). Each technology creates its own challenges and throws up particular barriers to successful implementation. Nevertheless there are common themes apparent from the preceding stories such as 'keep it simple' (eg Abbey National, and Queensland University of Technology).

However, looking beyond the mere technicalities of the innovation, it has been said that there is no such thing as technical change without social change (Juran, 1964). The technology of learning delivery and support affects the roles of both teachers and learners and in doing so may impact on the wider organizational culture, leading to resistance to change as individuals in the organization seek to stabilize the situation and defend their own positions within it. In addition to having unexpected side effects, changes in learning technologies may actually be regarded as the instruments of change by managers seeking a cultural paradigm shift, as described by Moran in the case study on the University of South Australia.

Strategies for the management of change are therefore an essential requirement for would be learning innovators. Textbooks on organizational culture abound (see Brown, 1995, for a review of models) and this book does not attempt to compete in that arena. However, the evidence from the case studies suggests that there are some basic concepts and rules that can be applied whether one is operating at the macro (strategic), or micro (pragmatic) level of the organizational system.

Technology

Open and distance learning is inevitably dependent on technology of some sort: for access to learning resources, for provision of instructions and guidelines to learners, for communications between learners and teachers. The technology need not be very sophisticated: printed materials for instance can be cost effective, as attested in the BT and Reuters case studies; or it may encompass the very latest 'gee-whizzery' of satellites (TSB), Intranet (Reuters), videoconferencing (Ulster), etc. The technical lessons emerging from these case studies concern:

- future proofing;
- infrastructure;
- technical support.

Future proofing

In any innovation there are bound to be some fundamental technical considerations and in the field of technology-based learning, future proofing has to be a primary concern. The rate of technological change means that hardware and software purchased to support a particular innovation may become obsolete within a short space of time (between three and five years seems to be the current cycle of obsolescence). The examples described by Hills (Lloyds

Bank) and Christian-Carter (Barclays) show how unforeseen developments in technology can affect investment decisions and block further development. There is a need to include technology upgrade paths wherever possible. Sometimes this can mean having to take a gamble, as in the case of Abbey National CBT Group's decision to invest in PCs ahead of the business, and sometimes it means waiting to see how a technology is going to settle down, as in Reuters' stance on the use of the Internet.

Infrastructure

Access is, in many of the cases described here, determined by the availability of infrastructure in the sense of learning centres (Reuters, Barclays, Lloyds, University of South Australia), computer networks (Abbey National, Reuters, Wirral Metropolitan College, University of Ulster) or broadcast receiver networks (eg TSB). Without adequate infrastructure and take-up, the innovation may be limited (eg BT). Standardization of infrastructure is also an important issue, allowing for standard interfaces and learner management software (Abbey National), standardization of training products (Lloyds, Barclays) and ease of support.

Technical support

Doughty *et al.* raise the issue of ensuring that the organization's technical support team is involved in and supportive of the technical innovation. This was not the case at Glasgow University where 'negotiation was needed to persuade the operators of an engineering computer cluster to mount the software on their machines'. Despite the objective nature of the objections raised – technical staff 'did not know, and had not evaluated the software, especially for compatibility with their ways of operating', 'had not previously served the needs of this group of students with so many machines over so long a period of time', and 'felt hard pressed for desk spaces and computer memory' – the fact that 'the promise of funding more server memory seemed to help, although this has not yet been claimed' suggests that the objections were more deep seated and emotive. Once the real objections of feelings of exclusion and professional trespass were overcome the promised recompense was probably not regarded as important any longer. Wakeley describes a similar phenomenon in the Abbey National, but on a larger scale, where he reports how the business IT team felt very uncomfortable about the activities of another group issuing PCs and influencing company policy on the use of IT. Computing is of course not the only kind of specialist support on which an innovation may depend. In the language learning case study at Glasgow, Harland *et al.* report how the sudden unavailability of the *leitora* or language specialist, threw the programme into similar disarray.

Human factors

Turning from purely technical considerations to aspects of use, Skelly and Hargis, describing the evolution of METTNET® at Wirral Metropolitan College, stress: 'At all times the key issues of access, ease of use and relevance were of paramount importance to the design process and controlled the evolution of the system.'

Access

Commenting on accessibility, Skelly and Hargis state, 'It was decided at an early stage at WMC that IT was not a classroom based technology... Being able to access IT at a time, place and pace suitable to individual needs seemed to be a fundamental prerequisite for the successful adoption of IT.' This theme is echoed by Christian-Carter (Barclays Bank), Moran (University of South Australia) and Cook (Reuters) and broadened to encompass accessibility for off campus learners by Winn (Queensland University of Technology) and McAleavy and Parr (Ulster). The BT case illustrates some of the problems concerning lack of acceptance and adoption that can occur when access to learning materials is restricted for technical or cost reasons. Only Harland *et al.* explicitly challenge the idea of completely open access, pointing out that in the context of undergraduate language learning at Glasgow University, the tendency of students to leave the computer-based elements to the end of their course negated the careful design and pacing of the course as a whole. The point here seems to be that to be successful, open and distance learning materials need to be accessible when and where learners will need them, but that in some cases learners will need to be encouraged to access them at times dictated by the requirements of the course.

Ease of use

Skelly and Hargis define ease of use in terms of software interface design and stress the importance of adequate learner support via a 'one stop shop' system of study assistants. The importance of the interface design issue is illustrated by the BT example of the sales training interactive video in which 'learners experienced difficulties in knowing where to start and what to do next. They also got confused about the differences between each of the various sections and what they were required to do in each section.' The importance of learner support is echoed strongly by Winn at QUT, Christian-Carter at Barclays, Hills at Lloyds, Cook at Reuters and Moran, University of South Australia. All these authors stress the role of learning centres as places for supported study.

Relevance

Relevance can be viewed as referring to the 'fit' between the learning materials and the learners, as defined by Skelly and Hargis, or it may mean relevance to the strategic objectives of the organization or its managers: 'focus on the business priorities' (Wakeley). The BT case study shows how important the learner/course fit can be in determining success or failure. Higgins in the TSB case study refers to the high degree of relevance perceived by learners and their managers regarding the Financial Planning Certificate and Wakeley points out the need to keep products updated to maintain relevance. This takes us beyond the narrow consideration of technologies and into the murkier waters of organizational culture.

Cultural change

It has been suggested (Nadler and Tushman, 1979) that there are three key components to organizational change: tasks, individuals and organizational arrangements. It is tempting to focus on the immediate practical tasks, eg developing a new course, setting up a network of learning centres, and on the formal organizational structure, eg creating a new unit. However, if the feelings of individuals are not taken into account and the informal communication and power relationships are not harnessed, there will be resistance to change.

> 'Every culture has its own system of motivation, status, values, rights, "way of life". Any proposed change is a potential threat to parts of this system and is therefore examined carefully to judge its social effects [by the members of that culture].' (Juran, 1964)

Therefore, even apparently minor changes, such as modifying the way a particular course is taught, can engender surprisingly strong reactions if members of the organization perceive the innovation as undesirable in terms of its impact on their way of life. This explains how rational arguments for change can be turned aside in favour of the *status quo,* or why apparently objective solutions to stated problems are not adopted. For example, the performance and comparative data collected within BT demonstrated quite clearly the significant advantages to the organization of maintaining a sophisticated internal distance learning development and delivery capability, yet the facility was disbanded. A similar fate awaited the distance learning group within Abbey National, for much the same reasons. Established staff felt threatened by the separate, non-conformist values of these groups, which operated outside mainstream formal and informal power hierarchies, and yet had considerable influence on the rest of the organization. By way of an example on the micro scale, the offer of more resources to the technicians at

Glasgow University overcame their objection that they did not have enough resources to support computer-aided learning, yet the additional resources were never actually taken up, suggesting that their true objections lay elsewhere.

Drivers

Doughty *et al.* observe that 'Change is usually sought when at least one stakeholder feels a mismatch between their current values and practice, or becomes aware of strengths, weaknesses, opportunities or threats, particularly economic and other social pressures.' In other words there are usually external factors in the environment that prompt or *drive* the change process. Sometimes drivers can be personal: ambition, infatuation with technology, boredom with existing methods, etc. However these are unlikely to be sufficient or sustainable to effect real change. A review of the preceding chapters shows that effective drivers are usually significant pressures on individuals that motivate them to seek to change things or to accept changes made by others.

Pressures may arise as a result of changes within the organization, or they may be driven externally. Examples in this book of internal drivers are the *changing expectations of learners* themselves (Glasgow University, Reuters), *mergers* between groups with differing values and practices (University of South Australia), major *staffing changes* caused by company *relocation* (Abbey National), major *internal reviews* of functions and structures (Barclays, Reuters) and *drives for enhanced productivity*, as at Sheffield University, Queensland University of Technology, Reuters and BT. They may even be as mundane as *timetabling changes* (Doughty *et al.*).

Internal reviews and productivity drives are themselves often prompted by changes in the external environment such as *increased competition* (Moran, Brown, Robertson, Wakeley), *legislative changes* (Wakeley, Higgins), or new *market sector trends* such the growing emphasis on quality referred to by Higgins, Robertson, Sharratt, Moran and Doughty *et al.* Other examples cited by the contributors to this book are: the need to improve *regional economic competitiveness* (McAleavy and Parr); the need to forge strategic *cooperative links* with external partners (Doughty *et al.*, McAleavy and Parr); the need to respond to *external criticism* (Skelly and Hargis; Doughty *et al.*); or to external *customers' requirements* (Robertson).

Champions

A vital ingredient of change seems to be the presence of enthusiasts in key positions within the organization with the authority, charisma and skills to both push and facilitate the change process, for example, Sharratt at Sheffield

University and Wakeley at Abbey National. If the scale of change is small, say just one element within a single course, the champions of change need not be high up the organizational hierarchy. In the case of changes made to languages and maths teaching at Glasgow University or to practices in associate colleges of the University of Ulster, the champions were the lecturers themselves and the AV technicians respectively. The point here is that because the changes were localized and small scale, the actors in the situation were able to control the necessary resources and communication channels themselves.

For larger scale changes, which have more impact on organizational culture, a necessary ingredient seems to be one or more senior managers prepared to stake their reputation on the innovation, for example: the Head of School of Computing and Information Systems, later Pro Vice-Chancellor with responsibility for teaching and learning support at Sunderland University; the Deputy Vice- Chancellor at Queensland University of Technology; the Personnel Manager and Training Director at Abbey National; the Head of Training at Barclays and the senior management group at University of South Australia. Interestingly, when the champions at BT and Abbey National left the organizations, the change process went into reverse and the specialist teams set up to implement the changes were disbanded.

Barriers

Barriers are those aspects of the situation that can frustrate the change process and they may be either *intrinsic* to the innovation or *extrinsic*, in the environment. Intrinsic barriers concern the design of the learning materials, the study arrangements, physical infrastructure, learning support and management systems, in other words, the obvious task and formal organizational aspects of change. Things to watch out for include ensuring learners have adequate time for study, do not feel isolated, have ready access to adequate, easy to use, learning facilities and relevant, easy to use, study materials. All these things are under the control, or should be, of the innovators.

Extrinsic barriers, on the other hand, lie beyond the control of the innovators but need to be taken into account in the planning and implementation. The effects of technology change, for instance, were discussed by Hills and Wakeley, leading to the conclusion that it is important to future proof developments as far as possible.

Brown, Cook and Harland *et al.* each refer to the expectations or 'mind set' of learners and the problems that can arise when these do not match the type of learning event offered. Resistance can also come from staff: reluctance to provide technical support (Doughty *et al.*, Wakeley), to undertake necessary staff development (Skelly and Hargis) or to adopt the innovation themselves (Wakeley, Brown, McAleavy and Parr, Winn, Robertson). Resistance can sometimes be the result of previous negative experience of IT-based learning (Doughty *et al.*, Cook), in which case competent design and planning will overcome the objections. More difficult is the sense of loss of ownership and control caused by having to adopt someone else's material; or seeing one's own material pass into other people's hands (Skelly and Hargis, McAleavy and Parr, Moran, Robertson); and the inferences made about future job quality and security (Winn, McAleavy and Parr, Brown).

Enablers

Despite the frequent recurrence of these typical barriers, the preceding case studies have shown that it is possible to establish preconditions for success, or to modify strategies to get the change process back on track after a derailment, through the harnessing of aspects of the situation that assist the process of change.

Resources are usually a limitation. The successful innovators here have taken advantage of technology changes that allowed them to exploit something that was not previously available, such as low cost, powerful desktop computing (Harland *et al.*, Wakeley, Winn), satellite TV (Higgins), or telecommunications infrastructure (McAleavy and Parr). External funding sources can be exploited, such as the Universities New Initiatives, the Teaching and Learning Technology Programme, BT University Development Awards. External funding is probably less appropriate in the private sector because it usually comes with strings attached, but internal resources can be found too: the general equipment budget at Queensland University of Technology, the training budget at Abbey National. The trick appears to be to look for recent changes in the environment that can be exploited in some way.

It seems that shifts in opinions and values are important enablers. The bottom up changes to languages and maths teaching introduced so successfully at Glasgow were carried out in the wider context of institutional culture change (the TILT project), itself a result of an explicit change programme in UK higher education: the TLTP. Hearts and minds can be won through judicious publication of evaluation findings (Harland *et al.*, Doughty *et al.*), favourable quality assurance reports (Doughty *et al.*) and timely cost comparisons (Wakeley, Hills).

Hearts and minds can also be won by enabling participation through awareness raising events (Robertson), workshops (Skelly and Hargis, Sharratt) and by making available tools, templates and resources that are easily used and obviously useful (Skelly and Hargis, Winn, Hills).

Rewards, in terms of promotion, consultancy payments, enhanced salaries, relief of other duties, etc have been successfully employed at Wirral Metropolitan College, Sunderland University and University of South Australia. The obverse of this approach seems to be the (compulsory) staff development programmes advocated by Skelly and Hargis and Moran. It is interesting that both sets authors have described a combined carrot and stick approach in their organizations.

Issues

Despite the commonality of themes, the case studies show that there is no simple algorithm that can be applied to the introduction of open/distance learning into a conventional, face-to-face context. There are a number of issues that need to be addressed in relation to the particular context of the proposed innovation.

Internal versus external development?

Is it best to set up an internal design and development team, on the grounds that specialist design skills will be needed in addition to the subject matter knowledge and classroom teaching skills of the existing tutors? The Barclays, Lloyds and Sunderland studies show the internal development team approach working effectively, while in the Abbey National case it led to severe problems downstream. Cook is one of several authors who point to a compromise: outsource generic material and develop in-house only company specific, mission critical, applications. This is an interesting concept in the context of education where the individuality of courses is highly prized by their institutions, even at first year undergraduate level.

Centralized versus local/distributed development?

Most of the examples cited in the foregoing chapters refer to centralized models of development and support. That is to say, special units have been set up, distinct from existing face-to-face provision, to service the needs of the rest of the organization. Winn shows how, at Queensland University of Technology, it has been possible to migrate from centralized production and support systems towards a more localized approach through the development of templates that can be used by non-technical subject matter experts to generate their own materials. This is similar to the philosophy employed at Wirral Metropolitan College and appears to offer a solution to the twin barriers of 'not invented here' and loss of control over one's own material by providing conventional tutors with readily usable tools, enabling them to play an active role in the process of change. Sharratt describes a half way house position at Sheffield University in which the central unit provides advice and consultancy only, on the grounds that it could never be adequately resourced to produce materials for all its customers and that control of development should be with the tutors anyway. The Glasgow University examples illustrate the opposite approach of local, 'bottom up' development in which the changes to teaching methods are developed and implemented by the face-to-face teachers themselves. In the language learning example Harland *et al.* describe how they developed their own computer-based learning materials from scratch. While this undoubtedly resulted in very high degrees of motivation among the staff involved and produced satisfactory results in terms of students performance, it has to be asked whether this approach would be the most efficient if replicated across all courses. The other Glasgow example, in which externally produced courseware is imported and adapted as necessary for use, is probably a more realistic model to adopt given the resource limitations within which most innovators have to work.

An alternative approach is offered by the TSB example. In this case the design and development of all courses was handled by a separate central team, quite distinct from the course tutors; a model with strong parallels in wholly distance learning institutions, such as the UK Open University, but otherwise rare in education and training. In this case resistance from established trainers was not an issue because they were not normally involved in decisions concerning course design and so were not in a position to erect barriers to change

Growth and integration

Harland *et al.* warn that success can breed problems. As awareness of the benefits of new approaches to teaching and learning spreads, rising demand can force the pace of organizational growth. At Wirral Metropolitan College the METTNET® team has grown to 14 people over a decade. Winn reports that central staffing for computer-based education at QUT grew from 16 to 58 staff in five years. At Lloyds Bank the growth was from one to 15 staff in eight years while at BT the numbers involved in distance learning production and support reached over 40 at their peak and at Abbey National they grew from one to 15 plus, absorbing the rest of technical training in just four years. Rapid expansion of a separate, distinct, unit can lead to problems of 'them and us' as described by Wakeley, particularly if the growth entails mergers or take overs of other, existing, units.

The METTNET® team at Wirral Metropolitan College seem to have acceptance of their growth, by taking care to involve users through local development centres and by developing readily accessible resource pools that tutors can easily draw upon to develop and enhance their own teaching materials. The staff development programme at Wirral is also an important instrument of change, helping tutors to develop the skills necessary to use and develop IT-based teaching and so integrate their activities with those of the METTNET® team. Integration seems to be the key concept here. The scale of the teaching and learning operations in each of the organizations described in this book is such that implementation of open/distance learning organization-wide requires large amounts of resource. The creation of a wholly separate production and support team appears to be unsustainable in the longer term, even though it may be justifiable in the initial stages to ensure the innovation is launched successfully. The various organizations covered by the case studies here have adopted different strategies for integration, including the 'carrot and stick' approach of Wirral Metropolitan and the University of South Australia; the process of merger and acquisition followed by Abbey National, QUT and Lloyds Bank; the self-effacing stance taken by Sheffield University and the position at TSB in which all course development is undertaken by a single integrated team.

Building on existing organizational teams and expansion via mergers with cognate units seems to have been a successful strategy at Sunderland University, QUT, University of South Australia and Lloyds Bank and is probably an inevitable consequence of the convergence of previously distinct media into a single digital domain. Video, computing and telecommunications technologies are increasingly interchangeable, encouraging and enabling convergence of traditionally separate teams involved in programming, video production audio-visual and IT support, libraries or information centres, graphic designers, desktop publishing teams and educational technologists. All these functions are natural allies for the would-be open/distance learning champion.

Learning support

The extent to which and the ways in which learners using new technology are supported varies from organization to organization, but most of the case studies here report on the need for an adequate infrastructure of learning centres, ie locations to which learners can go to access not only learning materials, but also help with technical matters, such as how to save their work or print files and with learning difficulties arising from the content of the learning materials.

Cook notes the irony of a situation where learning centres are regarded as too distant to be accessible and points out that even quite short distances can be a significant barrier to take up. The Abbey National tried to overcome this problem by making training available on the desktop of all potential users, but this obviously requires the existence of a suitable organization-wide infrastructure and sufficient discipline/license to concentrate on study amidst the normal working environment. In this context, the motivation to study needs to be very high and shared by the whole organization, such as the legal requirement for Abbey National employees to achieve accreditation.

Costing models

Change of any sort entails risks and in the case of open/distance learning, the risks tend to be loaded up front because of the need to invest in delivery infrastructure and learning materials development. Despite the potentially significant savings downstream, as shown by the figures in the BT case study, these high front loaded costs can be a serious deterrent to progression beyond the initial pilot or to further expansion and innovation (Hills, Brown, Christian-Carter, Doughty *et al.*, Wakeley). What a number of these studies show (eg Lloyds, BT, Barclays, Reuters) is that it is important to assess the entire life-cycle costs of alternative methods and to ensure that costs are calculated, if not paid for, at the point of delivery on a per person/study hour basis. It is also important to ensure that all possible uses of the necessary infrastructure have been included in the cost equation. For example the satellite TV receivers in TSB could not have been cost justified for training purposes, but once in place could be exploited. Wakeley and Cook make similar points in relation to PCs and Internet provision

Tips

Finally, arising from the experiences described and analysed here it is possible to draw up a list of 'handy tips' for beginners as follows:

1. Have a clear vision of change that relates to the needs of the organization and communicate this effectively (Hills, Wakeley, Christian-Carter, Moran).
2. Ensure you have at least one influential 'champion' on board who can ensure the support of key power groups and, where necessary, impose conditions such as compulsory staff development (Robertson, Winn, Christian-Carter, Moran, Wakeley, Brown).
3. Select external consultants carefully, they may not fit well with your organizational culture (Robertson, Winn).
4. Start with informal temporary organizational structures that bring together the players and keep these flexible enough to allow a transition to more formal structures later on as necessary (Robertson, Winn).
5. Ensure that *all* new course development proposals are subject to the same process of review, either by passing them through a single course development unit (Higgins, Hills) or by applying a common instructional design strategy (Christian-Carter, Cook).
6. Keep it simple, both in terms of the technology (Wakeley, Winn) and the educational design (Robertson, Winn) and don't set over-ambitious targets (Robertson, Doughty *et al.*).
7. Motivate people to want to change by building in rewards (Skelly and Hargis, McAleavy and Parr, Moran).
8. Offer partnerships and enable participation through templates, resource pools, adaptable modules, and tools for upgrading media to more sophisticated forms (Doughty *et al.*, Robertson, Skelly and Hargis, Winn, Hills).
9. Provide staff development events (Skelly and Hargis, Moran) and tools such as guidelines for materials development (Robertson), client packs (Winn), management guides (Hills).

10. Allay concerns about impact on teaching methods, workloads and job security (Skelly and Hargis, McAleavy and Parr). Don't threaten or advocate culture change openly (Doughty *et al.*, Cook), and plan developments that supplement rather than threaten existing provision (Winn, Wakeley). On the other hand do not dilute the impact of innovation by offering alternatives to your open/distance learning courses (Doughty *et al.*, Cook).

This list may not guarantee success, but, if followed, may help you avoid some of the frustrations and pains reported on here.

References

Brown, A (1995) *Organizational Culture*, Pitman, London.

Juran, J M (1964) *Managerial Breakthrough*, McGraw-Hill, New York.

Nadler, D A and Tushman, M L (1979) 'A congruence model for diagnosing organizational behavior', in *Organizational Psychology: A book of readings*, D Kolb, I Rubin, and J McKintyre (eds), Prentice-Hall, Englewood Cliffs, NJ.

The contributors

Stephen Brown BA, MSc, FRSA, MIPD is Director of the International Institute for Electronic Library Research at De Montfort University. Prior to that he worked for the British Open University and for British Telecom in a variety of positions including Head of Distance Learning in BT Training. He has produced learning materials in a broad range of media and published widely in the fields of distance learning, training and design education.

His teaching experience includes Royal Academy of Engineering Visiting Professor in Principles of Engineering Design at the University of Ulster at Jordanstown and at Queens University Belfast; lecturing in Design and Ergonomics at Leicester Polytechnic and at the University of Ulster at Belfast and tutoring for the Open University.

Contact: Learning Technologies, De Montfort University, The Gateway, Leicester LE1 9BH, UK.
Tel: +44 (0)116 257 7173; Fax: +44 (0)116 257 7170;
e-mail: sbrown@dmu.ac.uk

Judith Christian-Carter BEd, MPhil, FIPD is Director of Training and Development for Design for Learning Ltd, a company that designs, develops and delivers a range of bespoke training and development programmes across a wide client base. Prior to her current appointment, Judith spent six years in Barclays Bank, central training function as a Deputy Head of the Training Development Group, the Manager of Training Services, and the Manager for Training Strategy and Planning. Before joining Barclays she worked for the National Council for Educational Technology as Programme Manager for New Learning Technologies, having previously spent seven years running a large department in a comprehensive school covering the 11–18-year-old age range. She has written a number of books, produced more papers than she cares to remember, and has made numerous presentations at both national and international conferences.

Contact: Design for Learning Ltd, Talon House, Presley Way, Crown Hill, Milton Keynes MK8 0EE, UK.
Tel: +44 (0)1908 580460; Fax: +44 (0)1908 580546.

David Cook MBA has been involved in open learning since 1983, developing educational packages for the home computer market, an authoring and video control system for interactive tape and laserdisc, and interactive video, CBT and print-based learning packages for clients including BP, Lloyds Bank, Midland Bank and BNFL.

In 1988, he joined BT Training, where he was involved in the design and development of interactive video learning materials and research and development into new media including multimedia and the use of ISDN networks for the support and delivery of learning to remote locations. His 'Telephone Techniques' CD-ROM-XA disc won an award for the best new business training application at the Microsoft CD-ROM and Multimedia conference at Wiesbaden in 1991.

At Reuters UKI Training since January 1994, he is responsible for analysis and consultancy on business performance issues, and for the design and development of integrated, flexible learning solutions for Reuters staff, which have included both print and computer-based media. He was involved in specifying and launching Reuters first learning centre in UKI, and in evaluating and purchasing technical, management and personal development courseware packages for use in the centre.

Contact: Reuters UKI Training, 85 Fleet Street, London EC4P 4AJ, UK.
Tel: +44 (0)171 542 6343; e-mail: david.cook@dial.pipex.com

Gordon Doughty BA, PhD, CPhys, MInstP took an eclectic Open University degree while working in the optical industry, then joined Glasgow University's Engineering Faculty for optoelectronics research and a PhD. He is now a Senior Lecturer organizing the Bachelor of Technological Education degree, which produces teachers of Technology, Craft & Design and Graphic Communication. He is responsible for the Robert Clark Centre for Technological Education, an ITTI project 'Establishing Multimedia Authoring Skills in Higher Education', Glasgow University's 'Teaching with Independent Learning Technologies' project in the UK Teaching & Learning Technology Programme, and the Glasgow Centre of the UK Teaching & Learning Technology Support Network.

Contact: Robert Clark Centre for Technological Education, University of Glasgow, 66 Oakfield Avenue, Glasgow G12 8LS, UK.
Tel: +44 (0)141 330 4844; Fax: +44 (0)141 330 4832;
e-mail: g.doughty@elec.gla.ac.uk.

Jackie Hargis MSc, BA (Hons), Cert Ed (FE) has a Masters degree in Information Technology, a Bachelors degree in Librarianship and Information Studies as well as a teaching qualification. She worked in a variety of roles in industry before joining Wirral Metropolitan College in 1987. For several years she taught IT and since 1993 has worked on developing systems within the field of multimedia and materials development that enable staff to consider flexible curriculum delivery through the use of IT.

Contact: Wirral Metropolitan College, Carlett Park, Eastham, Wirral, Merseyside L62 0AY, UK.
Tel: +44 (0)151 551 7860; Fax: +44 (0)151 327 6271;
e-mail jhargis@wmc.ac.uk.

Mike Harland is Senior Lecturer in Portuguese at the University of Glasgow and started using computers in his teaching seven years ago, with HyperCard on Apple Macintosh machines. As well as teaching literature, he originally specialized in lexicography helping HarperCollins to update their Portuguese dictionaries, while experimenting with Hypertext dictionaries himself. For the past three years he has worked on two TLTP projects, as author and designer of 'De Tudo um Pouco – 'a little bit of everything': a year piloting integrated text and computer courseware for Portuguese for the TILT initiative at Glasgow, and a member of the Courseware team of TELL, the language consortium based in Hull.

Contact: Department of Hispanic Studies, University of Glasgow, Hetherington Building, Bute Gardens, Glasgow G12 8QQ, UK.
Tel: +44 (0)141 330 5306; Fax: +44 (0)141 339 1119;
e-mail: mch@lang.gla.ac.uk.

Peter Higgins MBA, Dip FS, ACIB formerly managed TSB's Design Team based in Birmingham where he planned, coordinated and controlled training development activities and managed a portfolio of key business projects. Prior to that he managed the bank's national Remote Autoteller network. In his previous role as an Area Manager he gained extensive experience in managing the delivery and achievement of Business Development and Customer Service objectives while managing the Training and Development activities of a large number of Sales and Customer Service staff.

He has designed and produced a wide variety of training solutions, with particular experience in designing Open Learning solutions and in Regulatory Sales Training and Assessment.

He completed an MBA at Sheffield Hallam University in 1994 and is a member of the Chartered Institute of Bankers, having completed a Diploma in Financial Studies and the institute's own ACIB examinations.

Peter Higgins now works for Mercuri Urval as a consultant.

Contact: Mercuri Urval, Peat House, 45 Church Street, Birmingham B3 2RT, UK.
Telephone +44 (0)121 233 4911; Fax +44 (0) 121 233 4977.

Howard Hills BA, FIPD is currently Head of Training Development at Lloyds TSB. He has worked with interactive training technologies since 1972, developing training programmes for the Royal Navy. From this early work in CCTV, large simulators and classroom technology, he moved to research for the Ministry of Defence into Human Factors, Artificial Intelligence and the use of computers in training systems.

Commercial reality followed with consultancy and training design for a wide range of industries. He joined Lloyds Bank in 1987 setting up the Distance Learning Centre and expanding the bank's use of technology in training, particularly multimedia. He has written several articles and given presentations on the development, and particularly the successful implementation, of open and distance learning.

Contact: Lloyds TSB Training Development Group, PO Box 57, Navigation House, Walnut Tree Park, Walnut Tree Close, Guildford, Surrey GU1 4XW, UK.
Tel: +44 (0) 1483 457272; Fax: +44 (0) 1483 457311.

Gerry McAleavy BA, Cert Ed, DASE, MEd, DPhil is Senior Lecturer and Director of the Further Education Training and Research Unit at the University of Ulster. He was a lecturer in Further Education for 15 years and he is currently involved in lecturing and research at the University of Ulster. He has published 50 articles on post-16 education and training and has been involved in a range of research projects with particular reference to technologies of learning. His research interests are vocational education and the application of communication technologies to learning.

Contact: Further Education Training and Research Unit, School of Education, Faculty of Social and Health Sciences and Education, University of Ulster, Shore Road, Newtownabbey, Northern Ireland BT37 OQB, UK.
Tel: +44 (0)1232 366911; Fax: +44 (0)1232 366825;
e-mail: gj.mcaleavy@ulst.ac.uk.

Erica McAteer MA, PhD, CPsychol is a psychologist whose research interests include communication, information design and education. A lecturer in the University of Glasgow's Teaching and Learning Service, she works with staff and students to design, integrate and evaluate computer mediated learning resources and to develop student-centred teaching practice.

Contact: Consultant Teaching and Learning Service, University of Glasgow, Information Technology Unit, Robert Clark Centre, 66 Oakfield Avenue, Glasgow G12 8QQ, UK.
Tel: +44 (0) 141 330 4997; Fax: +44 (0)141 330 4832;
e-mail: E.McAteer@udcf.gla.ac.uk.

Louise Moran PhD, Grad Dip Ed Admin, BA is currently Director of the Flexible learning centre and Associate Professor of Flexible Learning in the University of South Australia, and has over 25 years' experience in the design and implementation of innovations in teaching and learning. She has worked in continuing education, academic administration and distance education. She spent 15 years at Deakin University where she developed the course development and delivery programmes for distance education. Her doctorate was on the history and politics of distance education and she has published widely on policy, information technology, collaboration and student support issues in distance and flexible learning. She has conducted many consultancies and commissioned projects for international agencies, government and educational bodies in Australia, the Asia/Pacific region and North America.

Contact: Director, Flexible Learning Centre, University of South Australia, Holbrooks Road, Underdale, SA 5032, Australia.
Tel: +61 (0)8 8302 6368; Fax: +61 (0)8 8302 6767;
e-mail: Louise.Moran@UniSA.Edu.Au.

Gerard Parr BSc, Phd, MBCS, MIEE, CEng, MIEEE is the Director of the Telecommunications & Distributed Systems Group at the University of Ulster and has carried out a range of research and consultancy projects in the application of advanced communications to business development, industrial regeneration and education/training. He has a BSc(Hons) degree in Computer Science and a PhD in Telecommunications and Computer Networking, both obtained from the University of Ulster. His main research interests are Interworking Protocols, ISDN, Network Modelling, ATM Switch Fabric Analysis and Operating Systems. He has published widely in the fields of computing and electronics and sits on the Technical Committee of a number of international journals and conferences.

Contact: Telecommunications & Distributed Systems Group, School of Information Software Engineering, Faculty of Informatics, University of Ulster at Coleraine, Northern Ireland BTSZ 1SA, UK.
Tel: +44 (0)1265 324131/324366; Fax: +44 (0)1265 324916;
e-mail: gparr@causeway.infc.ulst.ac.uk;
www: http://www.infc.ulst.ac.uk/staff/gp.parr.

Maggie Pollock BSc, PGCE, PhD completed an Engineering Science Degree at Durham University, followed by a PGCE. She then taught Mathematics to 'A' and 'S' level for several years in English Grammar Schools, before going to Strathclyde University to study for a PhD in Bioengineering. She then spent a number of years in industry on the design and stress analysis of heavy rotating machinery. She joined the University of Glasgow's Mechanical Engineering Department with a special responsibilty for teaching on the Bachelor of Technological Education (BTechEd) Degree, which she organized and ran for two years. She was involved in the university wide TLTP programme (TILT) where she took over the Mathematics teaching for the BTechEd students. She is also heavily involved with teaching the mechanics and design courses on the degree. Her research interests include the evaluation of teaching methods for technology and mathematics to all age groups.

Contact: Department of Mechanical Engineering, Robert Clark Centre for Technological Education, University of Glasgow, 66 Oakfield Avenue, Glasgow G12 8LS, UK.
Tel: +44 (0)141 330 4976; Fax: +44 (0)141 330 4832;
e-mail: m.pollock@mech.gla.ac.uk.

Suzanne Robertson BSc is the Director of Learning Development Services at the University of Sunderland. She and her team are responsible for promoting new developments in teaching and learning and ensuring appropriate staff development so that initiatives are evaluated and embedded into learning strategies. Her experience teaching Microbiology for 22 years, in full time, part time, block release and distance modes, latterly to students without a strong science background has re-inforced her committment to resource-based learning strategies.

Directing a service with cross institutional responsibility for all copying and printing, audio visual development and support in large lecture theatres, telematic and multimedia developments, student study and maths skills support, optical scanning developments, the production of print-based open learning materials and management of European projects gives Suzanne opportunities to facilitate cooperation and collaboration in open and distance learning involving a full spectrum of technologies.

Contact: Learning Development Services, University of Sunderland, Hutton Building, Chester Road, Sunderland SR1 3SD, UK.
Tel: +44 (0)191 515 2280; Fax: +44 (0)191 515 2279;
e-mail: suzanne.robertson@sunderland.ac.uk.

Niall Sclater BA, Msc is the University of Strathclyde's IT Support Coordinator, promoting and supporting learning technology across the institution. At Glasgow University, he worked for three years with Mike Harland and Erica McAteer developing courseware in Spanish and Portuguese. He now manages Clyde Virtual University, which is delivering multimedia teaching materials over the Internet to Higher Education students in the West of Scotland.

Contact: IT Support Coordinator, University of Strathclyde, Glasgow, Scotland.
Tel: +44 (0)141 548 3496; Mobile: +44 (0)410 057562; Fax: +44 (0)141 553 4100;
e-mail: n.sclater@strath.ac.uk;
Computer Assisted Learning: http://www.strath.ac.uk/CAL/;
Clyde Virtual University: http://cvu.strath.ac.uk/

Ruth Sharratt BSc, PGCE is the Acting Director of the Distance Learning Unit (DLU) at the University of Sheffield. She has had many years involvement in distance education starting as an Open University student and then tutor-counsellor. She has worked in both Further Education in the Open Tech initiative and in Higher Education. Working in a variety of institutions, she has always been involved in the development of distance learning provision. At Sheffield, the DLU provides advice and assistance to staff across the university who are producing distance learning programmes. She also represents distance learning in the university's decision making structures. Her research interests include the cost-effectiveness of distance education.

Contact: Distance Learning Unit, University of Sheffield, Division of Adult Continuing Education, 196–8 West Street, Sheffield S1 4ET, UK.
Tel: +44 (0)114 222 7046; Fax: +44 (0)114 222 7001;
e-mail: R.Sharrat@sheffield.ac.uk.

Iain Skelly BA (Econ), Cert Tech Ed qualified with a degree in Politics and Sociology in 1969. Since then he has worked in Further Education teaching a number of subjects including Sociology and Business Studies. In the early 1980s, he wrote and had published a variety of educational software for the BBC micro. He became the Information Technology Manager at Wirral Metropolitan College in 1989.

Contact: Wirral Metropolitan College, Carlett Park, Eastham, Wirral, Merseyside L62 0AY, UK.
Tel: +44 (0)151 551 7860; Fax: +44 (0)151 327 6271;
e-mail: iskelly@wmc.ac.uk.

Ian Turner requalified as a secondary school teacher in Technological Education after an engineering career in chemical and civil engineering, being latterly most closely involved in biotechnology developments in waste water treatment. His interests in computer applications and interactive training led to a research post with the University of Glasgow and a commercial training position in CAD, computer systems and software. He has lectured in computing for the Bachelor of Technological Education degree and provided lecture and tutorial support for the mathematics course of the same degree. He is working towards an Open University degree which combines mathematical modelling and technology modules. He is a writer and computer consultant.

Contact: Graphics Resources Consultant, Robert Clark Centre for Technological Education, University of Glasgow, 66 Oakfield Avenue, Glasgow G12 8LS, UK.
Tel: +44 (0)141 330 4976; Fax: +44 (0)141 330 4832;
e-mail: i.turner@elec.gla.ac.uk.

Julian Wakeley formed the Distance Learning Group at Abbey National in 1985. Prior to that he had spent four years designing and developing end user IT training for Abbey National. From 1992 to 1993 he was Vice President of SATURN , the European Distance Learning Organization which enabled businesses and distance teaching universities and educational establishments to work on joint projects and share experiences. He left Abbey National in 1983 and joined NETG as Director of Technology, in charge of custom multimedia development and localization of courseware. He joined Unilever plc as World-wide Head of Distance Learning in 1996, working on Intranet and multimedia delivery of management training programmes and best practice initiatives.

Contact: Head of Distance Learning, Four Acres International Management Training Centre, Unilever plc, George Road, Kingston upon Thames, Surrey KT2 7PD, UK.
Tel: +44 (0)181 336 6051; Fax: +44 (0)181 949 9166;
e-mail: julian.wakeley@unilever.com.

Jenny Winn BA, Grad Dip IT, MEd has worked in tertiary education since 1977, with 12 years at the University of Southern Queensland, involved in set up and course coordination of the Department of External and Continuing Education and lecturing in Business Maths and Introduction to Computers in the Schools of Business Studies and Information Technology. In March 1991 Jenny joined the Queensland University of Technology as Deputy Manager/ Instructional Designer in the Computer-Based Education Department. In her current role as Acting Director, Jenny overseas the design, implementation and marketing of the numerous interactive multimedia projects developed by CBE.

Contact: Computer-Based Education Department, Queensland University of Technology, Gardens Point Campus, 2 George Street, GPO Box 2434, Brisbane Q 4001, Australia.
Tel: +61 (0)7 3864 2913; Fax: +61 (0)7 3864 1525;
e-mail: j.winn@qut.edu.au.

Index

Subject index